Developing Professional Memory

Studies in Professional Life and Work

Series Editor

Ivor Goodson (*Education Research Centre, University of Brighton, UK*)

Editorial Board

David Labaree (*Stanford University, USA*)
Sverker Lindblad (*University of Gothenburg, Sweden*)
J. M. Pancheco (*University of Minho, Portugal*)
Leslie Siskin (*NYU/Steinhardt Institute for Education & Social Policy, USA*)

VOLUME 13

The titles published in this series are listed at *brill.com/plwo*

Developing Professional Memory

A Case Study of London English Teaching (1965–1975)

By

Paul Tarpey

BRILL
SENSE

LEIDEN | BOSTON

All chapters in this book have undergone peer review.

The Library of Congress Cataloging-in-Publication Data is available online at http://catalog.loc.gov

ISSN 2589-6067
ISBN 978-90-04-38072-1 (paperback)
ISBN 978-90-04-38073-8 (hardback)
ISBN 978-90-04-38074-5 (e-book)

Copyright 2018 by Koninklijke Brill NV, Leiden, The Netherlands.
Koninklijke Brill NV incorporates the imprints Brill, Brill Hes & De Graaf, Brill Nijhoff, Brill Rodopi, Brill Sense and Hotei Publishing.
All rights reserved. No part of this publication may be reproduced, translated, stored in a retrieval system, or transmitted in any form or by any means, electronic, mechanical, photocopying, recording or otherwise, without prior written permission from the publisher.
Authorization to photocopy items for internal or personal use is granted by Koninklijke Brill NV provided that the appropriate fees are paid directly to The Copyright Clearance Center, 222 Rosewood Drive, Suite 910, Danvers, MA 01923, USA. Fees are subject to change.

This book is printed on acid-free paper and produced in a sustainable manner.

CONTENTS

Chapter 1: Motivations, Locations, Intentions … 1

    Introduction … 1
    Motivations … 2
    Locations … 4
    Approaches … 8
    Structure of the Book … 14

Chapter 2: Conjunctures, Contexts, Circumstances … 17

    Introduction … 17
    Progressive and Radical Traditions … 19
    Locating English into a Wider Genealogy of Context … 21
    The Changing Identity of English Teaching … 25
    Developments in Practice and Resources … 27
    John Dixon's 'Growth' Model of English … 28
    Some Wider Developments … 32
    Events and Developments in the ILEA … 34
    The Bullock Report … 36
    Contending Polarities in English? … 38

Chapter 3: Memories, Narratives, Relationships … 45

    Introduction … 45
    Collective Memory … 48
    Autobiographical and Historical Memory … 52
    Inner Speech and Speech Genre … 54
    Social Constructionism … 57
    Narrative Representation and PM … 59

Chapter 4: Constructing Identities and Attitudes … 63

    Introduction … 63
    English before School and English at School … 63
    Attitudes to English Lessons … 65
    The Teaching and Activities in English Lessons … 67
    Memorable Teachers … 69
    Being 'Bad' … 72
    University and Teacher Training College … 74

CONTENTS

The Learning Experience at University and Teacher Training College	77
So Why Become an English Teacher?	79
What Do These Memories Tell Us?	81

Chapter 5: Working in the 'Cauldron' 1965–1975   83

Introduction	83
Becoming an English Teacher	83
Building Positive Relationships	85
Developing Practice and Resources Collaboratively	87
Bringing Popular Culture into the Classroom	93
Developing Oral Work	96
A Focus on Children's Agency	98
Developing Curricula and Assessment	101
Insistence on Mixed-Ability	103
The Influence of ILEA and the English Centre	106
Professional Development in Other Areas	111
What Do These Memories Tell Us?	114

Chapter 6: From 'Cauldron' to Current Contexts   117

Introduction	117
Attitudes to Regulation and Prescription	117
Is There a Continuing Relevance of the Teachers' Practice?	120
What Defines This Generation of English Teachers?	122
Changes in Attitude	124
Has Something Been 'Lost'?	126
Perceptions of Professionalism and Accountability	130
Can Lessons Be Learned from This Generation?	132
Suggestions for Future Developments	136
Are They 'Progressive' Teachers?	139
What Do These Memories Tell Us?	142

Chapter 7: Making Sense of the Memories   145

Introduction	145
Identities and Working Cultures in English Teaching	145
Are There Alternative Speech Genres in English Teaching?	150
The Importance of Confronting Conjunctural Circumstances	155
Is the Teachers' Work Still Relevant?	157
Competing and Contested Currents in the Teachers' Stories	159
Teacher Memory and Teacher Nostalgia	160
Political English Teaching?	162

Chapter 8: Conclusions, Implications, Destinations	167
Where to Next?	167
What Is PM and How Might It Be Significant?	168
What Practical Contribution Might PM Studies Make?	169
PM and History of Education	173
PM, Teacher Education and Professional Development	174
PM, English Teaching and Collective Memory	176
More PM Studies?	177
References	179
Index	189

CHAPTER 1

MOTIVATIONS, LOCATIONS, INTENTIONS

INTRODUCTION

This book is about Professional Memory (PM) in English teaching. It tells the stories of six London-based English teachers who began their careers between 1965 and 1975. Their stories offer an alternative narrative, a different understanding of English teaching in the period. When set against the current background of performance management, external accountability and a fragmented education system, the teachers' stories foreground a different sense of accountability, professional agency and a strong co-operative ethos. Some histories of English teaching are limited because they fail to include practitioner voices. A central motivation of this book then, is to *write back in* teacher experience. Exploring practitioner memories from a collectivist perspective means that the various missions, motivations and priorities of English teachers from different periods can be recovered. In this way, this book generates a practitioner history of English teaching that can offer valuable lessons in current contexts.

Recent government interventions have framed the school subject English in divisive and elitist ways (Coultas, 2013), and for years practitioners have been coerced into technicist and functionalist practices (Robinson, 2000). English, of course, is not immune to broader educational developments and discourses, and aggressive marketisation, consumerism and individualism have helped re-define English teacher roles and responsibilities in recent decades. These developments have been intended to re-orientate social perceptions of education away from public service to competitive marketplace. Such interventions seek to efface alternative traditions in education, with teachers, parents and children constrained to compete in this so-called 'marketplace'. The problems and inequalities of competition and individualism in education are well documented.[1] But English has a long history of progressive, sometimes radical, collaborative and collectivist approaches – and valuable lessons can be learned by exploring the PM of practitioners from different periods. Starting as an English teacher in particular contexts provides resources (memories, values, identities, discourses, practices) that remain with practitioners for whole careers. The coming-together of different historical, social, cultural and political circumstances provides distinctive opportunities to develop practice and professional identity. The teachers represented in this book began their careers in a period that offered genuine opportunities to work collegially, with professional autonomy and agency.

CHAPTER 1

This period, 1965–1975, is contentious because it is sometimes associated with the development and sedimentation of 'progressive' or 'radical' sensibilities and practices in English teaching. For this reason it is useful to think of the period as a particular 'cauldron' in which radical understandings of English teaching were fertilised and fomented. But the period was chosen because it is book-ended by a number of significant developments. Comprehensive schools gained official support in 1965 (Circular 10/65, DES, 1965), and over the next fifteen years they grew rapidly, until by '1979 approximately 80 per cent of secondary school children attended such schools' (Goodson, 1983: 21). The Inner London Education Authority (ILEA) was established in 1965 and it set about providing networks and support structures for its teachers (Lowe, 2007). At the end of the decade, the 1975 Bullock Report promoted a progressive model of English influenced by the London Association for the Teaching of English (LATE), and in particular the work of James Britton (Burgess & Hardcastle, 2000; Gibbons, 2009). In 1975 ILEA also established the English Centre, which offered teachers centralised resources, collaborative working spaces and publishing opportunities. The teachers' memories foreground a strong collective identity formed in this period. However, the social, cultural and political effects of the period are not limited to these dates and the collective memories highlight attitudes and values that have remained for whole careers. The teachers began their careers in these circumstances, and this book locates their memories into a number of contexts.

The past couple of decades have seen a growing body of research that investigates teacher memory, experience and narratives, locating these into broad debates in educational history. Teacher narratives have been considered from a variety of perspectives, with studies making valuable contributions to understandings of practitioner identity, professionalism, motivation, nostalgia and so on. Researchers like Ivor Goodson, Peter Cunningham, Miriam Ben Peretz, Andy Hargreaves and Philip Gardner[2] have contributed to this developing, and potent, body of evidence that foregrounds teacher experience in explorations of professional life and work. Some of this work has a broad focus. This book has a very specific focus on a particular school subject: English. It offers a body of evidence, and analysis, of English teacher memories. The teachers' stories were generated through empirical research, combining life history and collective memory methods. As such, the book offers an approach to investigating the collective PM of practitioners in a particular school subject.

MOTIVATIONS

At this point I want to say something about my own experience as an English teacher. My motivations for writing this book, and my interpretations of the teachers' stories, are inevitably influenced by my experiences, attitudes and ideological perspectives: my 'positionality' (Lichtman, 2013; Thomas, 2009). I started as an English teacher in 1997. New Labour had won the recent election and Prime Minister, Tony Blair, had famously asserted his main priorities: 'education, education, education'. It seemed like an exhilarating time to be embarking on a teaching career. Newly qualified, I started at a school where a new head-teacher had recently arrived. It did not take long to realise the school was fast becoming an ideological battlefield. The new head arrived with a 'corporate' (her word) agenda and set about surrounding herself with colleagues of a similar outlook. Soon there was tension among senior staff. The head clashed with the existing deputy-heads, who belonged to an older generation of teachers. I was intrigued by the way the older generation seemed to operate in a different ideological universe. Their priorities were for student learning, negotiating the curriculum and equality. Teacher-accountability, standardised tests and league tables seemed secondary considerations. This was an all-girls secondary school in West London, where many of the girls came from working-class and ethnic-minority backgrounds. I was drawn to the older teachers and the methods and values they vehemently defended. But what were these methods and values? And why were they so vehement?

I developed an immediate rapport with Ann, the Head of English, and worked closely with her, becoming second in department in my second year at the school. She encouraged a student-centred, active approach and was uncompromising in her commitment to 'mixed-ability' teaching groups. We spent a lot of time each year organising these groups. The other teachers in the department generally bought into Ann's approach and most English lessons included lots of discussion, drama, presentations, filming, even dancing. It was common to see groups of students from different classes in corridors rehearsing for role-plays and the like. I consider this initial period to be the most important in developing my identity as an English teacher; Ann's experience had a lasting effect on my own thinking and practice.

What was fascinating about working in this particular school though was the brutal clash of ideologies and personalities that I was entangled with. I quickly realised the business of teaching was much more political than I had naively imagined on my teacher training course. After five years with quite a lot of conflict, the head-teacher eventually insisted on imposing 'ability sets' in the English department. This proved to be the final straw for Ann who resigned at the end of the year. I took over as acting head of department but followed her a year later. At the same time I was studying for an MA in English Studies at the London Institute of Education. This added a variety of theoretical and contextual perspectives that helped me to understand some of the circumstances my own practice was framed within. I started out with a strong commitment to social justice, but being opened up to the ideas of Raymond Williams, Paulo Freire, Lev Vygotsky and Mikhail Bakhtin (among others) helped me to be more critically reflective and reflexive in approaching the job.

These formative experiences influenced my thinking. I constructed a view that the collective is stronger than the individual, and that theory and practice must combine to challenge and reconstruct social realities. I suppose I am referring to a developing understanding of 'praxis' or what Freire (1970) calls 'Conscientization'. But these experiences also highlighted the complex nature of human relationships when looked at critically in their multifarious contexts. What motivates people to behave the way they do? I was forced to reconsider my own various roles framed within those working conditions. I realised I was attracted to characters who were

CHAPTER 1

prepared to challenge the status quo in order to try and improve their material circumstances. Similarly, I realised I was attracted to conceptions of the 'radical' and 'collective'. So, I have sought to try and understand something of the collective memories of 'radical' and 'progressive' English teachers. A key motivation for this book stems from my conviction that English teacher voices must be firmly located into the history of the subject.

I wanted to find out more about Ann's generation of English teachers' ideas and experiences. I wanted to know why her values and methods seemed to be at such odds with those of the head-teacher. Ann started teaching in the late 1960s and I was intrigued by what impact that particular historical period had on how she constructed her professional identity. When I started there were big structural changes in education and it seemed the experience of Ann's generation was being discredited. In the school there were big ideological differences between some of the older teachers and the new senior management. But by talking with the older teachers ('whingers' as the head-teacher would have it), I learned about methods of practice that seemed more progressive, egalitarian, and for me, *better* than the standards expected by the school management. I wanted to re-capture and 'give voice' to a generation of English teachers who seem to be discounted in current 'official' accounts of the subject.

LOCATIONS

I need to locate the teachers' memories into a number of contexts. This means understanding how various social, historical and political circumstances came together to influence their attitudes and identities. This is not a simple case of cause and effect, and to help understand these processes, I adopted the *Annales* concept of 'conjunctures'. In the twentieth century *Annales* historians re-orientated historiographical approaches away from linear, chronological accounts of past events, concentrating instead on long-term economic and social history: the *longue durée*. Alongside studies of economic cycles over long periods, *Annales* historians identified 'crises', marked turning points within the larger patterns, which they called 'conjunctures'. Braudel (1995: 118, originally published in 1958) describes the implications of these historiographical changes, where 'conjunctures' open up 'large sections of the past, ten, twenty or even fifty years at a stretch ready for examination'. Goodson (2004) argues that it is in these key moments, the conjunctures, that lasting change occurs,

> The most interesting points of inquiry and investigation are when the different layers of historical time coincide; for it is at these points that inclination towards, and capacity for, change and reform are strongest. Such co-incidences or conjunctures can be seen in key moments of educational history and change. (2004: 17)

The period under scrutiny here, 1965–1975, was one such period. So to understand the teachers' memories it is crucial to locate them into what Goodson (2003) refers to as a 'genealogy of context'. That is, it is necessary to trace the evolution of various trajectories, proclivities and convictions that constitute the teachers' collective identities. It also means analysing what Hardcastle (2008: 4) suggests are 'circumstances and the chance intersections that constitute the "milieu" in which events unfold'. But change does not happen because of 'chance intersections' alone, human agency is instrumental. For this reason the term 'conjuncture' can take on radical connotations. For example, Althusser (1969) suggests it is characterised by complex layers of tangled, changeable power relations in a given period. Understanding the complex relations within a conjuncture makes it possible to examine the effects of various structures, conditions and political interventions. Critical analysis of these effects can highlight contradictions, areas of weakness, which offer up exploitable opportunities to force through change. As Stuart Hall (1987: 16) argues, by determining 'what is *specific* and *different* about this moment', it is possible to understand 'how different forces come together, conjuncturally, to create the new terrain, on which a different politics must form up'. This means taking action to turn circumstances to one's own advantage. It appears some English teachers in this conjuncture, in the 'cauldron', did just this.

This conception of conjunctures is important in this book. The teachers present themselves as active agents of change, and they took advantage of existing circumstances to re-imagine English teaching in a variety of ways. Locating their narratives into the wider 'genealogy of context' helps to sediment their collective experience. But the book also has broader ambitions. By offering an example of how the PM of this generation of teachers, in this conjuncture, can be scrutinised, it is hoped that current practitioners might be provoked into a critical examination and discussion of their own circumstances. In this way, PM studies might have transformative potential – if English teachers can define their own priorities and motivations, it might be possible to highlight conflicts and contradictions between what they *want* to be doing and how they are forced to operate in existing circumstances.

Locating the Teachers' Experiences

The teachers have lived through various conjunctures that have influenced their conceptions of 'English', their professional identities, attitudes and practices. Being born during or immediately after World War Two, their early memories appear to have been constructed at a time of hardship, but also optimism. Cities were literally being re-built; there was rationing and widespread poverty. But it was also a time of 'make do and mend', a reliance on communities to 'muck in'. This period saw the development of the 'welfare state', which Ball suggests is characterised by 'post-war economic growth and the expansion of the middle class', alongside the move towards 'universalist welfare state education' (2008: 57). Yet, while the 1944 'Butler' Education Act finally provided secondary education to all children, it was implemented through the tiered and inequitable 'tripartite' system (Jones, 2003).

CHAPTER 1

And as John Dixon (1991: 149) says of the time: 'The taken-for-granted structure of education, you might say, was an echo of the class structure'. However, in a time of 'consensus' politics, the institutionalisation of the National Health Service and education system were seen as ways of improving ordinary lives and social justice. For some, education was crucial for the further democratisation of British society (see Simon, 1953, 1955; Williams, 1961). Indeed, Raymond Williams's prophecy in 1961 seems especially portentous in current contexts,

> It is a question of whether we can grasp the real nature of our society, or whether we persist in social and educational patterns based on a limited ruling class, a middle professional class, a large operative class, cemented by forces that cannot be challenged and will not be changed. The privileges and barriers, of an inherited kind, will in any case go down. It is only a question of whether we replace them by the free play of the market, or by a public education designed to express and create the values of an educated democracy and a common culture. (2011: 186, originally published in 1961)

In the 'cauldron' some teachers attempted to re-orientate the aims of English towards the advancement of 'an educated democracy'. But these groups were by no means dominant. Systemic segregation along class lines is an indelible aspect of educational history and school English in the period was influenced by these historic factors. There are examples of progressive practice in the 1950s, but for the majority of children tripartism resulted in very different experiences of English. Indeed, the distinct cultures of some grammar and secondary modern schools encouraged social inequality unashamedly. Medway argues English was designed for different outcomes in each context, and some secondary moderns 'unambiguously emphasised preparation for subordinate roles in life'. They promoted skills and values intended to 'produce a useful, responsible and inoffensive citizen with a respect, based on slight acquaintance, for literary culture'. English in these schools was defined by the 'school's socialising function' (1990: 5) rather than a comprehensive apprenticeship in the subject.

Yet some groups of teachers in the 1950s were dissatisfied with these circumstances and initiated reforms that re-conceptualised the subject in more democratic ways (see Medway et al., 2014; Gibbons, 2013). Lines of work emerged that gave school English a 'new' identity and templates were generated for future generations to draw on. Gibbons (2009, 2013) demonstrates how this new English was significantly influenced by a community of teachers in London, and particularly through the work of LATE. The new model aimed to negotiate and develop a curriculum that was relevant and responsive to children's experiences, backgrounds and cultures. Dissatisfaction with the tripartite system meant London County Council was supportive of the burgeoning comprehensive movement (Gibbons, 2009). Throughout the 1950s English in some London schools changed radically. Hardcastle and Medway (2013) foreground Harold Rosen's pioneering work at LATE, and at Walworth School, an early 'experimental' comprehensive.

In the 1950s however, because 'there had been no comprehensives there had been no English for comprehensives' (2013: 35), Walworth essentially had a streamed system. But Rosen initiated a series of curriculum developments to produce a version of English that 'owed much to the comprehensive school ideal' (2013: 34). Through the collaboration of colleagues at the school and in LATE, a model emerged that challenged existing conceptions of the subject: 'less about what's called "methods" than "aims", what English should be *trying* to do' (2013: 37).

Throughout the 1960s English teachers had increasing opportunities to work collaboratively and to engage critically with the aims and intentions of the subject. After 1965, ILEA encouraged collaboration between its schools and teachers and provided a network of local Teachers' Centres. Joint advisory and inspection teams meant good practice was circulated, with support and guidance readily available (Lowe, 2007). And in 1975 when ILEA established The English Centre, practitioners had unprecedented access to resources, publishing opportunities, courses, conferences and spaces to work co-operatively. The English Centre evolved through an organic desire to institutionalise arrangements for creating partnerships between teachers and different schools. It also aimed to put practitioners at the forefront of curriculum development.

These developments occurred against a backdrop of wider social change. Lowe (2007) highlights dramatic changes in social attitudes because of increasing affluence in the 1950s and 1960s. Organised social and political movements demanded solidarity for oppressed groups; there were protests against the Vietnam War, Civil Rights Movement, and 'Counterculture' which generated a sense of militancy that filtered into social institutions, including schools. Lowe suggests it is unsurprising that what was happening in schools 'should be seen to be changing swiftly and to be particularly controversial at this time' (2007: 40). By 1965 events culminated in various kinds of social, cultural and political change. Comprehensive education was promoted; popular cultural movements in art, music and film burgeoned; there was some political will to tackle issues such as racism, homophobia, capital punishment and abortion (Bray, 2014). A young generation of teachers engaged in political debate and with new theoretical perspectives on language and literature. The coming together of different circumstances in this conjuncture created favourable conditions for some practitioners to challenge the status quo. John Dixon puts it like this:

> These were heady days intellectually, for the young in spirit – and also for the combative, rebellious and iconoclastic: for respected authorities were challenged, of course. (1991: 175)

These two conjunctures appear to have enabled the teachers to construct attitudes and approaches that have remained with them throughout their careers. The period after WW2, which saw the development of the Welfare State, seems to have provided a resilient sense of solidarity. The period when they began teaching, the 'cauldron', presented them with opportunities and creative possibilities which they took up enthusiastically.

CHAPTER 1

APPROACHES

Generating PM is a collective enterprise. The evidence presented in this book is the result of collaboration between the teachers and me. To investigate their collective PM I used well-established methods. I adopted a life history approach and drew on Ivor Goodson's substantial body of work in this field.[3] Memories of professional practice cannot be isolated from other experience, identity, culture, language and so on. Nor can they be understood without being located into the various contexts and conjunctures that influence their construction – Goodson's 'genealogy of context'. This requires a study of depth that brings together different types of research. To understand the contextual background I carried out documentary research. I examined existing histories of English teaching, various policy documents, white papers, reports, text books, resources. The teachers' memories were explored through multiple semi-structured interviews and biographical questionnaires, which resulted in substantial life stories. Goodson and Sikes (2001) differentiate between life 'story', as told by informant, and life 'history', as created collaboratively between life historian, informant and resulting 'data'. The move to create life 'history' is a sensitive one and it requires careful and honest interpretation on the part of the researcher. But where life 'stories' might be told in personal, idiosyncratic narratives, life 'history' has to offer an insight into the intricate relationship between individual narratives and the wider social, political, historical and cultural contexts in which they are situated. I constructed life 'histories' through Goodson and Sikes's favoured (2001: 163) three-stage process of 'narration' (where interviews were conducted); 'collaboration' (where the teachers and I considered transcripts, checked meaning, identified gaps); and 'location' (where the individual stories were located into the wider contexts).

However, because I was interested in the teachers' *collective* PM I needed to broaden the methodological approach. I developed Goodson's life history approach by combining it with collective memory methods. Memory is often viewed from an individualist perspective but I wanted to explore the extent to which it is a socially distributed phenomenon. When individuals generate memories they become irreducibly social. Maurice Halbwachs (1992) conceptualises memory as a collective social construct that is coloured by a diversity of external influences. Individual memory is unintelligible without the skilful control of socially constructed communicative tools in a given culture. These tools supply templates for individuals to narrate and represent what they view as personal, subjective memories. But memory construction is a dialectical, trans-individual process. As such it is intensely ideological and submerged in issues of power, language, society, history and culture (Shotter, 1990). Memory allows individuals to envisage how they were in the past (Middleton & Edwards, 1990). But when the past is recovered and reproduced through social narrative it is done with particular intentions (Rosen, 1998). As Shotter (1990: 123) puts it, we tell our stories 'to constitute and sustain one or other kind of social order'. In this way individuals maintain identities and relationships by drawing on collective memory. In combining life history with collective memory approaches I have been able to generate collective narratives that allow for multi-layered interpretation. This approach can highlight the ways that teachers' personal and professional identities are mediated through various collective contexts. A collective memory approach to PM reveals how groups of teachers wish to be represented, their values, concerns and practices they promote.

Conducting the Research

Six teachers participated in multiple semi-structured interviews, lasting between seventy-five and one-hundred minutes. To understand how their memories, identities and working practices developed, I designed questions with Goodson's 'genealogy of context' in mind. The teachers were asked questions focussing on different aspects and stages of their lives and careers. First, questions about their early experiences of 'English', how they were socialised into the subject at home or school before becoming teachers. Next, questions focussed explicitly on early professional practice in the conjuncture 1965–1975. Finally, questions focussed on their attitudes to current circumstances in English teaching. This structure allowed me to produce holistic professional life histories, and made it possible to consider how the beliefs and attitudes they took into teaching influenced their early practice. It is also possible to consider how various circumstances in the 'cauldron' influenced their identities, memories, narratives and practices. Finally, after full careers, it is possible to consider how previous experience contributes to current attitudes. So, in the first round of interviews, questions were structured to focus on distinct 'phases' in the teachers' development: what I termed 'initial', 'developmental' and 'professional':

- *Initial phase*: teachers' memories of their own 'schooling' in English

  Questions designed to tease out information about teachers' own experiences of English at home, in the community, at school, teaching methods, teachers, any subsequent study, university, teacher training etc.

- *Developmental phase*: memories of early professional practice, career development

  Focus explicitly on memories of early professional practice, individual lessons, networking, collegiality, professional development, career development etc. Formative development of professionalism 1965–1975

- *Professional phase*: current attitudes to the profession

  Professional judgements and thoughts based on experience, current attitudes to English teaching, examples of practice which have stood the test of time, suggestions for future practice

CHAPTER 1

Following the first round of interviews, my early analysis looked to identify collective elements in the stories. Decisions made at this point informed the question design for the subsequent interviews. Follow-up interviews were deliberately less structured than the first. Some initial questions were rephrased and asked again to see if there was any consistency in the narratives. I was initially struck by the way the teachers referred separately to broadly similar events in their lives and careers. This prompted me to return with questions about those particular events and moments. A third set of questions were informant-specific, with each being asked questions about their unique stories in the earlier interviews. The reason for asking individualised questions in a study about 'collective' memory was to highlight areas of divergence as well as convergence.

When interpreting the teachers' stories I tried to understand how they make sense of their professional lives through narrative. All narratives are produced in particular contexts which affect ways of telling, motivations, intentions and so on. In that case I was interested in how various dialectical processes influence the teachers' narratives, which in turn shape their collective social reality. In analysing the narratives I was not seeking to reveal the 'truth', but I was trying to uncover the ways '…individuals make sense of their lived experience and how its telling enables them to interpret the social world and their agency within it' (Gill & Goodson, 2011: 160).

I was interested in how the life stories might relate to the realities of lived experience: to understand meanings in context. I avoided the impossible task of trying to recover and recreate what the teachers said or thought at the moments they constructed their memories. Rather, I tried to mediate the stories in an attempt to bring out what seemed significant. My interest was not that of a linguist, looking at underlying forms and structures, but rather in the textures and weightings of how the teachers express understandings of their professional lives. Themes and issues were selected that seemed significant because all participants referred to them and because they were reinforced multiple times. But I am also interested in how social power relations are evident in collective memories. So I was drawn to stories that appeared to run counter to dominant discourses around schooling and English. Examples include the teachers suggesting they were 'rebellious' at school, being drawn to teachers who challenged the status quo, or suggesting they learned nothing in their English lessons – they were 'self-taught'. They all point to events and episodes that seem to have had a lasting effect. Sometimes issues emerged that were quite independent of the interview questions. For example all the teachers suggest they could read before they went to school, and they enthuse about the opportunities offered by ILEA. Some of the stories share remarkable similarities, suggesting the narratives are indeed aimed at achieving a sense of collective identity. Despite coming from diverse backgrounds the teachers refer to broadly similar concerns in their work.

I hope it will already be clear that my interpretive approach has several intentions. To develop an understanding of PM the analysis considers how the teachers developed attitudes to English in their early years. These memories relate to their subsequent constructions of identity as particular types of practitioners. In turn memories of professional practice influence the teachers' attitudes to current contexts in English teaching.

The Teachers

The six teachers (Ann, Steve, Michael, Shaun, Liz, David) were recruited because they began their careers between 1965 and 1975. They all worked in London and they represent a range of backgrounds in terms of social class, education and political outlook. They are not representative of all English teachers in the 'cauldron'. They were recruited through purposive, snowball and convenience sampling. These methods are liable to produce particular effects: a degree of commonality, a level of homogeneity. Therefore they represent a particular *type* of English teacher in the period that might be described as 'progressive' or 'radical'. To generate their narratives now, they access memories from much earlier periods in their lives. But they are all skilled users of narrative, which has clearly been developed over the years. Goodson (2013) argues life narratives can generally be located on a spectrum of 'description to elaboration'. The 'descriptive' end of this spectrum tends to be populated by narrators with fairly low levels of reflexivity and agency. 'Scripted describers' seem unaccustomed to producing critical, transformative life narratives. At the opposite end 'focussed elaborators' are highly reflexive and flexible. Narrative is used self-confidently to implement a clear 'personal vision'. Elaborators have the ability to re-position themselves throughout life, with strong narrative identity continuously reconfigured. The teachers in this book are highly sensitive to the intentions behind their narratives, which can be read as representing narrators from the *agentive* end of Goodson's spectrum: elaborators.

Some of the teachers became high-profile figures in London English teaching. This presented an ethical dilemma. It became clear from the interviews that some of them knew each other. This made sense; they all started teaching around the same time; they all worked in London, for ILEA; they had networked and attended courses together at the Institute of Education and the English Centre. Some of them did other public work which meant they would quite easily be identifiable to colleagues from the time. For example, until recently, Michael still ran the English and Media Centre (originally the English Centre) and it would not take much to be able to identify him if I referred to this important aspect of his career. I felt it would be too convoluted to try and anonymise the English Centre with another name. This led to the decision that it would be better to name the participants. There is nothing particularly controversial about this research and on balance it seemed the participants would not come to any 'harm' by being named (BERA, 2011). But ensuring anonymity is a golden rule in human research and any violations of it must 'be made with the agreement of the participants' (Cohen et al., 2011: 91). So the teachers were asked to give written informed consent. The option of anonymity remained and there was no coercion. All the teachers are happy to be named.

CHAPTER 1

I invited them to complete biographical questionnaires. These were designed to help contextualise the teachers' backgrounds and elicit information about personal circumstances, the schools they attended, routes into teaching, schools they worked at and wider professional development. I used this information to construct brief biographies and generate a sense of the teachers' lives before interviewing them. This made it possible to map career development and professional identity alongside changes in different conjunctures. One way of contextualising professional development is by understanding what Goodson calls the 'personality of change', exploring how 'each teacher has to construct a personal professionalism that suits his or her life history, training, context and, above all, personality' (2003: 74). Some of these elements pre-date working age so biographical information helps to understand these processes. There are different 'personalities of change' for the individual teachers, as well as the collective personality of change for the whole group. This book will explore these issues. At this point however, I want to introduce the teachers:

Ann

Ann is a Londoner who was head of English in the first school I worked at. She attended a private, all girls' boarding school in Sussex, from where she gained O' levels and A' levels. From there she studied English at Reading University. Initially, Ann had no intention of becoming a teacher and left Reading to pursue a career as a potter. However, she eventually trained to be an English teacher. Her first teaching job was at Churchfields School in West Bromwich, which she describes as being very 'progressive and innovative' at the time (late 1960s – Ann did not want to specify dates). She moved from there to schools in Leicestershire, where she became second in department in two schools, then head of department in another. She moved back to London in the mid-1970s where she took up head of department roles. She eventually took a role as English consultant for an outer London Local Education Authority. She has now retired.

David

David is a Londoner who passed the eleven-plus and attended Grammar School from 1958 to 1965. He gained O' levels and A' levels. From there he studied for a Certificate in Education (Cert. Ed) at Christ Church College, Canterbury from 1965–1969. He started teaching in 1969 at Rutherford School in London, achieving various promotions during ten years there. He became second in English in 1970 and head of English in 1971. He maintained this role until 1980, but from 1979 he was also Acting Deputy Head. From 1980–1984 he was senior teacher at Battersea County School, where he was also Acting Deputy Head from 1982. In 1984 he was seconded by ILEA to be advisory teacher and local English Centre leader for Camden, Westminster and Islington. After this he was a senior lecturer in English at Roehampton University until 1988. Since then David has worked as English adviser for a London Local Education Authority. He gained a Master's degree from the Institute of Education. He has also published articles on English teaching and various resource books through the English Centre. David has since retired from all permanent roles and now works as an independent consultant.

Steve

Steve is a Londoner who 'failed' the eleven-plus and attended two secondary modern schools: first Balham Boys' School in London, before moving to Charles Chute Boys' School in Basingstoke. He gained O' levels and A' levels. From 1970 to 1974 he trained to teach at St Paul's College, Cheltenham, studying first for a Cert. Ed then a Bachelor of Education (B. Ed). His first teaching post was at Woodside School in London. He was a classroom teacher from 1974 to 1994, teaching English, drama, media, film and occasionally history. In his first decade as a teacher, Steve became 'heavily involved in trade union and Labour activity'. From 1983 to 1990 he was an elected member of ILEA. Steve has two MAs and a PhD from the Institute of Education. He has taught at Roehampton University and is currently a lecturer at the Institute of Education. He has worked in vocational training and assessing and he has written and published histories of professional football clubs. His main work is in History of Education.

Liz

Liz is a Londoner. She passed the eleven-plus and attended Ursuline Convent School in Wimbledon from 1950 to 1963. This was an all girls' Grammar School in an affluent part of south-west London and she gained O' levels and A' levels. From 1963 to 1966 she trained as a Drama teacher at Digby Stuart College, Roehampton. From there she taught drama and English at Holland Park School from 1966 to 1974. At the same time as teaching, Liz converted her teaching certificate into a B. Ed at the Institute in 1971/72. She became editor of London Drama Magazine in 1977, a job she continued until 1989. As well as editing, Liz taught English at Richmond-upon-Thames College from 1980 to 2008. She completed an MA at the Institute of Education between 1985 and 1987. Liz has edited a number of books, notably on drama practitioner Dorothy Heathcote. She taught English and Drama from 1966 to 2008. She has now retired.

Shaun

Shaun grew up in Lancashire, where his parents had settled after moving from Ireland. His father was an English teacher. Shaun attended a Catholic seminary, St Michael's College, from 1960 to 1967 where he gained O' levels and A' levels. However, he decided against joining the priesthood and left to study history at Lancaster University. He disliked the history course and transferred to English,

CHAPTER 1

developing an interest in sociolinguistics. He left Lancaster and studied for a PGCE at Nottingham University in 1970/71. From there he took his first teaching post at Holt Comprehensive in Liverpool from 1972 to 1974. In 1974 Shaun moved to Holloway School in Islington and worked there until 2001. He has since taught English at City and Islington College. Shaun studied for an MA at the Institute of Education between 1984 and 1985. He has published various articles about socialism and language, with a particular interest in the work of Volosinov. Shaun has been a long-standing member of the Socialist Workers' Party and has organised a number of high-profile campaigns.

Michael

Michael is a Londoner. He attended Merchant Taylor's school from 1955 to 1960 where he gained O' levels. From there he attended High Wycombe Grammar school to study A' levels, 1960–1962. He then studied English at Jesus College, Oxford from 1963 to 1966. From Oxford he briefly taught at the University of Tubingen before returning to complete a PGCE at Sussex University in 1966/67. He took up a teaching post at Wandsworth School and worked there from 1968 to 1975. During this time, Michael contributed to various courses and seminars through LATE, and at the Institute of Education. With colleagues he produced materials for a series of seminars called 'Teaching London Kids' in the early 1970s. These seminar groups evolved and he became a founding editor of the magazine of the same name in 1972. In 1975 he approached ILEA with the idea of setting up the English Centre, which provided resources, courses and support for teachers in Inner London. Michael ran the Centre from 1975 to 1990, when the abolition of the ILEA under the Thatcher government meant funding ceased. The Centre now runs independently as the English and Media Centre. Of all of the teachers, he has been away from the classroom the longest. He has now retired.

STRUCTURE OF THE BOOK

In the following chapters I will explore the teachers' collective PM from a number of perspectives. Chapter 2 examines a range of conjunctural circumstances and issues relevant to the 'cauldron'. The aim is to provide contextual backdrop to the teachers' narratives. In Chapter 3 I consider the concept of PM from a range of theoretical perspectives. These include conceptions of collective memory, social constructionism and narrative representation. Chapter 4 explores the teachers' early experiences of 'English' at home and at school. Chapter 5 focuses on their early teaching practice in the 'cauldron' 1965–1975. Chapter 6 considers their current attitudes to English teaching. Chapter 7 discusses and tries to make sense of the teachers' memories from a range of perspectives. Finally, Chapter 8 looks at the potential of PM studies for future developments in English teaching.

ACKNOWLEDGEMENT

Sections of this chapter have appeared, in other forms, in Tarpey, P. (2015). Professional memory in context: Can it help counter the "counter-revolution". *Changing English, 22*(4), 382–392; Tarpey, P. (2016). "Fire Burn and Cauldron Bubble": What are the conjunctural effects on English teacher professional memories, identities and narratives? *Changing English, 23*(1), 77–93; and Tarpey, P. (2017a). 'We not I' not 'I me mine': Learning from professional memory about collectivist English teaching. *Changing English, 24*(1), 103–117.

NOTES

[1] See for example Ball, Bowe and Gewirtz (1995); Ball (2008); Burgess, Briggs, McConnell and Slater (2006); Coffey (2001); West, Hind and Pennell (2004); Burgess, Propper and Wilson (2007).

[2] See for example Goodson (1992a); Goodson and Hargreaves (1996); Goodson (2003); Goodson (2005a); Goodson, Moore and Hargreaves (2006); Ben-Peretz (1995); Ben-Peretz (2002); Cunningham and Gardner (2004); Cunningham (2007); Gardner and Cunningham (1998); Gardner (2003).

[3] See for example Ball and Goodson (1985); Beynon (1985); Fliesser and Goodson (1992); Goodson and Walker (1991); Walker and Goodson (1991); Goodson (1992a); Goodson (1992b); Goodson & Mangan (1992); Goodson & Cole (1992); Middleton (1992); Butt, Raymond, McCue and Yamagishi (1992); Nelson (1992); Measor and Sikes (1992); Goodson (1994); Helsby and McCulloch (1996); Goodson and Hargreaves (1996); Goodson (1999); Goodson and Sikes (2001); Goodson (2003); Goodson (2004); Goodson (2005a); Goodson and Choi (2008); Gill and Goodson (2011), Goodson (2013); Goodson and Rudd (2016): some of these are in volumes edited by Goodson.

CHAPTER 2

CONJUNCTURES, CONTEXTS, CIRCUMSTANCES

INTRODUCTION

To contextualise the teachers' narratives I need to establish some of the circumstances and events in the conjuncture 1965–1975, to create Goodson's 'genealogy of context'. My intention is not to produce a comprehensive history here, but rather to offer a *sense of the time* by focussing on selected issues and developments relating directly to the teachers' early professional experiences. This conjuncture is sometimes depicted as a 'golden age' of teacher autonomy and progressivism. However, this mythology has been challenged (see Jones, 2003; Cunningham, 2007; Lowe, 2007; Goodson, 2005b). Lowe (2007) examines some of the systemic changes in educational approaches, practices and curricula in Britain since WW2. He argues 'progressive' education is 'dead', and the period most closely associated with it, the 1960s/1970s, should be viewed as a 'period of partial and timid change' (2007: 60), rather than one of wholesale radical and progressive development. Certainly, there are examples of progressive practice in this period. But Lowe suggests powerful voices from other traditions were not prepared to countenance change that militated against often narrow, hierarchical assumptions about educational processes and outcomes. Some of the fiercest opposition to democratic change came from those who had attended grammar schools. These include Brian Cox and Anthony Dyson, editors of the infamous *Black Papers* on education in the late 1960s (1969a, 1969b, 1971). These 'meritocratic elitists', Lowe argues, were symptomatic of existing circumstances, structures and traditions. But they contributed to an increasingly powerful discourse calling for a more rigid, controlling and interventionist attitude to education from the late 1960s. In short the conjuncture 1965–1975 is partly characterised by ideological clashes over educational processes, practices and structures. For these reasons, Lowe concludes,

> The picture which emerges of educational change during the 1960s and 1970s is one that is very complex and far from straightforward. (2007: 58)

Nonetheless, the period was one of significant educational change. And this appears particularly true of English teaching. The subject is a site of contestation and ideological struggle. To take one example, Deborah Cameron (1995) highlights the 'moral panic' of the 'great grammar crusade' in the 1980s. Formal grammar teaching has been a ubiquitous and thorny issue in the history of the subject. By

CHAPTER 2

the 1980s its supposed withdrawal in the 'cauldron' was connected with social and moral decline. Slapdash models of practice were attributed to progressive English teachers, who have been consistently derided. Debates have been 'liberally garnished' with 'scare stories about falling standards among pupils and ideological subversion among teachers' (1995: 89). In the 1970s, controversies like the 'William Tyndale Affair'[1] contributed to this narrative of 'subversion' and influenced broader debates about the nature and purposes of education. Stories of teacher radicalism, bad practice and falling standards provided a backdrop to James Callaghan's Ruskin College Speech in 1976. He argued for greater centralised control of education and policy directed by economic demand. So periods of change provoke conservative reaction. Indeed, political, cultural and structural re-organisation aimed at securing and maintaining long-cherished hegemonies is evident everywhere. In education, conservative re-organisation in these critical moments is well documented (see for example Ball, 2008; Jones, 1989, 2003; Goodson, 2005a; Lowe, 2007), and frequently vitriolic, with most venom aimed at supporters of comprehensive and progressive education. In these periods English becomes intensely politicised because it deals with language and fundamental aspects of national culture and identity. And, as Gramsci taught us – 'Every time the issue of language surfaces…it means that a series of other problems are coming to the fore'. The 'governing class' re-positions itself to preserve dominant relationships with 'the national-popular mass': actions intended 'to re-organise the cultural hegemony' (1985: 183–184).

Conservative criticism of English is common currency (see Allen, 1980; Marenbon, 1994; Cameron, 1995; Davies, 1996; Coultas, 2013), and policy interventions in recent decades (the National Curriculum, the focus on 'functional' literacy, the re-introduction of formal grammar testing and the downgrading of classroom talk) have re-orientated English away from the more democratic conceptualisation of the 1975 Bullock Report, to the culturally elitist curriculum of today. Much criticism focusses on the supposed excesses of the mythological 'golden age' in the 1960s/1970s: a period often stigmatised as having low standards, weak practitioners and high levels of 'failure'. However, there is abundant written evidence of positive, progressive development in education generally since WW2 (see for example Simon, 1953, 1955; Williams, 2011; Benn & Simon, 1972; Jones, 1983, 2003; Lowe, 2007). English in particular saw dramatic change in these periods (see Dixon, 1967, 1991; Rosen, 1972, 1981; Shayer, 1972; Medway, 1980, 1990; Ball, Kenny, & Gardiner, 1990; Burgess, 2002; Gibbons, 2013; Medway, Hardcastle, Brewis, & Crook, 2014). Curriculum, assessment, pedagogy, learning and children's agency were re-imagined by pioneering practitioners in new ways. There have been struggles over what English *is*. But no settled history of English teaching has been established. Some existing histories are so opposed that they risk de-stabilising coherent conceptions of the subject altogether. Here, I am interested in the controversial tradition of 'progressive' or 'radical' English teaching.

PROGRESSIVE AND RADICAL TRADITIONS

The roots of progressive education can be traced through various philosophical traditions (Howlett, 2013). Empiricism, Rationalism and Idealism offer different perspectives on the nature and acquisition of knowledge, and they influenced educational pioneers like Pestalozzi, Froebel, Dewey and Montessori who conceptualised learning in more 'child-centred' ways (Ornstein & Levine, 2000). In England in the early twentieth century, progressive education was mostly evident in private schools such as A.S. Neill's Summerhill, founded in 1921 (Watts, 2002). But the Hadow Reports of the 1920s and 1930s promoted a somewhat more progressive approach for state schools, insisting,

> We are of the opinion that the curriculum of the primary school should be thought of in terms of activity and experience rather than of knowledge to be acquired and facts to be stored. (1931: 140)

Hadow also proposed replacing 'elementary' schools with a primary/secondary model (Galton, Simon, & Croll, 1980; McCulloch, 2002a; Gillard, 2006). The development of state schooling in England, while not being necessarily *progressive*, is partly a story of progress. Gary McCulloch (2000) divides educational history into three distinct versions of the past: 'official', 'private' and 'public'. He demonstrates how the 'official' past, the version promoted by the state, is subject to change during different economic, cultural and political periods. From the 1920s to the 1960s McCulloch argues the 'official' past was recognisable for promoting a 'liberal notion of steady, gradual evolution towards social improvement' (2000: 9). Official policy documents in this period utilised educational history to justify developments and improvements to the system. However, by the early 1970s the 'official' past no longer corresponded with the perceived social realities of teachers, politicians or public, and this version of the past, as it had existed until then, was obliterated. Its absence from official discourses paved the way for various kinds of aggressive ideological assault. However, it resurfaces in the 1980s in a very different guise:

> This was the antithesis of the liberal-progressive version of the past that had been so potent a generation before. History became a story of failure and disappointment, even of betrayal. It was seen increasingly as part of the problem, as an explanation of failure, rather than as the basis for solutions. A hostile, negative view of history as the enemy of an improved future is a striking feature of education policies in the 1980s, representing in many ways an estrangement from the educational past. (2000: 11)

This re-framing of the 'official' past has helped those on the right to generate discourses that intensify this 'estrangement'. But in the first half of the twentieth century there was increasing momentum to replace 'elementary' schools with primary/secondary education. This change eventually came through the 1944 Education Act. Consequently, some primary schools in England developed strong traditions of progressive practice, despite in many cases being rigidly streamed (Simon, 1994; Cunningham, 2002). By the early 1960s the issue of streaming children was considered discriminatory, and a teacher-led movement brought about dramatic change, until 'by the early 1970s, you could hardly find a single streamed primary school in the country' (Simon, 1994: 175). The 1967 Plowden Report reflected these developments and progressive change that occurred in some primary schools was underpinned by particular principles, as Ken Jones argues,

> Progressivism was a diverse and complex movement, but it centred fundamentally on three assertions: children were unique individuals; learning was the product of the active relationship between individual and their environment; learning was best organised through collaboration between students and their teachers. (2003: 54)

These assertions influenced the identities and missions of some teachers in the 1960s/1970s. But some groups thought these developments did not go far enough. Educational processes were inevitably bound-up with issues around children's rights, fair competition, equality of outcome and seeking an improved society. This more 'radical' interpretation deliberately sought to locate educational practices into a range of political and ideological contexts. Howlett argues 'radicalism' is a diverse and complicated tradition, incorporating sometimes competing ideological perspectives. He offers 'levellers', 'diggers', 'suffragettes' and 'chartists' as examples of this. However there appear to be 'common factors' that give radical groups impetus, including, 'a desire to improve and better the lot of the disenfranchised and marginalised groups within society' (2013: 211). In different periods these might have included the working class, religious minorities, women, ethnic groups and so on. A conception of education as crucial for delivering emancipation is a common characteristic of radical movements. Howlett claims,

> Consequently, it is perhaps unsurprising that, in the context of radical social movements and amid deep-seated and often revolutionary calls for 'root and branch' change and reform, education has often had a central role to play. It is a common opinion, for example, of the 'left' in England that self- improvement stems from self-enlightenment, which itself, in turn, emanates from education. (2013: 211)

Progressive and radical movements in education are not mutually exclusive, each informs the other. But in the 1960s and 1970s they were neither unified nor universal. Jones (1989, 2003) suggests competing traditions meant progressive and radical approaches had no unifying rationale. This made them vulnerable to broader criticisms that ultimately eroded faith in progressive approaches, missions and values. Jones (1989) is particularly critical of progressivism's failure to develop coherent strategies for improving children's agency,

But progressivism, though it correctly stated the importance of building educational development upon the interests and motivation of the individual, did not sufficiently consider issues of curriculum content. Stressing 'discovery', 'relevance' and 'expression', it downplayed the enormity of the task of equipping non-privileged students with the knowledge and conceptual equipment they would need to improve their life-chances, still less to understand and change their world. (1989: 131)

Instead, Jones argues for radical 'socialist alternatives'. In English teaching progressivism was realised through different and sometimes competing traditions. But it was probably in secondary schools where more radical versions of the subject evolved. Different approaches emerged through the pioneering work of teachers like Harold Rosen, James Britton and John Dixon in the 1950s, 1960s and 1970s. Dissatisfied with the impoverished state of English, these practitioners attempted to generate a 'new' approach (Gibbons, 2013; Medway et al., 2014), through which they sought to make positive connections with students' social realities. Harold Rosen (1972) recognised the importance of understanding students' cultural backgrounds and encouraged the use of children's own language as a fundamental teaching resource.

The conjuncture 1965–1975 offered favourable circumstances for various kinds of change in English teaching, in terms of subject content, outlook and aims. Circumstances also meant that particular types of teacher identity could be constructed. And although progressive and radical approaches were never mainstream, many practitioners were attracted to their humane ideals and values. Some energetic young teachers experimented with new ways of working that ultimately broadened the parameters of English. The teachers in this book entered the profession during this period. They are sensitive to differences between 'progressive' and 'radical' traditions. For them, progressivism is associated with innovative classroom practice and child-centred approaches. Radical perspectives target the strengthening of children's agency and critical consciousness.

LOCATING ENGLISH INTO A WIDER GENEALOGY OF CONTEXT

School English has not evolved in a vacuum. It has been actively shaped through complicated developments in political, economic and cultural processes, by different events, attitudes and values throughout its history. Here I want to give a selected view of how English evolved alongside broader circumstances and developments. A century before 1965 there was no state education in England (Morton, 1997). In fact, there was strong opposition to it. Clyde Chitty argues this came mostly from a privileged elite who thought 'too much education or schooling would simply make the working poor discontented with their lot' (2004: 4). Educating the poor was neither desirable nor in-keeping with existing hierarchical social structures. But at the height of the Industrial Revolution the populations of cities were rapidly

CHAPTER 2

expanding, which increased pressure to provide education for various reasons. There were domestic concerns over potential rebellion among the working poor. As Simon (1994) points out, working-class movements gathered momentum with collectivist institutions, trade unions and organisations being established. There were also fears over Britain's economic standing internationally: some European countries and the USA were developing education systems. Raymond Williams (2011) argues three main factions influenced the eventual development of state education in England, with each group promoting different ends – from those advocating democracy, to those wishing to 'rescue the poor' from themselves, to those emphasising economic prosperity. Similarly, Simon highlights increasing pressure throughout the nineteenth century, with some 'educational measures undertaken and supported by the industrial and commercial middle class in England' (2005: 143). However, this support was not necessarily benevolent, and could be seen as a response to 'the rapidly growing and perhaps threatening independent political and educational activity of working people at that time' (2005: 143). A complicated mix of economic imperatives, class struggles and clashing ideologies influenced the eventual development of the elementary system (Aldrich, 1982).

The hierarchical social structure at the time inevitably influenced education provision. This is evidenced in three mid-nineteenth century reports. The Clarendon Report (1864) promoted the privileged position of the 'great public schools'. The Taunton Commission (1868) focussed on three 'grades' of secondary school, mostly for the middle classes, while the Newcastle Report (1861) was concerned with elementary education for the masses (see Williams, 2011; Wardle, 1976; Goodson, 1983; Gordon, 2002). Social divisions along class lines have dominated education in England. But the various debates at the time culminated in the 1870 Education Act, which ensured some form of education even for the poorest children (Goodson, 1983; Aldrich, 2006). Elementary schools focussed on the 'three Rs', with basic literacy, numeracy and bible study being the order of the day. But the decades following 1870 saw political, social and cultural change. Theoretical developments in psychology and social analysis also began to emerge. In terms of education, child-centred perspectives from the likes of Froebel, Dewey and Montessori began to find their way into debates in the early twentieth century (Ornstein & Levine, 2000). However, ideas around 'educability', 'intelligence' and 'aptitude' proved to be more potent (Jones, 2003).

Despite social and cultural change, most working-class children remained in elementary schools until they went to work at fourteen (Chitty, 2007). When a primary/secondary system emerged there were debates about the types of schools to be provided. Benn and Chitty (1996: 5) argue there was determination from 'decision-makers at the Ministry of Education' to implement a 'divided system' of secondary schools. Two reports highlight the thinking at the time. The Spens Report (1938) sketched a model for a tripartite system (McCulloch, 2002b) and the Norwood Report (1943) suggested a divided system based on long-cherished, class-based distinctions (Jones, 2003). Added to the mix now of course, were supposedly 'scientific' assertions about inherited 'intelligence'. Norwood insisted on three distinct 'types' of student with 'enough in common as regards capacities and interests' to justify being placed into 'certain rough groupings' (Norwood Report, 1943: 2). Both reports influenced the 1944 'Butler' Education Act and the resultant 'tripartite' system of secondary schools (grammar, technical, secondary modern).

The tripartite system caused opprobrium as soon as it was implemented. Although the 1944 Act provided secondary education for all, eligibility for grammar schools was decided through the 'eleven plus' test, which apparently tested levels of 'fixed' intelligence. Psychologist Cyril Burt influenced the development of these tests and insisted on the 'absolute determination' of intelligence by 'hereditary or genetic factors' (cited in Galton, Simon, & Croll, 1980: 36). The various schools were promoted as having 'parity of esteem', but this was never the case. Secondary Modern schools became associated with 'failure', as they catered for children who had 'failed' the eleven plus (Jones, 2003). Ultimately the tripartite system worked to reproduce class divisions in a stratified class-ridden society. It also perpetuated the damaging myth that working-class children were generally of lower intelligence than their middle-class peers. Such circumstances were anathema to some teachers and Gibbons (2009) argues that because LEAs were free to devise local models, there was opportunity in some areas for progressive change. McCulloch (2002a) argues that London in particular was in the vanguard of promoting alternative approaches, with a view to setting up a comprehensive system. But this was a long process.

Comprehensivisation occurred throughout the 1950s, 1960s and 1970s. But it became official policy in 1965 when Labour Education Secretary Anthony Crosland published Circular 10/65, which stated,

> It is the Government's declared objective to end selection at eleven plus and to eliminate separatism in secondary education...The Secretary of State accordingly requests local education authorities, if they have not already done so, to prepare and submit to him plans for reorganising secondary education in their areas on comprehensive lines. (Circular 10/65, July 1965)

Not all LEAs did reorganise. But in some areas comprehensivisation meant primary schools were freed from administering the eleven plus, allowing them more freedom to generate their own curricula and approaches. However, newer methods of practice immediately became a target for criticism (Cunningham, 2002; Sharp, 2002; Watts, 2002). And in 1970 Crosland's 'request' to LEAs was rescinded by the new Conservative government, which allowed LEAs to decide themselves whether or not to make systemic changes. This made the process of change inconsistent.

Ideological tensions throughout this period, in the 'cauldron', influenced wider developments and debates around education. Richard Hoggart's *Centre for Contemporary Cultural Studies* opened at Birmingham University in 1964 and generated research in a range of areas. New theoretical perspectives on education emerged through academic literature, magazines and pamphlets, which contributed to the 'spirit of the times'. Notable examples of 'progressive' or 'radical' approaches include Paulo Freire (1970a, 1970b, 1973, 1976), who deliberately attempted to 'conscientise' practitioners and learners. Postman and Weingartner (1969) encouraged practitioners to be 'subversive' and to equip students with the skills of 'crap detection'. David Hargreaves (1967) considered how school structures and negative labelling impacted on actual social relations. Nell Keddie (1971, 1973) investigated the construction of knowledge in classrooms, and the gap between teacher and student expectations. Similarly Michael Young (1971) explored the social construction of knowledge and power relations in the curriculum. Ivan Illich (1971) argued against the institutionalisation and ritualisation of formal education, suggesting schools be abolished. Such work was taken seriously by the teachers in this book and they refer to it in different ways. Series such as *Penguin Education Specials* also contributed to debates by making contemporary issues and new theoretical ideas available to practitioners through inexpensive 'pocket' books. Slightly later, Bowles and Gintis (1976), Willis (1977), Corrigan (1979) and Apple (1979), continued in the tradition of locating education practices and outcomes into wider social, cultural and political contexts. These publications provide a small picture of debates and developments at the time. Yet despite practitioners having access to more research into educational practices and processes than ever before, dominant discourses presented teacher professionalism in negative ways. Whitty (2002) argues the 1970s saw the role of teachers significantly re-imagined,

> ...a view emerged in the1970s that teachers had abused this licensed autonomy to the detriment of their pupils and society...[they were assumed] to be largely self-interested. Many professional groups and particularly the "liberal educational establishment" of the "swollen state" of post-war democracy came to be regarded as ill-adapted to be either agents of the state or entrepreneurial service providers in a marketised civil society. (2002: 66)

This view took hold. By the 1980s, according to Lowe (2007), the Conservative government successfully re-focussed attention from concerns about comprehensive schools and professional freedom for teachers, and orientated it on external accountability, measurable outcomes, market forces, consumerism and deliberate training for the economy. The 1988 Education Reform Act eliminated almost all previous legislation, and introduced a National Curriculum, more testing, league tables and more accountability through OFSTED (Jones, 1989, 2003; Lowe, 2007). The developments I have been describing highlight just some of the changes in policy, structure and philosophy in English education in very different conjunctures. Through these different periods the identity of English has changed. Contested ideas about social class, equal opportunity and 'intelligence' weave a common thread through many of these developments. Tensions about these issues came to a head in the 1960s/1970s when the teachers in this book entered the profession. This period is characterised by ideological clashes, but it is also significant for the amount of new practices and theoretical ideas that emerged in English teaching.

CONJUNCTURES, CONTEXTS, CIRCUMSTANCES

THE CHANGING IDENTITY OF ENGLISH TEACHING

School English is a hotly-debated subject. Because language is so integral to identity, advocating one or other approach can provoke all kinds of reaction. Politicians, the public and media quite happily pass judgement on curriculum content, pedagogy, assessment and expected outcomes. These discussions usually pay little attention to teacher experience or research on English teaching. Different groups promote different aims for the subject. Ball, Kenny, and Gardiner (1990) and Davison (2011) define four main traditions in English teaching: English as 'skills'; English as 'great literary tradition'; 'progressive' English; and 'critical literacy'. The 'skills' model emphasises functionality, prescription and direction. As it sounds, the 'great literary tradition' is a cultural-heritage model promoting a pre-determined canon of 'great' works. These models see learners as passive recipients of accepted skills, language and literature. Davison argues they teach children 'to appreciate rather than to critique; to acquire rather than to actively generate knowledge' (2011: 180). On the other hand a 'progressive' approach,

> ...places an emphasis on the development of the individual and the link between language and learning: the English of self-expression, the personal voice, of creativity and discovery. (2011: 180)

The 'critical literacy' model is highly politicised, counter-hegemonic and radical. It seeks to confront and challenge social realities. Unsurprisingly this version of English is controversial, even though it has never been dominant. Throughout the development of the subject different traditions have been in vogue at different times. And they are not exclusive, they overlap. For example 'creativity' in English is often associated with progressivism in the 1960s, but McCallum (2012) shows how creative approaches date back much earlier. George Sampson's *English for the English* (1921), and the Newbolt Report (1921) promoted a creative English curriculum as an entitlement for all children. Sampson criticises the failures of elementary education for thinking 'too much of children's heads and not enough of their hearts. Hearts are still out of fashion in schools' (1921: 3). But Sampson and Newbolt also suggest the need to 'cleanse' or 'purify' some children's 'evil' language habits. Sampson did not see all children as having 'creative' potential. The concept of creativity in English is important. McCallum argues that Sampson's model views literature as the primary conduit for a creative approach in English. Literature allows children to be 'creative' in varied but limited ways. It was not thought all children could reach the same levels of creativity that were found in the original literature.

McCallum argues these assumptions are also present in the work of F. R. Leavis, who creates an elitist dichotomy between those 'in the know' on one hand, and the rest of us on the other. This model views 'creativity' as coming from *within* the individual, a hereditary aspect of ability. From this perspective some children can be viewed as having a creative 'deficit' that well trained teachers can 'enculturate' through literature. McCallum argues,

CHAPTER 2

> If anything, [Leavis's work] sets creativity at a further remove from everyday life. It positions literature, the embodiment of creativity, not so much as a means to move individuals towards completion, but as a protection against the pernicious influences of mass culture, making anxious calls for citizens to "be trained to discriminate and resist"…Much of Leavis's work is directed towards training an elite corps of teachers, able to hand on the benefits of studying literature to the mass population (though the masses would never 'get it' to the same degree as the elite). Thus access to creativity becomes staged, teachers providing critical commentary in acting as intermediaries between writers and readers, guardians to the creativity locked within great works. (2012: 11–12)

Children are viewed as passive recipients of a given culture. This approach was evident in the development of secondary education after 1944, when there were marked distinctions between children's experiences of English. Those who attended grammar schools generally received a 'liberal' curriculum, based on canonical literature and Standard English grammar. In secondary moderns children's experiences varied considerably, depending on who taught them. Williams (2011: 171) argues the 1944 Act produced 'a new system of grading' children, predicated on the notion of innate, fixed intelligence. Deficit models of working-class culture and language were used to justify selection and ultimately implied social stratification was a 'natural' outcome of measurable difference in intelligence. This is reflected in the Norwood Report's different 'types' of children, with 'type 3' (those destined for the secondary moderns) supposedly being incapable of abstract thought:

> Because he is only interested in the moment he may be incapable of a long series of connected steps; relevance to present concerns is the only way of awakening interest; abstractions mean little to him. (Norwood Report, 1943: 3)

This labelling undoubtedly affected children's experiences, and such attitudes, or 'normalcies' as Medway (1990) calls them, promoted social inequality. Medway points out that by 1958 three quarters of children attended secondary moderns. English in some of these schools had very specific aims,

> Some secondary modern prescriptions unambiguously emphasised preparation for subordinate roles in life: the skills and values taught were seen to be such as would produce a useful, responsible and inoffensive citizen with a respect, based on slight acquaintance, for literary culture. In these schools the content of the English lesson might be determined by reference less to a conception of the subject than to the school's socialising function. (1990: 5)

The vast majority of children in these schools were working-class. Some teachers sought to defend working-class culture and language and their place in schools. Culturally salient indices of working-class identity (skilled employment, trade unionism, class politics), along with the gradual introduction of a more equitable comprehensive system, inspired small but influential groups of pioneering teachers to re-orientate English towards children's social and cultural realities (Medway et al., 2014). One teacher attempting to do this was John Dixon, whose *Growth through English* (1967, 1975), exemplifies a shift from conceptualising children as having innate 'cultural deficits', to locating learning into historic, social and cultural realities. Dixon was not alone and much work in this period confronted the aims and intentions of English teaching. It also changed conceptions of 'creativity'. McCallum again,

> Creativity no longer stems from drawing on inner resources to offer a representation of 'external reality', but through working with the material of that 'external reality' to give it shape and meaning to one's own life. Growth, then, no longer applies to a deficit model whereby the teacher's role is to provide for what is lacking in a young person's character, but to a process of building on what it already there, adding to, developing and extending. (2012: 13)

This reconceptualisation of learning and creativity as dialectical processes created opportunities for some practitioners to re-imagine the content and aims of the subject. And these developments occurred amid wider social and cultural change, which Lowe (2007) highlights,

> …it should not be forgotten that this was also to become a decade of social and political movements…protests against the Vietnam War, a greater realisation of the rights of oppressed minorities and ethnic groups, a liberalisation and secularisation of social values and a worldwide student protest movement. (2007: 40)

Yet the popular stereotype of radical change in the 1960s/1970s was not a widespread reality. Indeed, Lowe claims the stereotype itself partly increased the impetus for greater state control. In this period however, some working-class children were given a greater 'voice' in school than ever before. Some classrooms and curricula were genuinely 'child-centred', and some teachers paid much-needed attention to the particular needs of local constituencies. English itself was not defined by a particular 'version', nothing was off limits. But the democratic aspirations and ideological perspectives of some teachers significantly re-imagined the aims of the subject. But this period was short-lived, and less democratic conceptions of the subject have enjoyed a more enduring continuity.

DEVELOPMENTS IN PRACTICE AND RESOURCES

Throughout the 1940s and 1950s some English teachers in London started to direct local curriculum change themselves (Medway et al., 2014). London County Council's support for comprehensivism meant some schools were well placed to innovate. LATE members led discussions on the development of school English. One member, Harold Rosen, pioneered a series of developments at Walworth School in Southwark. He re-orientated the curriculum away from standard pre-war

CHAPTER 2

grammar exercises and comprehension, and introduced more discussion, improvised drama and a wider range of contemporary literature (Medway & Hardcastle, 2013). Rosen's work reconceptualised the intentions of English at the school. These intentions can be seen in the course-book *Reflections* (1963), produced by other English teachers at Walworth – Simon Clements, John Dixon and Leslie Stratta. The book targeted children's (mostly working-class) experiences, paying close attention to their backgrounds, cultures and languages. It included provocative texts, ideas for creative writing and images of inner-city environments. Compared with the 'Empire-building, character-forming...gendered stuff of the sort that attracted the scorn of LATE' (Hardcastle & Medway, 2013: 33), *Reflections* was a radical departure from existing models.

John Hardcastle (2008) argues *Reflections* was perhaps the first English course-book to show explicit concern for the social realities of working-class children. Students were positively encouraged to use their own voices and experiences. Dixon (1991) recalls actively thinking of ways to negotiate and reshape the curriculum to reflect the lives of his mostly working-class students. What went before *Reflections*, Hardcastle argues, were English course-books that 'typically concentrated on language tasks, passages for reading and comprehension exercises' (2008: 5). He examines one contemporary book, *Pleasure in English* (Yglesias & Holman, 1961), and criticises its decontextualized grammar exercises (identifying parts of speech), intimidating tone (children being 'instructed' rather than 'invited') and the class-biased content of selected texts (passages about skiing holidays were not really relevant to the constituents of inner-city London in the early 1960s). Such text-books paid little attention children's cultural backgrounds. Conversely, *Reflections* had the express intention of making English more relevant and responsive to the lives of working-class children.

Reflections appeared in a period when other course-books and practitioner research emerged – for example, Holbrook (1961, 1964, 1967, 1972); Abbs (1969); Newson and Mansfield (1965); Searle (1975); Richmond and Eyers (1982). These writers represent different traditions, but some of them were practising teachers when they produced this work. For some teachers curriculum development through negotiation and experimentation was a professional responsibility, and they had opportunities to design courses and publish them.

JOHN DIXON'S 'GROWTH' MODEL OF ENGLISH

Dixon published *Growth through English* in 1967. He was one of a number of British delegates to attend the 1966 Dartmouth Conference, held in New Hampshire, USA. The conference, sponsored by the National Association for the Teaching of English (NATE) and its American counterpart the National Council of Teachers of English (NCTE), debated what school English *was* – its aims, strategies, intentions. Dartmouth is sometimes presented as an important moment in the evolution of the subject. Joseph Harris suggests that for some optimistic teachers: 'Dartmouth has symbolized a kind of Copernican shift from a view of English as something one learns about to a sense of it as something one does' (1991: 631). However, Harris also claims that in reality much practice in English has continued as it had before. Dixon explains how discussions considered 'initial literacy' and 'cultural heritage' approaches. There were differences of opinion about curriculum content and the skills English should aim to develop. However, he suggests there was broad agreement on the notion of 'growth'. His aim in the book was to 'draw from the discussions and reports at Dartmouth such ideas as are directly relevant to my own work in class and to that of teachers I know'. This, he claims, was not intended simply to provide a neat summary of events, but 'rather to propose a new starting point' (1967: xi) for debate on the future direction of the subject.

Studying literature in order to 'enculturate' students was not part of the agenda. 'Growth' was re-conceptualised in more democratic and participatory ways, and Dixon foregrounds the role of language in learning – emphasising personal voice, innovation and exploration. 'Growth' is firmly located in children's social and cultural realities. Practice should focus on 'the need to re-examine the learning processes and the meaning to the individual of what he is doing in English lessons' (1967: 1–2). The idea was that children should 'grow' to have greater agency through dynamic classroom experiences. The suggested model for achieving this focussed on specific developments. There should be a much stronger emphasis on student talk, critical discussion and drama. Writing activities should be 'exploratory' and allow students to engage with ideas and negotiate the interplay of meaning in context. The processes of thinking and writing are of greater importance than end product. Children's real lives should be central to their learning and they should be freed from the 'limits of the teacher's vision' of learning outcomes (1967: 48). Similarly, students should be 'freed from the *disabling conceptions* of "correctness" and "dialect"' (1967: 77). Dixon's model encourages teachers to work in social constructionist ways, using children's own cultural resources as starting points from which to understand their own material circumstances.

This approach views all language use as fundamentally located in social processes and practices. From this perspective, traditional canonical literature is not afforded a privileged position, and popular cultural texts are equally as worthy of serious study. Also, because English is in constant flux, it is incumbent on teachers to be adaptable and critically alert in their practice. But Dixon's ideas evolved and 'growth' might also be conceptualised as having more radical connotations. Reflecting back on the 1960s, Dixon (1991) later claimed,

> ...there had to be a revolutionary break from defining language as reified object, towards observing social processes dependent on signs in use. (1991: 186)

This implies that language should be studied critically in its social, historical and cultural contexts. Dixon is writing this after the 'cultural turn' in English studies and he adopts a more confident theoretical position. But his evolving ideas can also be seen embryonically in the revised and updated 1975 edition of *Growth Through*

CHAPTER 2

English – set in the perspective of the seventies. He explains how changes in his practice were 'not confined to English teaching at all – that's just one microcosm of a far wider struggle' (1975: 111). This 'struggle' was about 'teacher and learner, parent and child, manager and worker. About the dilemmas of coercive authority and inescapable subordination' (1975: 111). Dixon claims to have had an 'uneasy awakening' in the aftermath of Dartmouth, when he began to recognise how he and other teachers were 'prone' to use 'language to dominate and constrict' their students in classroom interactions. These circumstances provoked him to re-consider the potential kinds of classroom relationships he created.

In developing his ideas about relationships and the role of language in learning, Dixon does not argue simply for 'progressive' or 'child centred' approaches to practice. This might make English lessons more interesting for students, but it essentially supports and maintains the status quo. Rather, he proposes a radical reconceptualisation of what school English should aim to do. Dominant conceptions of English impose particular limits and expectations on the subject – in terms of content, practice, expected outcomes. But this bears a false relation to the realities of lived experience. Instead, Dixon argues the fundamental concern of English is experience itself. As he claimed in the 1967 edition: 'a new model will be needed… to redirect our attention to life as it really is' (1967: 114). How is experience, and life, mediated through various contexts and factors – cultural, social, political, discoursal and so on? Dixon implies that by collaborating to engage critically with a range of dialectical processes, teachers and students might 'grow' to understand their influence on consciousness. He argues in the 1975 edition:

> The questioning of power and subordination in contemporary capitalism – or in so-called communism – is a running battle that I expect to reach beyond my own lifetime. What's hard to bear is the confusion inside ourselves. We are beginning to see how adults can learn from children, and maybe what kinds of social relationships would release fuller potentialities in the converse process. But the social models built into us, and within which we work, consistently pressurize and distort the effort to create such relationships. (1975: 112)

The restrictive power of dominant discourses and structures has a significant influence on consciousness. But by initiating genuine dialogic relationships, with teachers as 'listeners', there is the potential to work collaboratively so as to understand the 'confusion inside ourselves' by 'sharing the role of the learner'. Dixon discovered that when students 'were given the chance to talk among themselves' they made 'unexpected progress' (1975: 111). By allowing students to voice their concerns, initiatives and experiences, Dixon claims to have discovered 'quite unsuspected processes of feeling and thought, which class discussion dominated by the teacher's language had obliterated' (1975: 111). In learning together, teachers and students can generate alternative discourses and narratives that can open up new possibilities and expose contradictions in dominant perspectives. Dixon suggests the skills and critical abilities generated through these kinds of relationships and learning processes extend well beyond the English classroom, and across different temporal circumstances:

> Still, if we can understand people, ourselves included, in the process of formulating new perceptions and ideas at different stages in their lives, then we have a new basis for changing our roles as teachers. I believe that, over the past year or two, ideas have come to together in such a way as to transform my perceptions, first in learning and teaching, and second, in talking, writing, and reading well beyond the boundaries of the subject. (1975: 112)

Dixon argues that English cannot be limited to particular types of literature or static conceptions of language. It must be located into the various contexts, discourses, cultures and power relations that learners (including teachers) exist within. It should also be orientated towards confronting, understanding and re-imagining these circumstances. Dixon's developing conception of 'growth' aimed to make English more democratic by proposing an alternative theoretical base from which new ways of working might emerge. In this way, new discourses and narratives can be generated that can open up new possibilities and expose contradictions in dominant perspectives. Unsurprisingly, this approach was not universally approved.

Dixon's re-imagined landscape for English emerged during a period that Jones (1989) calls the 'heyday of progressivism'. And as progressivism has its critics, so does Dixon. For example Allen (1980) criticises Dixon's work, along with Harold Rosen and James Britton. Even Allen's book title (*English Teaching since 1965 – How much Growth?*) questions the validity of Dixon's 'growth' model. But Allen operates in a different ideological universe to those he criticises. He claims 'Britton's achievement has been great; but at very great cost' (1980: 67). He criticises Dixon's interpretation of events at Dartmouth,

> The selection that Dixon made of the voices at Dartmouth is strikingly clear. What he consistently omitted from his "map" were any that looked to a tradition, a transmission, a developed collection of values, for these were inert, moribund. (1980: 40)

Allen's focus on 'tradition', 'transmission' and 'values' betrays a number of assumptions about cultural heritage, pedagogy and society. But Dixon does not omit these aspects from his analysis. He challenges them by foregrounding the effects of social and cultural background in the construction of knowledge. English is in constant flux, and as Dixon claims, for it to be meaningful it should 'redirect our attention to life as it really is' (1967: 114). Allen's criticisms are aimed at maintaining a particular static conception of 'English', which is, of course, ideological. And these debates were not confined to English. Comprehensivism and progressivism were also part of a wider ideological struggle. Cox and Dyson's *Black Papers* gave prominent names from the time a platform from which to offer a succession of right-wing criticisms of education generally. But they held particular vitriol for

CHAPTER 2

progressivism and child-centred practice. Tory MP, Angus Maude, complained of 'The Egalitarian Threat' in 1969:

> It is necessary now to get very tough with the egalitarians, who would abolish or lower standards out of 'sympathy' with those who fail to measure up to them. We must reject the chimera of equality and proclaim the ideal of quality. The egalitarians, whose ideas of 'social justice' are prescriptions for mediocrity and anarchy, must be prevented from having any control over the education of the young. (In Cox & Dyson, 1971: 40)

Maude assumes a clearly defined set of 'standards', vague though they are. The fact he makes no attempt to fully define them points to his confidence in their universality. He associates egalitarian 'sympathy' with feebleness, insufficiency and incompetence. But his argument betrays a fear that ideas like Dixon's might actually result in more equal outcomes. Maude's 'standards' are punitive and mean some children will succeed while others fail. The *Black Papers* preyed upon perceived anxieties about comprehensivisation and the threat to 'traditional' teaching. But as Lowe (2007) argues they simply re-hashed older discourses, 'about de-streaming and new approaches to teaching. But they did not represent a sea change in the rhetoric around education' (2007: 56). Dixon, on the other hand, aimed to provide English with an alternative theoretical base from which new ways of working might emerge.

SOME WIDER DEVELOPMENTS

Practical and theoretical debates in English teaching in the 'cauldron' were framed within broader social and cultural change. Medway argues it is crucial to locate developments in English into wider circumstances,

> We can cautiously conclude that explanations for change in English which rest exclusively on changes in the material and institutional conditions of teaching are not enough. Influences from the wider economy and culture, though diffuse and hard to track through specific channels, appear at certain times also to be of critical importance. (1990: 33)

The conjuncture 1965–1975 embodied a number of these 'diffuse' elements that strengthened some English teachers' commitment to challenging the aims and identity of the subject. The wider political, social and cultural circumstances that Lowe (2007) refers to (counterculture, protest movements, secularisation and so on) influenced some practitioners to organise and generate new types of publications and initiatives. Here, I want to highlight only two notable examples: the magazine *Teaching London Kids* (TLK) and the *Centerprise* project. *Teaching London Kids* was one of a number of publications that encouraged teachers to take a critical and 'activist' approach to the job. It began as a series of meetings and seminars organised through LATE and run by practising teachers in 1971–1972. A group of teachers were sufficiently motivated to continue the critical debate through a new publication and the magazine was born. TLK became a successful magazine, and although its remit went beyond English teaching, it had regular features on literacy, reading, writing, sometimes publishing student work. It also located educational practices into a range of social, cultural, political and ideological contexts. One distinctive feature was its concentration on social class. TLK's 'activist' approach is evident in the 'mission statement' that appeared prominently in every edition:

Teaching London Kids is concerned with exploring among other things;

- the practice and dilemmas of progressive/socialist teachers in state schools, especially as experienced by new teachers;
- notions of 'progressive' teaching methods and their impact on the education of working class children;
- the concentration of educational problems in London schools;
- the ways in which the power structure of society affects the organisation and curriculum of schools;
- the potential role of the school in the community and vice versa;
- the critical importance of language in teaching and learning;
- ABOVE ALL, TEACHING LONDON KIDS IS CONCERNED WITH PRESENTING POSITIVE STRATEGIES FOR ACTION.

The magazine tackled serious, sometimes controversial issues such as racism, sexism or homophobia that affected teachers and students in London schools. It engaged critically with structural, theoretical and policy developments. And importantly, it was produced by practitioners. Existing circumstances meant opportunities were available for some teachers to broaden their professional experience and skills. Many practitioners contributed to the magazine in different ways, thus extending their professional identities beyond teaching. Other projects were also developed, including local publishing initiatives. Ken Worpole and the *Centerprise* project is a notable example. Worpole was an English teacher at Hackney Downs School in the early 1970s. He explains (1977a, 1977b) how *Centerprise* built a platform for the local community in Hackney to produce a 'people's history' of the borough. From this initial idea in 1971, the project grew to publish work by schoolchildren and other members of the community. The instigators of these initiatives, in the 'cauldron', understood and critiqued the contexts and circumstances in which they operated. Projects like *Centerprise* aimed to make meaningful connections between the cultures of school, home, parents, teachers, children and wider community, to give them a 'voice'. These projects foreground the crucial importance for individuals and groups to be able to story their own existence, to have a history. Worpole sums up this thinking at the time:

Yet even if Centerprise collapsed tomorrow, it is reassuring to think that in many homes, in front rooms, on bookshelves or on mantelpieces there would remain pieces of tangible evidence that the people who live in Hackney have a history, have written about themselves, have tried to describe and understand the world they have lived in, and which they have wanted to share with others. A society without a memory is like an individual without a memory: it moves without reason or purposeful direction, activated only by forces or pressures outside of itself. I have avoided as far as possible the word 'community'; it is properly the right word to be used, but it has been so distorted…that in some cases I think it is a word and an idea that we will have to re-appropriate at a later point in time, when it once again suits our needs and not the needs of those who are so concerned to impose the sense of 'community' upon us as a cheap substitute for a radically different, and better, society. Community, like history, is not something which happens by accident; not given, but made. (1977a: 20)

Worpole seeks connections between history and memory, individual and group. This work aims to equip individuals and groups with the critical tools and narratives to challenge dominant discourses, to assess and improve their life chances. Some English teachers in the period attempted this by locating practice into lived experience. For some practitioners in the 'cauldron', English had to provide opportunities for students to trace and explore various anchor points in their lives, identities and cultures. Taking children's intellectual lives seriously, especially working-class ones, was a fundamental concern. This aspect of the subject seems to be missing in current contexts.

EVENTS AND DEVELOPMENTS IN THE ILEA

ILEA was established in 1965 and provided resources and facilities for teachers, students, and wider communities. It established a network of London-wide teachers' centres and encouraged collegiality and collaboration. It employed a number of subject specialist inspection and advisory teams who worked with teachers to develop and share good practice. Teachers also had a range of professional development opportunities. Some foreground ILEA's commitment to innovation and experimentation. Peter Mortimore suggests,

> Much of ILEA's strength stemmed from its interests and innovation. With its economy of scale, the authority was able to develop a range of ideas, many of which were later adopted by authorities all over the UK. Initiatives such as its adult education service, specialist teachers' centres, joint inspection and advisory teams, and the research and statistics branch…influenced developments nationally and internationally. (In *The Guardian*, 3rd June, 2008)

ILEA did foster collegiality, but it was not a totally benign organisation and its relationships with teachers were not without tension. For example, Davis (2002) investigates its response to the 'Tyndale affair' in the mid-1970s, which created,

...divisions within the authority, between the authority and the teachers, between traditional and radical teachers, between teachers and managers, between teachers and parents, between different groups of parents and between the ILEA and the Borough of Islington. (2002: 275)

Ideological clashes exacerbated divisions between ILEA and the National Union of Teachers (NUT). In the early 1970s, Davis argues the NUT's inner-London branch was occasionally at odds with the national union. This caused conflict with ILEA over a number of issues. But it also led to a number of concessions. ILEA promoted greater equality in the running of schools, encouraging teachers to be involved in decision-making. Davis suggests this strategy was risky,

Devolution made sense as a means of demonstrating that ILEA valued its teachers, but it carried the obvious risk, in a period of high teacher turnover, of empowering individuals with very little professional experience. Some 14% of ILEA teachers in 1972–1973 were said to be in their first year of teaching, while in the more challenging inner-city areas the figure was much higher. (2002: 279)

High staff turnover meant some young teachers in London were quickly promoted with the apparent support of ILEA. An exodus of experienced teachers from inner-London schools in this conjuncture changed the demographic of its teachers. ILEA was concerned it would not have enough teachers to work in its expanding comprehensive schools. These circumstances forced it to recruit young teachers from training programmes and schools around the country. And while this might have contained an element of risk, as Davis suggests, it also created opportunities for some young teachers to develop new practices. The political will to expand the comprehensive programme, along with the changing demographic and economic circumstances, created favourable conditions for different kinds of change. Subsequently in some schools enthusiastic young teachers worked with energy and commitment, with some practitioners initiating radical developments. Jones (2003) claims some young teachers came out of training programmes with a degree of militancy,

Especially between 1968 and 1974, universities and colleges of teacher training were affected by, and themselves generated, movements of protest and attempts to develop new kinds of knowledge and new sorts of social identity. The teachers who graduated from these institutions formed a generation which sought to translate these experiences into an educational practice that could transform the ways in which schooling related to the majority of its students. From the perspective of many of them, comprehensive reform was important, but on its own it was not enough. (2003: 87–88)

Jones makes it clear that 'radicalism of this sort was never more than a minority commitment' (2003: 88). But ILEA's systemic structure allowed advisers, inspectors and teachers to develop and improve practice. The teachers in this book all claim

CHAPTER 2

to have had significant support. They also claim ILEA encouraged professional development beyond the classroom. Many teachers who worked in ILEA have positive experiences of the opportunities and working conditions provided. A *Teaching London Kids* editorial from 1982 claims,

> During its seventeen years of existence, it [ILEA] has developed an education service which is the envy of many. It spends more money on the education of each child than any other LEA in Britain. It has very favourable pupil-teacher ratios and class sizes. It provides high capitation allowances for schools to purchase books and equipment. It offers centralised learning resources and support services for teachers which are without parallel in this country. It organises a massive in-service training programme. (1982, no. 15: 2)

These comments were made in response to 'the Tory onslaught on ILEA' in a very different set of circumstances. Conservative attacks on ILEA were unsurprising because the authority supported many causes and campaigns opposed by those on the right. Jones claims, 'In 1982, the ILEA symbolised for the right everything it hated in state education' (1989: 151). Along with its support for teachers and commitment to collegiality, the previous decade saw ILEA promote a number of initiatives and ideological campaigns. Viv Ellis (2000: 216) highlights ILEA's 'Positive Images' campaign, which provided,

> ...a resources guide for teaching about homosexuality...This desire to provide 'positive images' for young teachers can be seen as a continuation of the struggle for equality initiated by the rights movements back in the 1960s. (2000: 216–217)

Similarly, Ball (2008) highlights a number of developments,

> The ILEA in particular was active in the development of anti-racist and anti-sexist strategies in its schools but, for the most part these were dismantled after its abolition. (2008: 160)

In 1990 the 'Tory onslaught' was complete when the Thatcher government abolished ILEA, providing a 'further blow to the autonomy of the educational establishment', according to Lowe (2007: 96). Despite this setback, ILEA had significant influence in London English teaching with the establishment of the English Centre in 1975. Resources and practices were developed at the Centre, which was also in the vanguard of publishing teacher-designed courses and materials for wider use.

THE BULLOCK REPORT

The Bullock Report (1975) is an important document in the history of English teaching. It provides a comprehensive discussion of approaches to classroom talk, reading and writing, monitoring and organisation. Davies (2000) argues it tackled language study in a 'more linguistically focused way, and carefully attempted to argue a case against an over-reliance on prescriptive language' (2000: 106). The central importance of language for both learning and identity is clear in the Report's title – *A Language for Life* – and it emphasised 'processes' of language learning over end 'product'. Wyse et al. (2013) argue Bullock, alongside the Plowden Report, stressed the importance of language relating to lived experience,

> Central to both the reports was an emphasis on the 'process' of language learning. From such a perspective, children's oral and written language would be best developed in meaningful language use. (2013: 11)

And 'meaningful language use' means skills must be developed 'in, and about, the daily experiences of the classroom and the home' (2013: 11). This means locating children's learning into a number of contexts, using their own languages and experiences as the fundamental starting-point for classroom interaction. The Report itself insisted,

> No child should be expected to cast off the language and culture of the home as he crosses the school threshold, nor to live and act as though school and home represent two totally separate and different cultures which have to be kept firmly apart. The curriculum should reflect many elements of that part of his life which a child lives outside school. (DFE, 1975: 286)

Bullock can be seen as a definitive document on English teaching in the 'cauldron'. James Britton's work at LATE and the Institute of Education was influential: theoretically, politically, pedagogically. The intention was to make English more democratic, inclusive and diverse, with the curriculum reflecting children's social and cultural backgrounds. The Report argues for 'appropriateness' in language use, insisting: 'Any one person belongs to a number of speech communities, and correctness therefore becomes a matter of conforming to the linguistic behaviour appropriate to that situation' (DFE, 1975: 143). Burgess and Hardcastle (2000) argue Britton's emphasis on language and context in learning was central to many of Bullock's recommendations,

> This perception of the fundamental role of language, in Britton's work and in the Bullock Report, gave English teaching in the schools its unifying rationale. (2000: 10)

This 'unifying rationale' suggested particular ways of working that were social, interactive and culturally diverse. And if diversity was to be taken seriously in practice then attention had to be paid to how English classrooms themselves were organised. For example, Bullock highlights the importance of mixed-ability classrooms. Despite claiming its intention was not to assess the merits of different groupings (setting, streaming) the Report suggests,

CHAPTER 2

> Speaking purely in terms of English, most of us have reservations about arrangements by which pupils are streamed or setted according to ability. However careful the process, classifying individuals in this way makes different pupils in the same group seem more similar than they are, and similar pupils in different groups seem more different than they are. Moreover, we believe that even if it were possible to grade children accurately according to language ability it would deprive the less able of the stimulus they so badly need. Less commonly acknowledged, but equally important, is the fact that it would steadily deprive the more able of opportunities to communicate with the linguistically less accomplished. (DFE, 1975: 224)

Bullock's support for mixed-ability challenges the taken-for-granted, historical organisation of educational hierarchies, based on 'ability' or 'intelligence'. However, it seems Bullock's timing was unfortunate. Goodson (2005b: 127) claims the 'conjuncture of the 1960s and 1970s aligns with the economic long wave upswing, which ended with the oil crisis of 1973'. Bullock emerged when momentum for radical conservative change and reform was building, and many of its concerns were lost among calls for greater accountability, functionality and standardisation. Yet, Bullock can still provide important lessons for current practitioners. Yandell (2011) argues current English teachers must 'make it their business' to find out about their students' uses of language and ways of learning in their different communities,

> Following the line taken by the Bullock Report, I am suggesting that part of the respect that teachers owe their students is to attend to their lives, cultures, histories and experiences beyond the school gates, to see these out-of-school identities as integral to the students' identities within the classroom. (2011: 162)

The teachers in this book worked in these kinds of ways.

CONTENDING POLARITIES IN ENGLISH?

Some critics argue that English in the 'cauldron' was characterised by a number of oppositions. Ball, Kenny and Gardiner (1990) compartmentalise several 'contending polarities' between different approaches to the subject in the period:

grammar schooling – comprehensive schooling
literature – language
elite – mass
cultural heritage – cultural relevance
transmission – participation
Cambridge – London (1990: 57)

These observations highlight a number of perceived tensions. Ball, Kenny and Gardiner suggest LATE, and James Britton, were successful in promoting a radical conception of English in London. Over time, they argue this approach influenced some London English teachers to critically re-examine their working practices and identities,

> ...the English teacher was no longer to be a missionary disseminating the values of civilisation but an anthropologist mapping and collecting the values and culture of subordinate groups, initially the working class (later girls and blacks). (1990: 58)

It might be true that some teachers did re-imagine their practice and reject the Leavisite 'missionary'. As Medway et al. (2014) demonstrate, there were indeed English teachers who re-defined the subject to make it more relevant to their students' own realities. But it was also true that English in many schools was moribund and uninspiring with 'radical' or 'progressive' approaches far from the reality. And were the 'polarities' in Ball, Kenny and Gardiner's model solely the preserve of each 'school' (Cambridge and London)? Gibbons (2009) argues that viewing London as operating in such an alternative way is unhelpful. Many early LATE members came through grammar schools and did not set out deliberately on a 'premeditated academic exercise' to overhaul English teaching. But new lines of work emerged, and Gibbons argues it is necessary to explore the contexts of post-war English teaching to understand why this was the case,

> An exploration such as this can begin to reveal the very practical conditions driving those involved in LATE work and cast light on why it was that core ideas about children's language and experience became central, and indeed over time, result in a reconceptualising of the subject English. (2009: 65)

Gibbons' (2013) history of LATE foregrounds the struggles some English teachers engaged in to re-define the subject from the late 1940s. By the 1960s/1970s this 'reconceptualising' of the subject helped create the 'practical conditions' for some teachers to work in more progressive ways. But this conjuncture also presented a complicated mix of developments and counter-developments, policy initiatives and clashing ideologies. Ball (2008) argues an 'educational settlement' existed from 1944–1976. This was 'a shaky, unstable settlement...that displayed a continuation of the entrenched, historic social divisions and class competition that had defined English education from the outset' (2008: 72). However, broad support for the welfare state meant social attitudes, at least in part, promoted collective, mutual endeavour – this can be seen in the developing comprehensive movement, new theoretical perspectives and changes in English teaching. These circumstances made right-wing criticism less potent. However, wider economic circumstances began to influence change. Between 1964 and 1973 Lowe (2007) argues there was an '11 percent fall in industrial production' and by '1975 manufacturing lost almost one third of its labour force' (2007: 62). The late 1960s/early 1970s saw an 'irretrievable trading deficit of over five billion pounds by 1974' (2007: 62). These desperate circumstances were exacerbated by a world oil crisis in the early 1970s that 'culminated in the quadrupling of world oil prices by OPEC in December 1973' (2007: 62). This created rising inflation, social discontent and widening ideological divisions. Those on the right seized opportunities to attack supposed weaknesses in different institutions, including education. The *Black Paper* arguments of the late 1960s now seemed more plausible. Ball (2008: 72) claims the *Papers*, 'together with a variety of linked and overlapping neoliberal or New Right think-tanks and advocacy groups…clearly gained a considerable influence within Conservative education policy thinking during the 1970s and 1980s'. The influence of these groups was echoed in dominant discourses around English teaching, as Cameron (1995) suggests of the period.

David Shayer (1972) argues that right-wing commentators claimed English was being 'sacrificed on the altar of egalitarianism', and on the 'altar of pupil-centred creativity with its mixture of self-expression and *Reflections*-like "social awareness"' (1972: 185). Shayer quotes a concerned Sir George Pickering, from *The Challenge to Education* in 1967:

> Britain is obsessed with the function of education as an instrument for levelling society and for eradicating the privileges of wealth and ancestry. (Cited in Shayer, 1972: 185)

If only. Pickering's hyperbole highlights the clashing ideologies that the likes Dixon, Britton and Rosen were evidently keen to confront. Shayer dismisses *Black Paper* arguments, claiming practice in English improved immeasurably in this period. Despite concerns about,

> …'standards', classroom procedures, or specific teaching practices, there is no disputing the fact that English teaching priorities are now (theoretically) more thoughtful, humane, far-sighted, imaginative and worth while than they have ever been before. (1972: 185–186)

For Shayer, this 'humane' approach to English evolved out of the struggles that the likes of Rosen, Dixon and Britton engaged in. He predicts an exciting and progressive future, where practitioners might generate a 'body of theory' for English teaching,

> …advances which have taken place in English teaching in this country since 1945 are tremendously exciting, and we have gone at least some way to make up for the stagnation which has distinguished the subject in the past. Out of the present intense soul-searching will at least come a body of theory for future decades which will be distinguished by its positive rather than by its conservatively negative qualities…English has at last got its heart in the right place. (1972: 185)

Such a 'body of theory' has never materialised. Gibbons quotes Tony Burgess, who claims,

> Relatively few people think of trying to create an overall body of theory for English teaching. Or, if they do, then it's the job of government or public report. (Cited in Gibbons, 2009: 73)

Any underpinning 'body of theory' for English teaching must emerge through the collaboration and negotiation of practitioners: a 'government report' is insufficient. Gibbons claims such a theory should include,

> ...a notion that the subject was a place for children of all backgrounds, in particular those whose culture might be furthest from the culture of the school, to tell their stories, relate their experience and use their language. (2009: 73–74)

In the 1960s/1970s some practitioners prioritised these ideals. But, as Gibbons claims, these priorities have been 'increasingly eroded over the past twenty years' (2009: 74). Indeed, such approaches have been contentious for decades. In 1978 Gerald Grace claimed English departments, especially in inner-cities, were singled out as hotbeds of radicalism. Dominant discourses damaged social perceptions of teachers: 'Anarchy is seen to be realised in these schools in the form of progressive education' (1978: 67). Grace argues critiques of progressivism formed part of broader economic arguments insisting that individuals needed a 'tougher' education to succeed in a 'competitive' society. He highlights Rhodes Boyson's concerns, a former English teacher, Black Paper author and Conservative MP. Boyson was particularly critical in *The Crisis in Education* (1975), over a perceived lack of discipline, declining standards and the like. Grace argues, 'Particularly singled out as a context for extremists are English Departments in inner-city schools' (1978: 70). English teachers became,

> ...the focus of an ideological struggle concerned immediately with conflicting notions of appropriate educational experience for working-class children and more widely with socio-political issues. A conservative critique calls for the restoration of 'standards', 'discipline' and 'structure' and insists that the central activity of schools and teachers is the advancement of learning, not socialisation, community regeneration or political consciousness. (1978: 86)

Of course as human activities educational practices mean all teachers remain the focus of an 'ideological struggle', with 'discipline, 'structure' and 'standards' still very much at the forefront of conservative critique. The discourse of radical, 'extremist' teachers fomenting revolution contributed to the 'ideological struggle' Grace refers to. But even in the 1960s/1970s the supposed 'extremists' were not ubiquitous. Burgess dismisses the 'radical' stereotype,

> Today, I find it puzzling to read about the trendy theorists of the sixties who are supposed at that point to have been corrupting literature into relevance and turning writing into creativity. They do not figure in my memory. Revolution was not on offer, but there were lines of work and new interests. (1996: 57)

So no revolution. But some of these 'lines of work' meant children's agency was a driving concern for some teachers, who sought to celebrate the culture and language of working-class children. These new 'lines of work' were influenced by

CHAPTER 2

contemporary theoretical developments. Sociolinguistics challenged conceptions of 'correctness' in language, promoting 'difference' and 'variation'. For example Labov (1969, 1972) explored non-standard varieties and different vernaculars; Chomsky (1965) examined tensions between competence and performance in language; Halliday (1973, 1975) explored language in use, concepts of 'appropriateness' and discourse; Hymes (1972) promoted 'communicative competence'; and Trudgill (1974, 1975) explored language and class, race and gender, as well as accent and dialect in schools. Bernstein's (1971) concepts of 'restricted' and 'elaborated' codes attempted to explain a perceived achievement gap between working-class and middle-class children. Some argue this implied working-class children arrived at school with a number of 'deficits' to be rectified. Harold Rosen was particularly unimpressed, especially after much work had been done to counter these assumptions,

> No serious writer could go on asserting that working-class speech was ungrammatical, lazy, debased and so forth. Bernstein's theories made it possible to bypass all that and to suggest a much more profound and intractable deficiency...The theories pointed to a basic cognitive deficiency. (1972: 3)

Nonetheless Bernstein's work was influential in the 1970s and Rosen's argument begs the question of whether teachers linked 'restricted' codes to this 'basic cognitive deficiency'. Rosen is critical of Bernstein for not sufficiently exploring how cultural and social background influence the ways in which children are able to learn – as in Shirley Brice Heath's (1982, 1983) ethnographic studies of literacy development in different communities. For Rosen (1975) children's 'social contexts' are not simply the settings in which events occur, but the whole process of active participation, of living. Context is people 'in action with one another and against each other improvising the text as they proceed' (1975: 338). Hardcastle (2016) provides a concrete example of this in relation to English teaching. He writes about his experiences as a young teacher in the early 1970s, and his realisation that children's social contexts are not simply the circumstances in which the daily dramas of life unfold – they are 'the dramas themselves'. Understanding the implications and complexities of the 'social context' is crucial for understanding the intellectual lives of individuals and groups. For some English teachers in the 'cauldron' this conception provided a theoretical underpinning for practice. I want to leave the last word here to Rosen, who poses a challenge for English teachers to be critical and decide where they stand in relation to a more urgent and fundamental set of 'contending polarities':

> It is becoming increasingly difficult to refuse to take sides. We have to choose between theories of cultural deprivation and assertions of a popular culture, between descriptions of an impoverished restricted code and the unearthing of a living oral tradition, between visions of school as a civilised and well-ordered island in a sea of barbarism and anomie and the aspiration that they should be

reincarnate through the nourishment of neighbourhood and community, between reading 'schemes' and literacy through critical consciousness. (1975: 338–339)

***

English in this conjuncture was immersed in debates about the nature of the subject, its theoretical base, competing traditions and ideological perspectives. All of this was framed by wider social, political and economic circumstances. The teachers in this book entered the profession during this complicated period, and their professional identities were formed in these contested and competing currents. Circumstances in the conjuncture influenced decisions about the types of teachers they wanted to be, their accounts of practice and beliefs about English teaching. The rapid turnover of teachers in London saw many young teachers enter the profession. It was possible for the teachers to see their own progression through a career structure that did not conflict with the ideas, values and interests they espoused. Dixon's 'growth' model was influential. So were wider theoretical developments in sociolinguistics, historical and social analysis. The ideological struggles of the time forced them to define their own positions and they all dismiss the *Black Paper* arguments for example. The teachers began in a period of social, cultural and political change: circumstances that offered possibilities to challenge traditional methods and existing orthodoxies. They claim to have done this through their practice and in other areas. Their work in this conjuncture had broad support from ILEA and the English Centre.

ACKNOWLEDGEMENT

Sections of this chapter have appeared, in other forms, in Tarpey, P. (2015). Professional memory in context: Can it help counter the "counter-revolution". *Changing English*, *22*(4), 382–392; Tarpey, P. (2016). "Fire Burn and Cauldron Bubble": What are the conjunctural effects on English teacher professional memories, identities and narratives? *Changing English*, *23*(1), 77–93; and Tarpey, P. (2017a). 'We not I' not 'I me mine': Learning from professional memory about collectivist English teaching. *Changing English*, *24*(1), 103–117.

NOTE

[1] The 'William Tyndale Junior School Affair' is described by John Davis as 'probably the most embittered educational controversy in post-war Britain' (2002: 275). In 1974 and 1975 the majority of the school's staff were radical, hard-left activists. Head teacher Terry Ellis and deputy-head Brian Haddow rejected the traditional curriculum and experimented with more a democratic approach to classroom interaction – children had freedom of choice in activities they wanted to do. This approach caused problems in the school with more traditional staff, who were concerned that educational 'basics' were not being met. Internal disputes erupted and the events led to a national media scandal. ILEA stepped in to try and resolve the situation. This caused divisions between many different groups – teachers, parents, managers and ILEA. See for example, Gretton and Jackson (1976); Ellis et al. (1977); Simon (1991); Davis (2002); Cunningham (2002).

CHAPTER 3

MEMORIES, NARRATIVES, RELATIONSHIPS

INTRODUCTION

I want to tell you a couple of stories. When I was four or five, I found myself in the hallway of our maisonette in the middle of the night. I think it was the middle of the night anyway, it was dark and neon light streamed through the front-door window at the bottom of the stairs. I think I must have been sleep-walking because I do not remember walking downstairs. I was suddenly just there. I started crying, I think, until one of parents came and took me back to bed. Around the same time I started in the 'admissions' class at my primary school. My teacher was Mrs Campbell, and one day she asked the class what 'god' had given us. Children gave lots of answers: 'animals', 'trees', 'chocolate'. I put my hand up and said, 'he gave us *you* Mrs Campbell'. At which point she struggled to hold back her tears, she was so affected by my honesty. Well that's how the story goes.

It will be obvious that these stories are memories. But they are different kinds of memories. You see, I 'remember' being at the bottom of the stairs, but cannot tell you with any certainty anything *specific* about it. I do not know how old I was, what time it was, if I cried, how I got there, which parent came to my rescue. In fact, I am not sure the incident happened at all. The events in Mrs Campbell's class I have absolutely no recollection of whatsoever. So how are these stories sedimented in my memory? I had the experience of being at the bottom of the stairs, but the narrative I have to make sense of it is inconsistent. I asked my parents about the event but they could not remember it. I 'remember' Mrs Campbell's class because my Mum told me the story when I was older, and it has been repeated occasionally over the years. Mrs Campbell apparently told my Mum what I had said and how 'touched' she was by it. And being proud of her son, my Mum told her friends and relatives. While she was doing this they generated a narrative about my supposed 'sweet' nature as a child. This narrative eventually found its way to me and I can draw on it if I want to impress on people how nice I am. Neither of these memories represents the reality of the events themselves. But what I am saying is that we need other people to help make sense of our experiences. The sleepwalking incident had little resonance, just a little boy needed to be put back to bed, and it was quickly forgotten by my parents even though I 'remember' it. The Mrs Campbell story, on the other hand, had social and cultural clout for my Mum, who no doubt exploited it in subsequent conversations. But who does the memory belong to – me, her, both of us? Our memories are constructed to large extent through our social interactions

CHAPTER 3

and the narratives we generate out of them. In that sense, it is not useful to think of memories as produced 'in our heads', but in the stories and narratives we construct and learn with others about our experiences. So language plays a crucial role in 'remembering'. Without it we cannot sensibly story our lives. And as social constructs, language and the narratives we produce make the process of memory construction primarily a social activity.

So I need to say something about how I am defining PM. In chapter one I said it is part of the collective memory of English teaching. It can be understood as a social, relational process. Yet I did not start out with a pre-determined conception of 'memory'. This evolved through my engagement and interaction with the teachers, which forced me to consider the connections between them. I drew on cultural and social understandings of memory as an aspect of 'mind'. So PM is a way of recovering and analysing collective lived experience. To explain this I need to draw on different theoretical perspectives. Conceptions of 'self' or 'mind' have tended to be constructed from an individualist perspective in different traditions. This is true of 'constructivism', which Gergen argues is a tradition where 'each individual mentally constructs the world of experience' (1999: 236). From this perspective the individual 'mind' functions to 'create the world as we know it', meaning there can be as many 'realities as there are minds to conceptualise or construe' (1999: 236). For constructivists the 'process of world construction is psychological; it takes place "in the head"' (1999: 237). But Gergen highlights a key distinction between 'constructivism' and 'social constructionism':

> In contrast, for social constructionists what we take to be real is an outcome of social relationships. This is no small matter, either intellectually or politically. Constructivism is allied with the individualist tradition in the West, the individual mind is the centre of interest. Yet, many constructionists are deeply critical of the individualist tradition and search for relational alternatives to understanding and action. (1999: 237)

Both traditions emphasise human construction in the generation of what we take to be 'real'. However, through a social constructionist lens 'mind', 'self' and 'memory' can be conceptualised as collective, social phenomena that are influenced by an intricate mosaic of contexts, discourses and practices ('relational alternatives'). Gergen (2001) insists it is impossible to escape the influence of historical context in the construction of 'mind'. History does not simply serve to give 'conditions of expression to an otherwise fixed domain of psychological functioning', but rather: 'the historical is the origin of the mental. That is, mental processes – both the ontology of the mind and the specific manifestations – are byproducts of antecedent historical conditions' (2001: 87). Through social relationships individuals acquire models for appropriate types of public performance and utterance, and the templates for these are always historical constructions. Gergen (1999) even insists that what appear to be personal emotions are constructed in this way: 'We gain much by replacing the image of private "feelings" with public action; it is not that we *have* emotions, a thought, or a memory so much as we *do* them' (1999: 132). Action and performance are 'constituents of relationship' that are 'inhabited' by a history of relationships, and shaped by 'the relationships into which they are directed' (1999: 132). From this perspective Gergen makes the radical claim,

> There is no creation of an independent mind though social relationships...We don't have to worry about how the social world gains entry into the subjective world of the individual...there is no independent territory called 'mind' that demands attention. There is action, and action is constituted within and gains its intelligibility through relationship. (1999: 133)

This does not mean human agency, identity and individuality are dismissed. But when considering who we 'are' it is essential to think about how memories, beliefs, values and ideological perspectives are constructed in relation to the various material contexts in which we live (also see Berger & Luckman, 1966). This understanding of mind and memory as social, relational constructs sits uneasily alongside dominant individualist discourses. There is a long tradition of memory being regarded as an internal, individual process. Studies in memory trace back to ancient civilisations. Russell (1984) examines how Orphic sects in ancient Greece drew symbolically on the myth of 'Mnemosyne' (remembrance) as the 'well-spring to drink from' to gain spiritual redemption,

> The soul in the next world, if it is to achieve salvation, is not to forget, but, on the contrary, to acquire a memory surpassing what is natural. (1984: 39)

This concept of memory works on the philosophical proposition that the individual 'soul' or 'spirit' precedes physical life, and lives on afterwards. It can of course be seen in religious ritual today. But I view memory from a materialist, dialectical perspective. Circumstances at any given point will influence how and why we remember experiences the way we do, and how we narrate them. But does all experience become 'memory'? Not necessarily. For instance, when Henri Bergson published *Matter and Memory* (2004, originally published 1896) at the end of the 19th century he defined two types of memory: 'motor mechanisms' and 'independent recollections' (or reflex and voluntary action). He gives the example of learning a 'lesson by heart', a poem for instance. Once committed to memory an individual might be able to recite the poem at will. However the process of memorisation is long and drawn-out and each 'reading' occurs in a different set of circumstances, a distinct point in a person's history. Simply reciting the poem without necessarily being able to remember the contexts in which it was learned, separate readings, different meanings, or other occasions it was recited, means the performance is habitual. This, according to Bergson is 'motor' memory, and not really *memory* at all. Russell (1984) picks up on this and argues that 'independent recollections' on the other hand form part of,

> The second sort, which alone really deserves to be called memory, is exhibited in recollections of separate occasions when he has read the poem, each unique and with a date. (1984: 760)

CHAPTER 3

There is no suggestion of *habit* here because events and contexts must be reconstructed each time they are accessed. In short, individuals must act upon past experiences to contextualise them and reproduce them into social narratives. Although helpful, Bergson's focus is on individual experience. I am interested in how groups are enabled to construct memory to represent the past. I foreground the material, social, historical and cultural contexts in which it is located. Over time, memory studies have diversified into different traditions and disciplines. Psychology seems like the obvious place to start. But I am not interested necessarily in the 'workings' or 'mechanics' of individual memory in the ways that cognitive psychology or neuroscience might be. Rather, I am interested in how memory is constructed and represented by particular groups at certain points in history. So I draw on the work of French sociologist Maurice Halbwachs (1992) who pioneered the concept of 'collective memory' in the early twentieth century. PM is part of this tradition.

COLLECTIVE MEMORY

Collective memory is a term applied to the socially shared memory of particular groups. It emphasises the irreducibly social character of memory. Individuals converge with the collective through relationship, social action, discourse, semiotic systems and so on – all of which influence memory construction. Halbwachs (1992) examines how memory is constructed by specific groups, including family, religion and social class; but also sub-groups, including nation, occupation, clubs/associations. In fact any group that shares common interests, values or beliefs. Each group has specific memories that help its members to interrelate and maintain identity. Individuals draw on collective contexts to recall and re-present past events. But, as Coser argues (introduction to Halbwachs, 1992), the past can never be recreated as it was, only reconstructed in the present by group members working to 'imaginatively re-enact' it. What is omitted from these 're-enactments' is as important as what is included. Halbwachs insists memory can really only function within collective contexts. Different social groups will have different collective memories, and depending on which they select, their behaviour and conceptions of reality will be differently affected. Many factors influence the construction of collective memory – class, religion, education and so on. Temporal and spatial factors also have a significant influence on this process. Various traditions, myths and ideologies, constructed through dominant cultural perspectives, are perpetuated both individually and collectively and are constantly re-configured. Halbwachs insists that cultural tools are essential for recovering, structuring and representing memory,

> No memory is possible outside frameworks used by people living in society to determine and retrieve their recollections. (1992: 43)

Our ability to shape and represent memories is impossible without specific kinds of cultural tools, with language being the most fundamental. But there are tensions and contradictions in the interrelations between the individual and collective, between memory and history. Anna Green (2004) differentiates between 'oral' and 'cultural' history, with cultural history represented through pre-existing ways of telling. Linguistic templates exist beyond the individual, even though we may use them quite happily and confidently to talk about past events. Green argues 'individual recollections fit (often unconscious) cultural scripts or mental templates' (2004: 35). The interrelation of individual and group can be analysed as a rich site of pre-existing cultural templates that help produce particular types of narratives. It is also a site where individual identity and agency struggle to remain intact. Cultural tools and frameworks (most significantly language and narrative) not only allow individuals to represent experiences and memories socially, but influence the construction of memory in the first place. Language plays a crucial role in thinking, memory and narrative representation (see Vygotsky, 1978, 1986; Volosinov, 1973). Bakhtin's (1981, 1986) concepts of dialogism, heteroglossia and speech genre highlight the complexities of human relationships and the impossibility of distilling language and memory into a single unity. The irreducibly social nature of memory construction makes it inevitable that we speak, think and remember with 'echoes' of others' voices.

So collective memory is a complicated phenomenon. My definition of PM draws on the sociological explanations of Halbwachs and social constructionism. Middleton and Brown (2005) highlight the limitations of traditional psychology in explaining memory phenomena, arguing instead for it to be located into social contexts. They critique both Bergson's focus on individual memory and Halbwachs' collectivist perspective. Differentiating between terms such as 'history' and 'memory', or 'individual' and 'collective' is pointless, they argue. These terms are not 'opposing forces' or 'mutually exclusive', but are 'necessary partners' in the complicated processes of remembering, forgetting and representing. These are processes whereby, 'remembering and forgetting are caught up in an endless dynamic of the spatialisation of experience, the actualisation of the virtual' (2005: 232). Memory is the complex process of representing experience in context, time and space. In that case memory cannot be located in any single place, and can only be analysed through the social, cultural and material contexts in which it occurs. Middleton and Brown argue,

> What we have been at pains to emphasise...is that – to the extent that remembering is a spatially located activity – the greater part of that activity occurs collectively, in the engagement of people with their material environments. However, more importantly, memory, and experience itself, is fundamentally a matter of time, of duration. As such, it is not located anywhere at all, so to search for a way to catch hold of memories themselves within the brain is, as Bergson puts it, to risk tiring one's hand in the attempt to crush smoke. (2005: 232)

What is needed instead is a 'social' psychology that engages with the broader social sciences of anthropology, sociology and history to understand how 'personal experience becomes afforded by and recruited to organised settings' (2005: 232). Individuals remember experiences, but what is remembered is shaped by social activity, dealings with others and expectations in material contexts. Misztal (2003) claims memory is highly inter-subjective, with various 'communities' constructing social boundaries that contribute to collective identity (also see Freeman, 1993). From this perspective memory construction is intensely ideological. An interesting way of conceptualising collective memory is to consider how social power relations influence it. Radley (1990) and Billig (1990) show how collective memory is intricately bound up with ideology. Billig argues if memory is 'collectively determined' then it is also 'ideologically determined'. The cultural tools that mediate memory construction must also be part of 'wider ideological patterns'. As a result,

> Ideology itself will be a form of social memory…it constitutes what is remembered and also what is forgotten…In this way, memory will be both a part of ideology, as well as being a process by which ideology, and thereby the power relations of society, are reproduced. (1990: 60)

Billig demonstrates how particular ideologies are present in the memories of British families towards the monarchy. Royalty is part of national collective memory; royal history is taught in schools; royal events reported; there are many narratives of royal genealogy, palaces, portraits, statues and so on. Billig argues royalty represents the continuity of a particular historical narrative. For royalty to be commemorated and revered in these ways, social groups must have 'historical consciousness, which is more than a memory for historical events, but which is a consciousness, or ideology, of history itself' (1990: 74). As a result, 'history' is about royal events, hierarchy, pomp and circumstance, rather than 'ordinary' people's lives. This profoundly ideological construction of 'history' forms part of a national collective memory. But all memory construction is intensely ideological. When we produce testimonies and narratives, we do so from certain perspectives, value positions, assumptions. Shotter (1990) puts it like this:

> My argument is that it is because our ways of talking about our experiences work, not primarily to represent the nature of those experiences in themselves, but to represent them in such a way as to constitute and sustain one or other kind of social order. (1990: 122–123)

What kinds of 'social order'? Exactly how much influence do shared 'ways of talking about experiences' have on people's memories? The teachers in this book have constructed memories of English teaching in the 'cauldron' that are in ideological opposition to 'official' versions of the subject. To understand these memories they need to be located into various historical circumstances, into the social, cultural and material contexts in which they were both constructed and now mediated. Groups intentionally represent themselves in particular ways through collective memory. Bakhurst (1990) uses Vygotsky's work to help define some of these processes.

Vygotsky insists that individuals can only become proficient in the 'higher mental function' of memory by mastering, or 'internalising' semiotic systems. He differentiates between 'elementary' and 'higher' mental functions. Bakhurst argues the former is a state of 'involuntary recall' occurring through external stimuli, and over which we have little control. However,

> In contrast, the higher mental function of memory permits us to search at will for an image or an account of the past. In such voluntary or 'logical' memory, it is not that the mind is just prompted to 'go and get' an image by some encounter in the present; rather, the past is deliberately recalled for a determinate reason. (1990: 209–210)

We deliberately shape our narratives to represent the past in particular ways. These narrative representations are influenced by participants, intentions, contexts, settings, previous utterances, events and so on. As a result Bakhurst claims that for Vygotsky, 'no form of adult memory can be rendered intelligible without essential reference to the concepts of "society", "community" and "culture"' (1990: 212). Bakhurst adds the work of Volosinov, who shared the belief that memory is socially and semiotically mediated. For Volosinov, individual memory cannot be a 'private mental image of the past' (1990: 220). Rather, 'images' only become memory when they are reproduced into narrative. Both Volosinov and Vygotsky insist that the foundations of 'mind' are 'social' and 'cultural'. Thought, consciousness and memory are developed by individuals through social interaction. These higher mental states can only be understood socially and culturally as ideological constructions. 'Mind' can only be understood in this way, and not through physical and natural science. To illustrate this, Bakhurst uses the analogy of TV drama: the *content* of the drama cannot be understood through the medium of TV alone:

> Just as it would be hopeless to look for law-like relations between the physical states of television and the semantic content of the programmes it transmits, so the search for laws relating to the states of mind and brain is, for Voloshinov, equally in vain. (1990: 220)

Bakhurst's discussion distils into three main points – the functions of memory are 'essentially social in origin'; 'memories are socially constituted states'; and collective acts represent forms of social memory that are 'irreducible to the happenings in any individual mind', but are at the same time 'essential to the continuity of the mental life of each individual' (1990: 223). Bakhurst carefully points out that these ideas 'will seem wild and unscientific from the perspective of contemporary cognitive science' (1990: 224). Nonetheless, he insists the construction of memory is reliant upon the skilful control of socially constructed semiotic tools available in a given culture. These tools, bound by history and ideology, supply templates for individuals to narrate and represent their personal, individual memories. This is not to say individual memory is dismissed as unimportant, subordinated always to the collective. But to understand individual memories it is important to place them into the various contexts and circumstances that contribute to their construction. The PM of English teaching is constructed in these ways.

AUTOBIOGRAPHICAL AND HISTORICAL MEMORY

Halbwachs (1992) divides collective memory into the 'historical' and 'autobiographical'. Memory and history are different processes for making sense of past events. Social, collective, popular memory and tradition all cease to function at a certain point, when 'history' begins. Only a small number of specialists practise 'history', whereas collective memory is everyone's. There are countless collective memories that do not necessarily contribute to an official history. An ambition of this book is to locate the PM of English teachers more firmly into the collective memory of the subject, both historically and autobiographically. According to Halbwachs, both types rely on commemoration to be sustained, but 'historical' refers to memory reproduced through officially sanctioned cultural artefacts – written documents, records, histories, photographs, statues, portraits and the like. So individuals have 'memories' of events, people or circumstances they could not possibly have encountered (Billig, 1990; Schudson, 1990; Schwartz, 1990). For example, in the UK Remembrance Sunday and Bonfire Night are commemorated and maintained in national historical memory. Smaller 'special interest' groups might have things to remember too: John Lennon's death might be commemorated by some music fans, Shakespeare's birthday by theatre goers. If individuals have no access to the artefacts that reproduce historical accounts of events, they are less likely to want to remember them. So, while England football fans might sing about 'thirty years of hurt', others might say 'so what'. This appears to be the case in different settings. Wertsch (2002) illustrates how official Russian interpretations of WW2 influence collective understandings of contemporary teenagers learning 'history' in schools – understandings that are very different to his own 'western' perspective. Schwartz (1982, 1990) considers how the 'iconography of the Capitol' and Abraham Lincoln help create a collective identity in the USA through portraits and statues. Schudson (1990) similarly analyses the way Ronald Reagan is 'misremembered'. Pierre Nora (1989) argues different 'sites of memory' exist in the various social contexts and institutions of France that influence national and individual identity. Nora's ideas are interesting because they highlight the fallibility of memory, suggesting it is inconsistent and easily influenced by factors such as nostalgia, space and time. Legg (2005: 487) analyses Nora's ideas and argues that as 'memory became envisioned as a representation of the past, rather than its repetition, it became amenable to nostalgic desires provoked by sociohistorical change'. So, 'historical' memory is socially, culturally and ideologically powerful. But what about everyday experience?

'Autobiographical' refers to memories of lived experience. For example, a couple might construct a narrative about their first date, or friends might remember teachers at a school reunion. A key difference between both types for Halbwachs is that only members of the immediate group can have autobiographical memories because they experience events and construct the past themselves. But both types originate in social, inter-personal contexts, and when reproduced into narrative they become irreducibly social because they rely on semiotic systems. The complexities of these processes mean that individual and group identities are constructed and maintained in a continuous struggle between historical and autobiographical memory, and in wider social, cultural, historical and ideological contexts. So how useful is memory for making sense of the past?

Gardner confronts the tensions between memory and history. He argues that 'official' versions of 'history', those written by 'historians', 'may be seen as permanently threatened with collapse into the realms of fable, myth or fiction' (2010: 14). Historians rely on various assumptions for claims of 'truth' or 'reality' they make about historical events. These assumptions include the belief that by seriously engaging with 'evidence' and using rigorous,

> ...interpretive procedures, the past may indeed be known in ways that might legitimately be called true, that there can be a knowledge of past time which might, in principle, fairly match the reality it constituted when it was yet present time. (2010: 4)

Gardner is suspicious about this. He suggests some historians are too comfortable with the notion of 'interpretation'. Textual production of histories involves analysis of past events. But also the imagination and intentionality of the historian, who is located in a variety of contexts: historical, social, personal, geographical, ideological. In that case epistemological claims made through written histories are relative, not universal. But assumptions about the concept of historical 'truth' allow claims of universality to be made. In this way some historians 'involve both terms, "truth" and "interpretation", in the same breath without evincing very much in the way of anxiety [or] self-doubt' (2010: 6). Gardner argues a major methodological re-think is essential if history is to escape accusations of relativism. 'Interpretation', as a key tool, and a search for 'truth' are incompatible and contradictory. So history, like memory, is a contested terrain and far from straightforward. This is an important point. I do not claim my analysis of the teachers' collective memories represents the 'truth'. I acknowledge my own positionality in the interpretive process. But by locating the collective memories into various contexts, and by foregrounding characteristic themes and concerns, it is possible to produce an alternative layer of narrative about English teaching in the 'cauldron'. This of course can be held up to scrutiny for others to decide how believable the narrative is.

English teaching is located in both historical and autobiographical memory. Official policy documents, histories, heritage, tradition and the canon all constitute the historical. The millions of teachers and students, who have experienced the subject, remember events in their own particular autobiographical contexts. Both types are commemorated in arguments, debates and continuous changes in policy and focus. But the historical memory of English in current contexts is predicated on culturally elitist conceptions of the subject. Versions of English as 'radical' or 'progressive',

CHAPTER 3

particularly between 1965–1975, tend to be depicted negatively in official discourses (Coultas, 2013; Yandell, 2013). Yet the collective, autobiographical memories of the teachers in this book tell a more positive and nuanced story. Their experiences of working in the 'cauldron' have helped them construct potent memories and narratives to maintain a clear sense of professional identity throughout their careers. They inevitably draw on official discourses about English in the period. Sometimes their own memories are dramatically different to official versions. Narratives about their working lives have been discussed, considered, presented and re-configured over decades in the processes of remembering and telling. Their engagement with policy initiatives or theories of practice will also have influenced their attitudes. Middleton and Edwards (1990) suggest that in remembering together, groups and individuals set precedents that influence future memories:

> For example, when people reminisce about family photographs, or recount shared experiences of times of happiness and trauma at weddings and funerals, what is commemorated extends beyond the sum of the participants' individual experiences: it becomes the basis of future reminiscence. (1990: 7)

Collective memories and narratives form the basis for future action. Yet there are tensions between the historical and autobiographical memory of English teaching. This makes it crucial to recover practitioners' lived experience through autobiographical memory. Locating it alongside the 'historical' memory of English can create a more comprehensive collective memory for the profession. Generating PM can recover versions of English that form the 'basis for future reminiscence'. PM can contribute to the collective memory of today's practitioners by providing alternative critical accounts from teachers in different conjunctures. The critical examination of narrative, collective memory and lived experience in various conjunctures can help practitioners forge more distinct professional identities and a greater sense of agency.

INNER SPEECH AND SPEECH GENRE

Vygotsky (1978, 1986) and Volosinov (1973) argue that external, social action is transformed into 'inner speech' through 'internalisation': a dialectic and dialogic process. Vygotsky insists 'the true direction of the development of thinking is not from the individual to the social, but from the social to the individual' (1986: 36). When re-introduced in social contexts, through 'outward expression', these internalisations are reproduced into 'speech genres' – ways of talking in particular contexts. All signs are socially constructed, and are organised into 'repertoire[s] of speech forms for ideological communication in human behaviour' (1986: 20). Like Vygotsky, Volosinov (1973) foregrounds the fundamental role language plays in understanding lived experience: 'experience exists even for the person undergoing it only in the material of signs' (1973: 28). Any experience has the potential to gain semiotic significance, therefore becoming expressive. Individuals select and express experiences that are socially and culturally relevant. And the 'word', as 'the skeleton of inner life', allows individuals to develop 'inner speech'. Volosinov insists,

> Any psyche that has reached any degree of development and differentiation must have subtle and pliable semiotic material at its disposal…that can be shaped, refined, and differentiated in the extra-corporeal social milieu in the process of outward expression. Therefore, the semiotic material of the psyche is pre-eminently the word – *inner speech*…Were it deprived of the word, the psyche would shrink to an extreme degree; deprived of all other expressive activities, it would die out all together. (1973: 29)

Thought and memory are developed through these same transformational processes. Vygotsky insists all 'higher' mental functions 'originate as actual relations between human individuals' (1978: 57). This means, as Gergen maintains, 'we are all made up of each other' (1999: 138). Conceptualising the 'self' as 'relational' is crucial for individuals to consider how these processes occur. In terms of English teaching it seems some of these ideas influenced the pioneering practitioners who re-imagined the subject following WW2. As Dixon claimed: 'there had to be a revolutionary break from defining language as reified object, towards observing social processes dependent on signs in use' (1991: 186). Particularly useful here are Bakhtin's concepts of dialogism, heteroglossia and speech genre. If thought and memory are semiotically mediated, then how are they influenced in both their construction and ultimate representation in discourse? Bakhtin's (1986) concept of *speech genres*, and in particular the *utterance,* is helpful. He argues grammar, words and sentences serve no meaningful communicative function because they are,

> …not demarcated on either side by a change of speaking subjects; [they have] neither contact with reality (with an extraverbal situation) nor a direct relation to others' utterances; [they do] not have semantic fullness of value; and [they have] no capacity to determine directly the responsive position of the *other* speaker, that is, [they] cannot evoke a response. (1986: 74)

The 'utterance' on the other hand does all of this. When selected by a speaker in context, utterances can be manipulated into an infinite number of appropriate *genres*. The utterance presumes a history and other speaking subjects. There must be a level of 'addressivity' because utterances respond to, and expect response from, previous and subsequent ones. Inner Speech, like the verbal utterance, is influenced by these same forces and has a particular 'addressivity'. Bakhtin (1986) insists all individual utterances (verbal or written) contain 'echoes' of others' voices, which lay templates for genre and narrative structure, often from particular ideological perspectives. Individuals act appropriately (or not) in different contexts by drawing on these templates, or 'speech genres'. Like Gergen's 'relationships', utterances are made in response to a history of previous ones, and projected into subsequent ones with intent and expected outcomes. Depending on how we evaluate the influence of the 'echoes', chosen genres will be orientated either towards or against dominant

CHAPTER 3

ideological perspectives. And although we imbue our utterances with 'individual style', based on convictions, ideological perspectives and so on, we are influenced by 'expected' forms of language and behaviour that are suitable for the social contexts we operate in. Bakhtin suggests,

> Each separate utterance is individual, of course, but each sphere in which language is used develops its own *relatively stable types* of utterances. These we may call *speech genres*. (1986: 60)

Speech genres are simultaneously constraining and enabling. Utterance, speech genre and memory will be influenced by social, ideological and cultural circumstances in a particular conjuncture. This process is further complicated by the dominant effects of *heteroglossia*. Human existence is determined by complex dialogic and multi-voiced processes that are un-limitable and transformative. An utterance's meaning is governed by a range of factors (physical, cultural, social, historical) that will vary with context. The continuous interplay of meanings through dialogue sees individual utterances merging with, challenging and re-shaping others' utterances. For this reason language, and life, cannot be resolved into a single unity: an individualist conception of human consciousness is impossible. As a consequence there can be no 'monologue' because it would be 'cut off from the fundamentally social modes in which discourse lives' (Bakhtin, 1981: 259).

However, dominant social groups frequently use 'monologic' discourses to give the impression that one ideological position is closely related to social reality. Bakhtin argues such discourses are deliberately intended to evoke 'a silent responsive understanding…with a delayed reaction', and sooner or later what is heard and understood will 'find its response in the subsequent speech or behaviour of the listener' (1986: 69). In this way individuals are debilitated in a continuous struggle between external, monologic conceptions of reality and the dialogic realities in which they live. Bakhtin insists 'standard' languages work in this same monological way. Individuals are given 'mandatory forms of the national language' (1986: 80) which limit opportunities to engage with the heteroglossial realities of ordinary talk. 'Standard' English of course is presented in such monological terms. In current contexts English teaching is dominated by monological conceptions of curriculum, pedagogy, aims and outcomes: think of the National Curriculum, various 'strategies', grammar tests, Ofsted inspections. These interventions promote a limited, and limiting, conception of the subject which is 'cut off from the fundamentally social modes' in which it operates. From a 'relational' and 'heteroglossial' perspective, the aims and intentions of English must emerge from the collaborative voices of stakeholders (teachers, children, parents) who exist in their various material contexts.

For Bakhtin, critical individuals learn how to challenge and repudiate authoritative discourse, taking from others' utterances ideas that correspond with their own experiences, missions, values. For some practitioners in the 'cauldron' English lessons aimed to give students the skills to understand how the narratives they are born into ultimately influence how they story their lives. Understanding these processes makes it possible to restructure dominant narratives and potentially change one's life trajectory. But this has to be a collective endeavour – an exploration; a negotiation; an agreement. But different speech genres in English teaching exist. This is evident in the ways the subject is discussed socially, politically, in academic discourse and policy interventions. But the utterances, genres and narratives that groups generate contribute to their collective memories, identities, actions. By sharing stories individuals are immersed in shared community and shared memory (Orr, 1990). Understanding how collective memory is constructed through speech genre and inner speech can empower practitioners to re-configure dominant discourses in English teaching.

SOCIAL CONSTRUCTIONISM

I have suggested memory is irreducibly social and relies on semiotic systems both for construction and meaningful representation. As Bakhtin (1986: 26) puts it, 'consciousness is never self sufficient…it always finds itself in an intense relationship with another consciousness'. We are always in dialogue and always addressing someone. Consciousness is immersed in a history of social relationships and culture. But how are conscious memories 'played out' socially? One explanation comes in Goffman's (1959) 'dramaturgical' metaphor, which suggests individuals, as social 'actors', play different dramatic roles in different contexts. Expectations of behaviour influence individuals to take on roles, personas and performances depending on other people involved and the objective of the situation. The world is organised in particular ways to provide the setting, props and costume expected in different contexts. Acting out these 'roles' constitutes a type of memory. Individuals learn how to 'perform' in different contexts and produce the right 'moves' from memory, verbally, kinaesthetically, spatially: memory as social action. But Gergen (1999, 2001) argues this idea of 'performance' in Goffman's work is 'deeply unsettling'. Goffman's 'actors' can only be manipulative, insincere and disingenuous because they have intent. Gergen claims,

> Goffman's analysis suggests that just beneath the surface of our actions there is manipulative agent who is continuously conning others. Sincerity itself is just a con, which might succeed in duping the actor. To accept such a view leaves us with an enormous distance between ourselves and others, a prevailing sense of distrust, a doubt in all support, gratitude, or affection. (1999: 78)

This is clearly unsatisfactory. All utterances are 'performances within some social group, serving let us say to establishing hierarchies, set agendas, welcome one form of action as opposed to another' (1999: 132). Gergen argues the same is true for psychological states, emotions and memory. All conscious aspects of mind are socially mediated, and performed in concrete circumstances with expectations of language and action. If we scratch the surface, or 'challenge the taken-for-granted ways of indexing our world – even momentarily – the social fabric quickly unravels' (1999: 80), and the ways in which we 'con' ourselves and others are laid bare. Gergen argues that a social constructionist understanding of mind, self and memory can reduce the 'debilitating gap between self and other' (1999: 137). The 'relational being' or 'relational self' should have no need to be 'self-seeking' as 'we are made up of each other' (1999: 138). Memory is a way of doing or acting, forged in social relationships, and Gergen insists: 'The challenge we now confront is generating an understanding of memory as a relational phenomenon' (1999: 134). He argues a student 'writing a paper', someone 'being rejected by a friend', or an actress 'preparing her lines' are essentially 'public actions'. That is, thinking, reproducing appropriate emotions and imagining are all socially constructed ways of acting. Individuals cannot extricate themselves from the grip of semiotic systems. Gergen rejects traditional psychology's view of memory as 'quintessentially individualist'. He is critical of psychologists or neurologists who, 'presume that the word "memory" stands for a specific process in the head of the individual, a process that is neurologically based and universal in its functioning' (1999: 134). Similarly, Vivien Burr argues for a 'discursive' psychology that 'both reframes the status of language in psychology and also considers psychology's usual subject matter, i.e. internal states and structures, somewhat irrelevant' (2003: 131–132). Gergen's and Burr's ideas have relevance here. There are ways of discussing English teaching in the 1960s/1970s that transcend individual recollection. A relational and discursive conceptualisation of memory can help generate understandings of how collective memories are formed, defined and reproduced. This makes it possible to consider how the values, concerns and traditions of English teachers are handed from one generation to the next, by examining the 'relational alternatives' they draw on. To do this means taking seriously what Young and Collin argue are social constructionism's key concerns:

> ...social constructionism asserts that knowledge is historically and culturally specific; that language constitutes rather than reflects reality, and is both a pre-condition for thought and a form of social action; that the focus of enquiry should be on interaction, processes, and social practices. Corollaries of the social construction of knowledge are indeterminacy, polyvocality, the need for contextualisation, and "pragmatics"...Importantly, social constructionism does more than say that something is socially constructed: it points to the historical and cultural location of that construction. (2004: 377)

A social constructionist understanding of memory makes it possible to consider how teachers draw on existing social, cultural and historical templates to generate a collective picture of English teaching. Michael Crotty insists knowledge and meaning are constructed through social interaction. But individuals do not construct new knowledge in an original way; they do it from pre-existing social, cultural and historical material. Crotty argues constructivism 'points to the unique experience of each of us' (1998: 58). Alternatively, social constructionism 'emphasises the hold culture has on us' (1998: 58). This cultural 'hold' is positive because it 'makes us human'. Understanding how culture influences social action allows for greater critical understanding. Indeed, Crotty argues, 'constructivism tends to resist the critical spirit, while constructionism tends to foster it' (1998: 58). Critically examining the influence of discourse and speech genres in the construction of identity can help us understand the narrative realities we create. In doing this, practitioners might generate alternative narratives to challenge dominant discourses in English teaching. For instance, PM studies might provoke critical engagement with 'monologic' conceptions of English to generate new ways of conceptualising the subject. Might it be possible to answer Gergen's question:

> Could we generate a new family of metaphors, narratives, images and the like that can reconstitute meaning as a by-product of persons within environments? (1999: 138)

NARRATIVE REPRESENTATION AND PM

PM is the act of re-telling, the process of constructing stories about past events. But it is separate from historical realities themselves. It is coloured by ideology, bias, omissions, emphases, embellishments and so on. Narrative helps construct both history and memory (Laszlo, 1997). And although coloured by individual tastes or dislikes, and by available semiotic tools, Padden (1990) argues that all languages and social narratives are fundamentally collective memories. Verbal language and inner speech enable individuals to story their experience. Narrative representations of autobiographical memory reveal the ways that individuals wish to be viewed and past events remembered. From a collective memory perspective, recall is not spontaneous or individual, but is rehearsed and carefully constructed in social and cultural circumstances. Rosen (1998) follows the sociological tradition of Halbwachs in claiming memory representation is a collective act. Individuals engage in a 'social struggle' to gain ascendancy over their memories. This involves telling and re-telling until, in collaboration with others, acceptable versions of past events are produced. Indeed,

> A memory becomes collective because it emerges from the constant negotiation of conversation…memories must be saturated with social meaning as soon as they are turned into texts, spoken or written. They may have been formulated already in inner-speech but when they are externalised they must draw on memories of existing texts…every text is a complex intertwining of social meanings encoded in language. This can be seen in the central device of autobiography – narrative. (1998: 132)

We practise our narratives until we are happy with them, until memory can be represented in ways we find comfortable and appropriate. Depending on audience and purpose, as Bakhtin (1986) suggests, individuals move between genres to construct narratives. Learning how to 'narrate' competently is essential to maintaining social and cultural relationships. It is crucial to be able to construct sensible (not necessarily 'true') versions of past events and conceptions of reality. Bruner suggests,

> Once one takes the view that a culture itself comprises an ambiguous text that is constantly in need of interpretation by those who participate in it, then the constitutive role of language in creating social reality becomes a topic of practical concern. (1986: 122)

Language is the primary tool through which history and memory are represented through narrative. According to Bruner, experience becomes meaningful through a 'narrative mode' of expression which draws on the conventions of storytelling. Narratives operate in 'two landscapes simultaneously' – 'action' and 'consciousness'. Characters, motivations, situations and so on must be present for narrative coherence in the landscape of 'action'. However,

> The other landscape is the landscape of consciousness: what those involved in the action know, think, or feel, or do not know, think, or feel. The two landscapes are essential and distinct: it is the difference between Oedipus sharing Jocasta's bed before and after he learns from the messenger that she is his mother. (1986: 14)

Bruner argues 'psychic reality' dominates narrative and the landscape of consciousness requires experience, interpretation and empathy for it to begin to be understood. We need to understand how narratives can be deliberately authored for 'dramatic effect' and then fill in the gaps. Bruner (1990) argues that narrative enables individuals to explain discrepancies in what they perceive to be normal, everyday events and those that are more unusual. By operating in the separate landscapes of action and consciousness, drawing on 'psychic reality' and using embellishments for 'dramatic effect', individuals construct narratives to make sense of wide-ranging, often disordered and misunderstood experiences. Narrative serves a number of important functions, including the ability to solve problems, reduce tension between experience and reality, or find resolutions to predicaments. Bruner (1996) develops these ideas and defines nine 'universals of narrative realities'. These include aspects of 'performance' – how and why individuals narrate the ways they do; 'interpretation' – what happens in the gap between saying and hearing; 'identity and self' – how and why particular versions of 'self' are created. Bruner suggests,

> We construct a 'life' by creating an identity-conserving Self who wakes up the next day still mostly the same. We seem to be geniuses at the 'continued story'…we impose coherence on the past, turn it into history. (1996: 143–144)

How can 'life' be understood? How is 'self' constituted through narrative? Bruner insists on a 'meta-cognitive sensitivity needed for coping with the world of narrative reality and its competing claims' (1996: 147). PM studies have potential to help create this kind of meta-cognition about English teaching. If it is possible to understand how narrative influences the collective identity of practitioners, it will be equally possible to confront these identities and generate new narrative accounts of English. Bruner urges a conscious recognition of the workings of narrative,

> It is not that we lack the competence in creating our narrative accounts of reality – far from it. We are, if anything, too expert. Our problem, rather, is achieving consciousness of what we so easily do automatically. (1996: 147)

Gaining such consciousness is difficult. But what I have been seeking to foreground is that this is fundamentally a social process. So while agreeing with Bruner, I stress the social, collective dimensions of PM. Bruner teaches us about the business of constructing a 'life', but we do this in relation to other people and through the various cultural artefacts available. PM is made up of the several perspectives discussed in this chapter, and it provides a way of understanding and interpreting the complexities of lived experience. The teachers' memories presented in the following chapters contain narratives that can be understood in these ways.

ACKNOWLEDGEMENT

Sections of this chapter have appeared, in other forms, in Tarpey, P. (2017a). 'We not I' not 'I me mine': Learning from professional memory about collectivist English teaching. *Changing English, 24*(1), 103–117; and Tarpey, P. (2017b). Disrupting continuities: Re-thinking conceptions of 'growth' in English teaching. *English in Education, 51*(2), 157–169.

CHAPTER 4

CONSTRUCTING IDENTITIES AND ATTITUDES

INTRODUCTION

Before examining the teachers' PM in the 'cauldron', I need to consider their early development, schooling and socialisation in 'English'. I want to understand how the identities and attitudes the teachers took into the job were affected by various conjunctural circumstances. This can highlight what Gill and Goodson refer to as 'the social construction of subjectivity in relation to dominant discourses' (2011: 160). It can also encourage reflection and reflexivity, because by 'telling' their experiences, individuals can 'interpret the social world and their agency within it' (2011: 160). Locating memory into conjunctural circumstances can unfold the ways that individuals and groups understand experience. In the context of this book, exploring early experiences creates a genealogy of context for the teachers' subsequent work in the 'cauldron'.

To analyse the teachers' narratives I draw on the theoretical perspectives discussed in the previous chapter. The issues I focus on emerged through constant comparison of the interviews (Glaser & Strauss, 1967; Thomas, 2009). I explored this 'initial' phase in the teachers' development with questions focussed on 'formal' encounters with the school subject 'English'. However, it transpired that they all referred to pre-school experiences, at home with the family, wider community and other social contexts, certainly before 'formal' schooling. This was spontaneously volunteered, and I was struck by the ways they referred to similar events in their lives and school experiences. For example, all of them claim to have had basic literacy skills prior to school. They suggest classrooms were mostly silent, restrictive spaces and lessons were repetitive and formulaic. There are exceptions however to stories of moribund practice, and the occasional lesson or teacher stands out vividly. These early experiences influenced the attitudes they took into the classroom as practitioners. I focus on what appear to be identity-shaping moments, covering a range of experiences from pre-school to teacher training – so the memories are viewed through a broad lens. An interesting starting point is that, despite questions focussing on school English, in all cases they spoke strongly about pre-school experience.

ENGLISH BEFORE SCHOOL AND ENGLISH AT SCHOOL

All the teachers claim they could read before going to school. This is variously described, and if anything, they suggest getting to school was a hindrance rather than a help. Here is a selection of their stories:

CHAPTER 4

> I think I could probably read fairly well before I went to school, but when I got to school it didn't matter of course because you all got wheeled through Janet and John. If you got beyond that it was Wide Range Readers, and I sort of whipped through that sort of stuff. The other thing I remember about reading was sort of outside school, and that was sort of books like Jennings and Just William and Billy Bunter and things like that, because they were about schools I didn't recognise. (David)

> Er, I have absolutely no memory of having been *taught* English, although I have vague ideas…of phonetic teaching. I could read before I went to school. So maybe I never paid any attention to what was being taught? I also have a book which when I did it, it seemed very big, but now it's quite small. I must have been four, and I copied out the Ladybird Book of Birds. And my handwriting goes up and down and across-ways and everything, and it was my first attempt at writing. And it seemed to be, from memory, to teach me the letters and all that. And I think I was self-taught…I sort of coasted through school as a sort of social experience, and I don't remember learning anything at school whatever. It was fun but it wasn't a place where I went to be educated. It seemed to me to be more of a joke and a laugh. (Steve)

> Well, in terms of primary and secondary I really don't remember anything because whatever was being taught in the classroom I wasn't listening to it! I had my own agenda, my own supply of books, and I always made sure I was at the back of the class…But I taught myself. (Ann)

> My Dad was an English teacher, so we were imbued in the spirit of reading, you know, we'd be walking along the promenade in Morecambe and he'd be pointing out signs to us and, you know, always looking at different forms of language. So we read very widely from a very early age, so er, you know you'd hide under the bedclothes and read, all sorts of things. I had a very happy primary education, er, and as I say, we were imbued with the spirit of English and reading. (Shaun)

These memories foreground the high value of literacy in the teachers' families. Self-reliance, self-learning and resourcefulness emerge strongly. But the timing and contexts are significant. The importance of literacy is emphasised in the immediate post-war context. The teachers were raised and went to school under the volatile shadows of WW2. They are sensitive to this. Some of them recall teachers who had fought in the war: 'I think they saw it as an extension of the army in some cases, you know, it was all about drill' (David). They recall a sense of 'post-war gloom' (Michael), or being taught by 'lots of women who'd lost men in the war. I was taught in a very bleak time I think' (Liz). So these memories were constructed in tough circumstances of general hardship and struggle. But it was also a time of optimism because this period saw the evolution of the welfare state, the NHS and an expanding education system. There was optimism that a better society could

CONSTRUCTING IDENTITIES AND ATTITUDES

be built amid the 'gloom' and 'bleakness' (Dixon, 1991; Lowe, 2007; Ball, 2008). The concept of shared ownership and the provision of services for the benefit of all was a driving motivation. Community, solidarity and co-operation were important for national unity in the post-war period, and there was the determination to tackle unemployment, poverty and health. As the welfare state was built, education, and literacy in particular, were considered crucial for social justice and democracy (Simon, 1955; Williams, 2011). Education was viewed as a way of improving children's life chances, maybe especially so among working-class families. This is not new of course, there is a long history of working-class self-education, writers' groups and co-operative movements (see Woodin, 2005, 2007, 2008, 2009).

The teachers refer to these wider circumstances in different ways but they seem to have influenced their constructions of identity and attitudes to English. Social justice, equality and a commitment to the egalitarian potential of education emerge as major collective characteristics. In the memories presented the teachers are mostly critical of their 'formal' schooling in English. Shaun is the exception, suggesting a happier experience. However, the memories build a collective picture of how attitudes to English were formed, and which they have retained as adults and teachers. Literacy is important and they all claim to have read widely outside school. At school however, there is the suggestion of going through the motions; being 'wheeled through Janet and John' is presented as unsatisfactory. Some of them claim to have no memory of English lessons, suggesting a resistance to school and having one's 'own agenda'. The strong emphasis on 'self-teaching' foregrounds a sense of confidence in the teachers' own abilities and resourcefulness that remains undiminished. All the teachers were 'imbued with the spirit' of reading from an early age which influenced their abilities and decisions made later in life. There are stereotypical aspects – the 'love' of reading, reading 'under the bedclothes' and being 'self-taught' – and these highlight some of the socially constructed 'relatively stable types of utterance' Bakhtin refers to.

There is a sense of optimism and the teachers suggest even at an early age they could critique the education they received. It is unlikely they had such advanced critical skills at the time, but their reflections now indicate they were capable of such analysis then. They present themselves as serious, capable and critically aware. Despite coming from diverse backgrounds, they describe their early experiences in strikingly similar ways.

ATTITUDES TO ENGLISH LESSONS

The teachers present school English with varying degrees of frustration or anger. They claim to have become more dissatisfied as they progressed through school. Again, Shaun is the exception, claiming he enjoyed what appears to be a more progressive approach at his seminary. The other teachers remain critical. They highlight de-motivating and belittling experiences. Liz describes having to have 'marks' at grammar school. She, and her friends, 'would be called out to stand on

CHAPTER 4

the line, where you were a B plus or a B minus…and in a way once you'd fallen from grace there was nowhere to climb back up really' (Liz). Michael highlights similar experiences, describing English as 'extremely dry and somewhat intimidating.' He shares Liz's sense of shame, claiming, 'whatever I wrote about, my teachers never seemed to quite understand what it was I was writing about. So there was a certain amount of shame attached to my own imaginative writing' (Michael). Ann suggests certain types of writing were more valued than others. She claims her teachers 'were simply drilling us through exercises that would produce the best results at the end of the day' (Ann). She recalls being 'very angry' because there 'was no private time at boarding school' to develop her own thinking and writing –

> And er, the net result was that having done lots and lots of writing in my early years, when I was a young child, pre-eleven…my opportunity to write was zero, and therefore I didn't write! And so although I could write the formulaic stuff that was required for the assessments you know, the creative stuff, the things that I would try out…at home mostly you know, I wrote all sorts of things which subsequently were interesting to look at, but they were from long ago, but there was no development. My development stopped, in terms of a writer, when I went to boarding school! (Ann)

Ann suggests these experiences influenced her to offer students a better deal when she started teaching. Steve comes from a very different background but appears to have had similarly negative experiences,

> I remember English being stunningly boring. It was one of the deadly lessons. It just literally knocked us out and killed us off. And you had to endure it, otherwise you'd get the cane or the slipper. And it was a killer, it was an absolute *killer*, and we all hated it. (Steve)

Steve is working-class and is sensitive to his schools' low expectations. His comments echo Medway's suggestion that the content of some secondary modern English lessons was 'determined by reference less to a conception of the subject than to the school's socialising function' (1990: 5). Class-consciousness is striking characteristic in all the teachers' memories. But Steve consistently foregrounds a struggle to negotiate his own approach to 'English'. David, also working-class, passed the Eleven Plus and attended grammar school. He is conscious of tensions this caused, claiming, 'I don't have good memories of secondary school…I went to the grammar school and I was the only kid off our estate who went to the grammar school that year…there were very few of us from a working-class background at the school.' (David) This caused problems in itself, but it appears English lessons were no better,

> I don't have particularly good memories of English. It was just being wheeled through the canon…there were things you had to learn by heart, which are still taking up part of my brain which I could use…I could do with that space really now! (David)

The teachers question the aims and values of English in their schools. There were struggles for identity and they claim there were few opportunities to engage critically with their own experiences and interests. They express negative attitudes to English, their teachers and schools they attended. Still, they all became English teachers and have enjoyed successful, enduring careers. Some of them insist they deliberately went into teaching 'to do a better job' than their own teachers. They claim they turned early negative experiences into positive aspects of their classroom practice. The contexts and conjunctures are important, and it seems the teachers understood some of the educational debates of the time. They perceived the unfairness of the tripartite system and rigidity of the class-structure in the post-war environment. These experiences influenced their subsequent professional identities.

THE TEACHING AND ACTIVITIES IN ENGLISH LESSONS

The model of English on offer is described as unimaginative and stultifying. Except Shaun, none of the teachers claim to have been inculcated into being independently critical in English. They describe classrooms as mostly silent, with talk only allowed to answer a teacher's occasional questions. Reading round the class was evidently a common activity, along with de-contextualised grammar exercises – 'box analysis' and 'parsing' (David). Other frequent activities included 'comprehension', 'composition' and 'précis! Endless précis!' (Michael). Shaun recalls 'sitting in the exam hall in the seminary…doing a précis…and you had to read three or four pages of dense text and reduce it to *exactly* three hundred words' (Shaun). They recall uninspiring practice with most activities described as pointless. Curriculum content was very traditional, with students paraded 'through the canon'. English was a heritage subject, with respect demanded for 'great' literature and 'correct' language.

The teachers recall negative secondary school experiences in the 1950s/early 1960s. But innovative and progressive work did exist in some schools. In chapter two I referred to the course-book, *Reflections*, published in 1963. Hardcastle (2008) suggests its authors promoted alternative aims for English. *Reflections* resulted from ways of working developed at Walworth School in the 1950s, which Hardcastle and Medway claim 'owed much to the comprehensive school ideal promulgated by the LCC and enthusiastically adopted by the school' (2013: 34). Some teachers directed curriculum change themselves. Texts like *Reflections* provided alternative templates for teachers to use if they were unhappy with existing resources. These developments set precedents for the teachers to draw on when they started out in the job. And they took them up enthusiastically. A major concern that emerges is their commitment to classroom talk. Steve claims he had no opportunities to speak with other children in English lessons,

> No, no, you got the slipper or the cane if you spoke. You got detention, you were shouted at. And I have vague memories of exercise books, you had a passage of writing and you answered questions and you couldn't go to lunch,

CHAPTER 4

> or go home, or to play-time until you'd finished them all...And it was one of the deadly, killer lessons...year after year, that's all it was, each and every lesson you just worked through the book, that's all it was! (Steve)

Steve was not the only one to suffer in silence. I asked about opportunities to talk in lessons. Liz appeared shocked – 'In my school? Good heavens, no!' (Liz). David recalls militaristic 'serried ranks and the teachers would be at the front. I can't remember a teacher ever moving round the room' (David). Ann's teachers did ask questions, but 'they were questions that the teacher expected to get the answers that they already knew. So no, it wasn't discussion' (Ann). Ann evokes a sense helplessness at being thrust into the traditions of boarding school; even the furniture seemed to bear the weight of expectation, institution, and establishment,

> It was mostly novels and you'd get a page at a time...it was usually up and down the lines. It was almost entirely predictable. You can imagine the typical English classroom, this was boarding school, these were wooden desks right, the desk and the chairs all in one. They were old fashioned *then*, and generations of kids had carved their names in the desk-tops. It reminded me of *Hard Times* right, that old wooden furniture. So we were in lines...talking in the classroom you know, that was not part of the agenda at all. (Ann)

English is recalled as remedial and hierarchical, as something that was 'done' to them, rather than participatory. But at least Ann had novels to read. Michael claims, 'I never remember reading a novel at all! Never a novel. I'm pretty sure we never studied a novel' (Michael). Again however, Shaun is the happy exception, claiming he enjoyed English and history. Although the seminary was very 'rigid and inflexible', his English and history teachers 'were absolutely outstanding, and encouraged discussion and debate and encouraged you to think for yourself' (Shaun). Context is important and Shaun's experience is unique, given the school's purpose was to produce priests,

> Obviously we boarded there, and when you say how was it different to grammar schools, or to secondary schools, well, er, a number of very obvious differences, I mean, er, you were locked away with a group of boys and twelve priests for much of the year, er, number one. Number two, it was out in the countryside, which was a *big* plus...lots of beautiful scenery, mountains, lots of walking, climbing, lots of sport, so that was fantastic. (Shaun)

The small size, location and ethos seem to have produced a more open and questioning culture. But only in English and history. Shaun claims other subjects were 'absolutely dire, er, maths and science were appallingly taught...a really quite a bizarre and very unbalanced curriculum'. It might seem unusual that they sought to become English teachers after their mostly negative experiences. However, they all agree that once they got to post-compulsory level things improved dramatically. Of course, they were older, developing their own interests and ideas. But English emerges as a subject that provides something personally inspiring, either through literature or language that forced them to pursue the subject further. This is true for Steve and Shaun who initially wanted to study and teach history. When they eventually became teachers different conjunctural circumstances encouraged them to seek broader possibilities for English than the narrow, heritage models they had experienced. Popular cultural movements in art, film, TV, literature and theatre (Bray, 2014; Lowe, 2007; Donnelly, 2005), alongside burgeoning work in sociolinguistics and cultural studies (Hoggart, 1957; Williams, 1958, 1961; Labov, 1969) encouraged some practitioners to challenge conceptions of 'English'. And some working-class teachers had come through grammar schools with different sensibilities. These circumstances provided an impetus for some groups of teachers to challenge existing orthodoxies. The teachers developed professional identities and attitudes in this milieu.

MEMORABLE TEACHERS

The teachers are mostly critical of the people who taught them. Yet they all remember at least one memorable person who stood out and inspired them in some way. They recall teachers from compulsory schooling (David, Shaun), at A' level (Ann, Michael), or teacher training college (Liz, Steve). Positive relationships appear important and it is unsurprising the teachers recall people who respected them, challenged them or simply made them laugh. Mutual respect, equality and dialogic relationships feature largely in the teachers' own examples of practice. These priorities seem to have been influenced by examples from their own time at school. David's teachers were not particularly enlightened and would 'be sort of sarcastic if kids pronounced words wrong and things like that' (David). Yet his English teacher was a published poet and mountain-climbing enthusiast. David recalls an incident when a boy asked, 'Sir, why do you write poetry?' Only to be asked in return, 'why do you shit?' This teacher, who the students 'all loved and who was brilliant', was an eccentric character. David remembers him affectionately,

> And his other thing he was into rock-climbing and you knew that you could get him off on something, you could distract him you know. And he'd demonstrate rock-climbing moves. He'd climb up the blackboard…and he'd go along and he'd get on the door-jamb. He'd be on the top of the window over the door. And one day he did this and the Head came in. And he came in and he said "You're being very quiet. Mr [Name] isn't here, you seem to be very quiet". Then there's this terrific thud, and he looks round and old [Name] has jumped off the top of the door and he's standing there behind him! (David)

The other teachers have similar stories. Michael recalls his A' level English teacher, who got him interested in Shakespeare,

> Our teacher…he has a reputation, er, I think he's written something, and er, he very interestingly began *questioning;* he was *definitely* interrogation, er, based on the text – "what's going on here?" "Why is this?" You know? (Michael)

69

CHAPTER 4

For every positive story there are many about teachers who are at best uninspiring, at worst bullies. The reasons for liking particular teachers are varied. Ann recalls being encouraged by an A' level teacher with more 'vivacity' than her previous English teachers. Having 'coasted' through O' levels doing 'formulaic' essays, Ann was surprised by a different approach, which was 'a bit of a revelation that suddenly I was expected to be thinking for myself'. She recalls handing in her first piece of work,

> The first bit of work I turned in for her, I can't remember what text it was on, I thought I'd done extremely well. I'd worked really hard because for once the teaching had become, what was happening in the lessons had become relevant to me. I'd become more engaged than I'd ever been before. And I got the essay back and she'd written something at the bottom to the effect – "I haven't found anything here interesting, because this is just what I said in the lessons, are you going to be giving me your own opinions at some point?" Question mark! There was no grade, nothing, just that. I thought *right*! I suddenly realised what the agenda was and it was totally different you see. I'd simply done what O' level teaching had prepared me to do – regurgitate. To turn out the correct answer, in nice paragraphs, well-structured and well concluded and nicely introduced and you'll get the top mark. (Ann)

Ann's feedback was completely negative, but seems to have provided a stimulus for her to improve and work harder. This indicates something about Ann's struggle for identity and she claims to have been incentivised rather than de-motivated. All the teachers suggest they had significant agency in their own development, and that they could critique social situations even at a young age. Ann remembers another young teacher she sympathised with and had her 'ears attuned to'. The teacher took 'a lot of stick from the class' and Ann wanted to know why. She concluded 'I reckoned that in fact she didn't like teaching in that formulaic way'. The teachers demonstrate critical interest in the people who taught them and do not seem content to dismiss or accept them on face value; they want to understand something about their motivations.

Again, Shaun's experiences stand out. He refers to the emotional and social 'stunting effect of the seminary on my own development'. Also, 'there was something, er, I hate to use the word unnatural because, er, unnatural about being closeted away with a hundred other boys and priests' (Shaun). But he seems to have had some of the more enlightened teachers. Shaun was animated when talking about his English and history teachers and is evidently fond of them. He recalls how his English teacher 'sat at the feet of FR Leavis and taught Leavis…as if it were the gospel'. And while this approach had 'its downside', Shaun argues he was taught to critique literature well,

> I mean if you put aside the moralism and the dogmatism, there was this notion that you had to engage with the text, that you have to look into the text for exemplification for the point you wanted to make. But more importantly than

that, er, there was, you know, we had tremendous opportunity for discussion…
we were really encouraged to discuss literally anything. (Shaun)

It was Shaun's history teacher who left the most emphatic memories however. He recalls events after decades of his own professional practice and political activism, so his narratives have been honed over a long period. Yet he consistently refers to the teachers in strikingly similar ways, emphasising the same points. Shaun's memories of these teachers appear to have been formed at a time when he was questioning his own identity and involvement in the Catholic Church. He suggests his 'break' with the church came in his mid-teens 'precisely because of these discussions'. After he, 'asked questions *about* certain things and questioned the church's authority', he concluded he was 'slightly naïve'. Crucial aspects of his identity were developed at this time,

Based on an analysis of the world, which even at that age I could see was divided into haves and have nots! So a strong sense of social justice, and a *strong* commitment to anti-racism. (Shaun)

He suggests these commitments were encouraged and developed by his history teacher,

And history again, as I've said, was probably my favourite subject. The teacher was a catholic priest…who managed to teach history from a materialist perspective, which is quite astonishing for someone who's a devout catholic. And so we did the Reformation from the perspective, er, not of the Catholic Church, but the perspective of, er, the development, or the shift if you like from feudalism to capitalism, and an understanding of how the Reformation had come about because of political reasons as well as religious reasons. And, er, he used to say to us, "oh, I expect the roof to fall in on me for teaching you all of this", you know. So he was that kind of guy. And, you know, brilliant, brilliant teacher and we really loved the guy. So, yes, a very, very happy secondary education, in terms of English and History, but not in terms of anything else, and certainly, certainly not in terms of the social aspects of it. (Shaun)

Memorable practitioners figure in all the teachers' narratives. Michael, Liz and Steve tell similar stories, although Liz and Steve refer to lecturers at teacher training college who exposed them to new, challenging ideas. Social templates exist for publicly sharing fond memories of teachers – even the *Times Educational Supplement* has a section where 'celebrities' discuss their 'favourite teacher'. As Bakhtin suggests, speech genres influence the construction of individual and group identity. The teachers draw on existing narrative templates to present their memories and they foreground people with particular characteristics. For instance, teachers are recalled who were challenging or eccentric. The teachers highlight 'love' or 'respect' for them. These narratives extend beyond individual recollection. They are shaped by speech genres and socially constructed ways of remembering school.

CHAPTER 4

BEING 'BAD'

The teachers present themselves as rebellious in different ways. Even Shaun, with the most positive memories, suggests once he discarded Catholicism, 'they, you know, they thought I was a bad influence'. He told the rector he no longer wanted to be a priest: 'he said that I could stay and my do A' levels as long as I didn't try and influence the others!' (Shaun). This is fairly benign, a joke even. But the other teachers present themselves more combatively. Liz suggests after 'falling from grace' through the ritual humiliation of 'marks', she became de-motivated and resentful. When pushed she said,

> Well I became *bad* really, it was a way out. I mean not *terribly* bad, but I mean by convent school standards bad! (Liz)

The competitive nature of the school, which prioritised sciences ('chemistry, physics, forensics, stuff like that'), meant Liz's interest in literature and drama – the one area she could be 'good' – was viewed less seriously. Liz claims she consciously engaged in what might now be called 'low level disruption'. There was an interesting moment of recognition for Liz. She suggests she coasted until going to teacher training college, where she was 'subject-zoned' into English and drama with like-minded people. Here she began to feel more enthusiastic. When explaining this she sat back in her chair suddenly and said, 'Ah! There's the breakthrough you see!' It was as if the interview process had awakened some moment of clarity. Michael tells a similar story about his A' level teacher who 'redeemed the course' and wrote 'interesting reports' on him,

> I remember one report in particular that said "wayward but able"…I liked that. I thought the idea of being *wayward* [Laughs] er, was a plus! And I wasn't really the conforming type or ideal student. (Michael)

The teachers suggest they were prepared to challenge expected behaviour. Like Michael, David suggests that he was slightly rebellious. He claims he has 'always been an irreverent sort of person and I still am.' He wrote 'parodies' of teachers – 'I used to write send-ups of teachers you know, they used to get passed around in the sixth-form and we'd all laugh about them' (David). These ways of presenting themselves as 'irreverent', 'wayward' or 'bad' are common in the narratives. But are these examples really bad? Maybe we like to think we were 'bad' at school? No-one likes to be too clean-cut and it seems there is a desire from these teachers to present as rebellious, however slight it may be. More extreme examples did emerge though. Ann had her 'own supply of books' at boarding school. Even 'during morning prayers' she would ignore everything but her 'own agenda',

> You remember I was as boarding school, so we had chapel every day and I discovered that the hymn books that you had to take in were the same size as one of the Everyman editions, so I had a whole host of books ready to take into

chapel. I knew all the hymns off by heart, so I'd be mouthing them away but my eyes would be reading the text. (Ann)

Ann claims to have a 'subversive' nature. She connects this with her developing sophistication in English – 'I began to realise that English sort of matched my own subversive tendencies' (Ann). Her 'subversive tendencies went from strength to strength', she claims, through critical thinking in English and challenging dominant discourses. I asked if she could exemplify this and she told a story that critiqued the internal politics of her school and its out-dated practices. Apparently rumour abounds at boarding school: a 'hothouse of internal gossip'. Rumour had it Ann 'was going to be appointed head-girl in my final year at the school.' She was summoned to the head-teacher's office, but she 'did not want to be head-girl, I did not want to represent the school, which seemed to me in many ways such a *hideous* structure you know, politically, ideologically and in every way, especially educationally!' (Ann). Ann attended the meeting, was admonished and informed she would *not* be head-girl. This, she claims, was 'affirmation that I'd survived.' She was given a dressing-down:

> At which point I was meant to break down in tears. But at this point this great wave of self-satisfaction came over me and I thought '*yes*! This is confirmation that I have survived'. This woman knew quite well that I was not one of her products! And so I said nothing, I didn't burst into tears of course, I was absolutely delighted! And she continued by saying that I had demonstrated subversive attitudes that she felt were not appropriate for someone to represent the school. It was terrific, great news! (Ann)

Ann links this incident with a struggle for her own identity; it influenced how she came to understand herself –

> So it's sort of, in this small period of about two years, I moved to being *me* really…I suddenly realised that it was all actually about survival, and it was also about asking questions, and it was about not accepting hierarchical structures, which the school was absolutely perfectly based upon, not accepting hierarchical structures, er, per-se you know for what they appeared to be doing, but always to question the ways in which they were undermining individuality. (Ann)

Ann's attitude to English teaching is partly influenced by her reaction to the old-fashioned ideas she was confronted with. Some of her friends 'survived' by being 'expelled', but Ann suggests she fought her battle for identity by critically confronting the opportunities and expectations presented to her. It seems something of the 'sprit of the times' is evident in the teachers' memories. There is an evolving critical consciousness. They developed identities and ideas about English during a period when some were prepared to confront old institutions and expectations. Remember Dixon's claim,

CHAPTER 4

> These were heady days intellectually, for the young in spirit – and also for the combative, rebellious and iconoclastic: for respected authorities were challenged, of course. (1991: 175)

Steve claims he had 'tremendous struggles' with authority at school and as a teacher. He recalls numerous run-ins with teachers, and one particular head-teacher. I asked why he wanted to study A' level English,

> It was a punishment for me; the head-teacher hated me! He was one of these Christian evangelicals and we used to have a sixth form lesson with the head-teacher. And most of the boys just kept dumb. And I thought the guy was an absolute prick so I just told him what I thought, and he hated me because I used to explain that his version of Christianity was very narrow, very restrictive, irrelevant and old-fashioned, and I just said it to his face in front of everybody and he hated me, absolutely hated my guts! (Steve)

Steve claims he became 'very political as a teenager'. This has remained throughout his life. Whether these confrontations were as aggressive as they sound is impossible to know. But the stories indicate a collective dissatisfaction with existing social power relations and a determination to challenge them. They highlight a struggle for identity that was carried into the teachers' work. Steve recalls 'major problems' throughout his career because of clashes with authority. He suggests he is not content to allow reified social expectations, or existing power relations to go unchallenged. The teachers suggest they were (and still are) rebellious in various ways, some more so than others. But these experiences appear to have influenced their attitudes and collective identity. They express a confidence in their own critical abilities. The words they use to describe themselves – 'bad', 'wayward', 'irreverent', 'subversive', 'hated' – suggest they enjoy the role of the outsider. However, they also claim they were exemplary teachers. Their conception of a 'good' teacher appears to be one who is prepared to challenge dominant structures and orthodoxies.

UNIVERSITY AND TEACHER TRAINING COLLEGE

The teachers are generally positive about post-school studies. They took different routes into teaching and are split between university (Shaun, Michael, Ann) and teacher training college (Steve, Liz, David). Interestingly, the teachers who attended university all went to private/boarding school (the seminary in Shaun's case). These contexts produced different kinds of experiences and expectations. Liz recalls general disappointment from teachers and family members because she wanted to teach: 'I went along to teacher training college instead of university and I think I felt, from the point of view of the school, a complete failure!' (Liz). Steve and David, both working-class, claim they were not even aware university was a possibility. They claim they succeeded despite little encouragement. David attended grammar school but received little help or advice. Indeed, he claims his main motivation to teach was a reaction to the way he was taught himself. He also had nobody in his family to advise him about higher education,

> I mean there wasn't anybody in my family who'd been into higher education, so I didn't get much advice there. And the careers service was utter crap! So I, I'd always been interested in teaching and it was largely a reaction against the way I'd been taught because I thought, I still do think, that what I received wasn't called teaching. I could do better! (David)

Steve and David were victims of the tripartite system. David lacked the various forms of 'capital' (Bourdieu, 1986) that helped his contemporaries take advantage of their grammar school opportunities. Social attitudes might have influenced how they were perceived by their schools. David suggests he was sold short,

> No-one told me you could do a three-year degree and then do a year's PGCE. I didn't know anything about it. Which was really stupid on reflection, because I had three A' levels, I could have gone to university! So when I went to college, I went to Christchurch, Canterbury, and really enjoyed it. (David)

David, along with Steve and Liz, made the most of opportunities at teacher training college. The university graduates are less positive. Shaun went to Lancaster to study history but found the course uninspiring and operating in an unattractive ideological arena. The main professor was 'a former colonel in the British army and, er, although a bright guy, he had a very narrow view of history. It was about military and the sea, er, an imperialist history of, er, England and Europe' (Shaun). Despite elements of social history, 'the rest of the history degree course was dire'. Shaun became 'very friendly with people in the English department', discovering they had much in common. He was drawn to 'one lecturer in particular who was a communist and who was very much into a kind of Marxist literary critique'. Shaun transferred to English and claims he rapidly developed a range of new skills and perspectives. He presents himself as independently critical, claiming he was not 'remotely sympathetic' to his new lecturer's 'Stalinist' perspectives, because his own 'socialism and… commitment to working-class power relations were from a totally different tradition' (Shaun). He also found continuity from his seminary in his new surroundings. His lecturer was,

> Ironically another Leavisite, who sat at the feet of Leavis at Cambridge, and who, if you like, there was that continuity, er, one of my Leavisite teachers became a bishop, and the other was a communist lecturer at Lancaster University! Er, but he was a lovely guy and I got on very, very well with him. (Shaun)

Typically, Shaun is the most positive. Ann and Michael were disappointed. Ann attended Reading University, or rather, did not attend very often. She became 'distracted' after the 'closed life of boarding school', and often 'hitch-hiked to London' and 'was missing off campus a lot really.' She received a 'couple of

CHAPTER 4

warnings', but still 'did masses of reading.' Her 'own agenda' was apparent to her tutors,

> But my tutorials were usually a bit on the personal side in terms of "why aren't you fulfilling your potential, we're getting disappointed in you" type stuff...I was expected to do very well I think in terms of my initial showing, but it became clear very early on that I had a wider agenda. It didn't mean not enjoying English but there were too many other things to catch up with. I mean let's face it seven years in a very closed environment like boarding school, you just need to, er, get out and about (laughing)! (Ann)

Ann succeeded despite her 'wider agenda'. Michael claims he made the 'natural' progression to university. But he was also the first member of his family to go. He likens his situation to Neil Kinnock's 'first person in a thousand generations' speech. He was unprepared because he was 'not familiar, er, there was no expectation, you know?' He studied English at Jesus College, Oxford, but even attending private school did not prepare him for what lay in store. His story evokes Raymond Williams's (1958) claim of being oppressed by the 'teashop' at Cambridge – the 'culture' was alienating. Michael claims the course was a 'complete let down' and he never focussed with any real commitment. He regrets his decision to go: 'it was a terrible, I mean a *terrible* mistake, er, going to Oxford!' The English programme appears to have been very traditional and deliberately esoteric. Teaching methods created a 'very uncongenial learning environment'; tutorials a 'complete waste of time'. He describes the monotony, 'you know, you spent half your time listening to everybody reading their essays out. I mean, how daft is that?' And not only the curriculum and pedagogy proved uninspiring. Michael claims he was intimidated by the arcane atmosphere. He describes seminars as 'fearsome places'. His contemporaries seemed self-assured, 'incredibly incisive, instant talkers', creating a 'very alienating environment'. He recalls never having 'any experience of an unthreatening environment to think aloud and to, er, debate literature at all!' He recalls some of his fellow students, their behaviour and attitudes, which he could not get along with,

> But probably the other thing that you were least prepared for, I mean it sounds daft, but in this particular place, people go to rehearse their future careers, at least the visible element are there. And that took a long time to get my head round. Literally, people were here to become actors, politicians, civil servants, you know? And that was a bit, you know, disorienting. But I had some good friends, but I don't think I entered fully into the life of the place. I never knew where it was. You know, this is the extraordinary thing, you know I remember being in the common room of this place, and people coming back, public-school guys, smashed out of their *minds* and breaking up all of the furniture. They'd have been put in jail, or they would have spent a year on probation, you know if it had happened elsewhere. It was a very alienating place. (Michael)

Michael presents Oxford as a training-ground for elitism and his memories are the most negative. But there is a collective dislike of social hierarchies and inequality. These various experiences have influenced a shared commitment to social justice.

THE LEARNING EXPERIENCE AT UNIVERSITY AND TEACHER TRAINING COLLEGE

Michael aside, the teachers' learning experiences were generally positive. Three teachers initially studied subjects other than English (history for Steve and Shaun, drama for Liz). Eventually they gravitated to English. Like Shaun, Steve found history uninspiring, claiming he fell into English by default,

> When I went to teacher training college I actually opted for history and not English. And then when I came back from the initial teaching practice I was so taken aback at the lack of intellectual content in the history course that I asked, I can't imagine how I had the nerve to do this, I asked to change course. And I opted for a double English course…So that's how I ended up, by accident, doing English at teacher training college. I had no intention, *no* intention, when I went I went to do history. (Steve)

Steve initially gained a Certificate in Education but stayed on to complete a Bachelor of Education degree. His 'double English' course was a 'straightforward literature course, mimicking what was done for an English degree in a university, and then the second part was the initial teaching and English in education' (Steve). Again, like Shaun, Steve claims he was attracted to particular characters, who 'just by accident, a few people arriving at the college the same time in the same year, for very different reasons, and a small collection of highly committed lecturers who wanted to do something different and who reflected elements of modern, challenging thinking'. It might be that these circumstances did not arise by 'accident'. Circumstances in this conjuncture influenced the attitudes of some teachers to be iconoclastic in the ways Dixon (1991) suggests. Lowe claims,

> As the sixties progressed, it began to seem in a range of areas that society was throwing off the austerity and social attitudes which had marked the whole of the early twentieth century. Changes in fashion, in popular culture and in the mass media might have been the icons of these developments, but it should not be forgotten that this was also to become a decade of social and political movements which appeared worldwide in their scope. (2007: 40)

Some of these issues resonate in the teachers' narratives. One lecturer stood out for Steve who 'wanted to make English relevant', who was 'very much part of a new wave of socially aware, committed teachers'. The lecturer was 'a Communist Party supporter, working in a Church of England college.' There are remarkable similarities in Steve's and Shaun's narratives, with almost identical elements in their descriptions of how and why they were attracted to English. There is of course the

CHAPTER 4

attraction of like-minded people. But 'English' itself seemed to offer possibilities for wider social, cultural and political issues to be confronted through critical thinking and collective action. All the teachers insist the subject goes far beyond simple curricular and pedagogic concerns. They were excited and challenged by ways of working at university and teacher training college. Steve highlights one term where his group worked exclusively on *King Lear* 'in every imaginable focus you could dream up as a piece of literature, it was something there to be *used*'. The group also spent time outside lectures preparing Brecht's *Threepenny Opera* to perform at the Edinburgh Festival. Steve foregrounds intensity, commitment and comradeship on the course, alongside a belief in the socially-transformative potential of literature,

> And it became much more than a course. There was a core of us and we drew a secondary group in and it became almost a, sort of a hobby, a way of life, a kind of obsession. And so we saw literature as a way of radicalising people. It was good, it was really strong and powerful, and the college authorities did not like us! (Steve)

Steve again suggests he was 'disliked'. He draws on radical discourses, presenting himself as confrontational, as all the teachers do. They represent themselves as highly committed, politically alert and capable of critiquing social structures. Steve suggests he was 'trouble' for some of the more traditional lecturers, claiming they penalised his work. He suggests he has 'always been a sort of person that's maybe had a habit of rubbing up authorities the wrong way'. But he maintains a commitment to English as a way of promoting agency and critical consciousness.

David comes from a similar perspective. His Cert Ed/B Ed exposed him to alternative methods of practice. He worked closely with two lecturers who 'opened me up to areas of literature I'd not come across before and they were open to all sorts of alternative approaches to things and I really took off'. Rather than write traditional essays, David was encouraged to develop creative writing for assessments. Like Steve, he claims he 'fell foul' of authority on teaching practice. He was teaching Stan Barstow's *A Kind of Loving* (1960) when the head-teacher warned him 'he didn't want anything used in his school where a parent could open any page at random and find something objectionable'. David confronted the head with 'Shakespeare, Chaucer, the Bible! This didn't go down well. I think he thought I was a smart-arse, which was probably right!' He stresses his motivations for wanting to teach,

> It was certainly a reaction against the way I was taught. And everything I've experienced in Education since then has reinforced that. The way I was taught was crap and there were better ways of doing it, better ways of relating to people. In particular, I mean ok, there's sort of a political thing, because I went in and I suppose my mission was to give working-class kids a better deal. Because I knew what it was like ok, at the time very few working-class kids, about six per cent went on to higher education. It's not a great deal more now. (David)

CONSTRUCTING IDENTITIES AND ATTITUDES

Teacher training in this conjuncture is presented as an arena where the realities of practice, relationships and responsibilities could be confronted and problematised. The teachers decided where they stood in relation to these issues. David is clear about his concern for working-class children. Experiences on their respective courses influenced the teachers' concerns, attitudes and collective outlook on English. Liz went to college to study drama, suggesting 'It was fabulous. It was like being in heaven!' The course combined 'theoretical-work, the text-work, the exploration-work, the voice-work that was incredible!' Her excitement changed her attitudes and motivations,

> The whole thing became very inventive. So you'd find the music to do something, you'd find a prop to go in, do you know what I mean? And I was working, I was learning to teach in a totally different way from the way I'd been taught. And it turned me round, if you see what I mean. And I worked hard, whereas I'd not really, I'd lazed for thirteen years really. (Liz)

When the subject became stimulating and relevant the teachers threw themselves into it. Liz's account is typical of how they found motivation through learning experiences. But their changing attitudes were not arrived at individually. They were socially mediated through negotiation and collaboration. The discourses generated mean the teachers have constructed similar attitudes to English that have had a lasting effect on their working practices. Conjunctural circumstances seem to have cemented a commitment to social justice, making English relevant and democratic.

SO WHY BECOME AN ENGLISH TEACHER?

Steve, Shaun, Liz and David are clear about always wanting to teach. Liz initially wanted to teach drama, but the departmental structure at Holland Park meant she 'had' to teach English,

> I found myself in this enormous English team and I wanted to teach drama. And the only way I could teach drama there was to be in the English team. That's how it worked. It was lumped together, and you did drama if you felt like it you see. (Liz)

At least Liz wanted to teach. Ann and Michael were less sure. Michael claims he 'fell into it by default'. After Oxford, he took a lecturing job at the University of Tubingen. However, after a year he 'suddenly took against the Germans' and left. He claims he was 'a bit at sea' on returning and though he 'never imagined myself doing this…I became a supply teacher'. His first job was a baptism of fire at a girls' school in North London: 'it was an absolute horror show!' He recalls a difficult initiation, which seems to have motivated him,

> I think I became an English teacher because I didn't know what had hit me! I thought blimey, you know, this is another world. You can't just be anywhere

like this where you're so insulted and so, er, there were so many challenges. So I, er, I thought I'd go for it. (Michael)

While Michael seems to have enjoyed being insulted, Ann had more practical reasons for teaching: 'I had no inclination to do teaching whatsoever really, but I was basically starving!' Ann worked for a local potter, occasionally teaching at a hostel. But poor conditions and pay influenced her to do a PGCE,

> I went into teaching just basically to have an income, it meant I could eat! It was a means to an end, because I vowed to myself that I'd do it for a couple of years, save some money, then do the pottery thing. I suppose in a way I was quite enjoying the teaching, but it was teaching in this art framework in the pottery context, not teaching English and not teaching classes, I mean I never imagined myself teaching classes. (Ann)

Her attitude changed when she got her first job in the late 1960s, in a 'progressive' English department,

> I got a job in a school which was really exciting as far as English teaching went, and that's when things changed. That's really when I got interested in teaching English, and the whole multi-faceted questions surrounding the business. It was really exciting and it raised so many interesting, absorbing questions and I'm still trying to answer them now. (Ann)

This experience cemented a particular outlook on English, shared by all the teachers, which is characterised by a commitment to respecting and foregrounding children's wider social and cultural backgrounds. The teachers' early experiences significantly influenced their identities and attitudes to the job. Shaun claims he 'went into teaching very deliberately, because I wanted to work with working-class kids'. He was also committed to trade unionism and 'in working-class struggle, if that doesn't sound too grandiose!' Steve claims he wanted to politicise those he taught to improve their life chances,

> Well we thought obviously that children have rights. And that's based on an idea that a person grows and develops and they're *free*! And that it was wrong for schools to imprison and to structure and to limit people, and schools needed to be liberative! So that means that when we chose a piece of literature, it was because we thought that it had some potential for that. (Steve)

Despite their different backgrounds and experiences, the teachers all claim they sought to increase children's agency. They share a commitment to collaboration and a belief that their work had positive effects on children's lives. Again, conjunctural circumstances influenced these attitudes. The spirit of the times, and ideas promoted by the likes of Freire (1970, 1972) and Postman and Weingartner (1972), seem to have found their way into the teachers' attitudes, identities and motivations.

WHAT DO THESE MEMORIES TELL US?

The memories indicate how the teachers constructed identities and attitudes towards English. Placed alongside other evidence, teacher memories can highlight gaps or contradictions in memory and history. For example Cunningham (2007) shows how popular interpretations of the Plowden Report's influence do not necessarily hold up when practitioners recall what it meant in practice. He foregrounds tensions between individual narratives, collective memory and historical events. But he insists on the necessity of locating oral testimony alongside existing histories. Doing this can generate new narratives that offer different possibilities,

> To improve the future, we must strive to learn from the past, a past that is not a simple narrative of policy but also a complex layer of individual and collective memory. (2007: 30)

PM studies can contribute to an improved future. In this chapter I have considered the evolution of the teachers' attitudes to the subject 'English'. Some of these attitudes include a commitment to promoting children's agency and challenging existing orthodoxies. Sometimes they take care to distinguish their own particular political allegiances. However, the individual recollections reveal a PM of *shared* ideas, values and commitments. The construction of these began in the contexts and circumstances they encountered when growing up.

Collective aspects of the teachers' PM can be distilled into a number of issues. Despite coming from very different backgrounds, they foreground similar aspects of their lives and educational experiences. They mostly highlight negative experiences of English at school, but suggest they had the ability to understand and critique how and why bad practice existed. They claim negative experiences spurred the development of positive practice in their own classrooms. Some elements appear stereotypical: having an 'inspirational' teacher; teenage rebellion against authority; not learning anything of value at school. The speech genres they draw on create a sense of group identity, and enable them to re-construct past events in particular ways. The narratives allow individual subjectivity and group identity to be represented simultaneously. Collective life histories cannot match the 'reality' of lived experience. But Goodson and Sikes argue, 'they are perhaps as close as it is possible to get' (2001: 56).

The teachers' narratives constitute social reality for them. Even when their experiences and opinions differ, the teachers appear concerned to represent themselves in particular ways. For example, Shaun is mostly positive about his early experiences while the others are largely negative. Yet their attitudes to English appear remarkably similar. They foreground a range of collective concerns and characteristics: a dissatisfaction with traditional, didactic approaches; a commitment to 'progressive' or 'radical' methods; an insistence that educational practices must be located in wider social and cultural contexts; a commitment to promoting student agency; an ability to critique and challenge authority. These formative experiences

CHAPTER 4

help to create a genealogy of context for the teachers' work in the 'cauldron'. Born at the time they were, into the circumstances they were, the teachers have constructed a collective identity that transcends their individual backgrounds and experiences. Their utterances are open to interpretation, but these teachers want to be taken seriously. They highlight a concern for social justice, equality and professional integrity. So how did these elements translate into social action in the 'cauldron'? This will be explored in the following chapter.

ACKNOWLEDGEMENT

Sections of this chapter appeared, in other forms, in Tarpey, P. (2016). "Fire Burn and Cauldron Bubble": What are the conjunctural effects on English teacher professional memories, identities and narratives? *Changing English, 23*(1), 77–93.

CHAPTER 5

WORKING IN THE 'CAULDRON' 1965–1975

INTRODUCTION

This chapter focuses on the teachers' early professional practice in the conjuncture 1965–1975. I have suggested this period can be thought of as a 'cauldron' in which progressive and sometimes radical approaches to English were developed. Conjunctural circumstances provided fertile ground for some teachers to re-imagine established practices. These circumstances emerged out of deliberate attempts to democratise English throughout the 1940s and 1950s. The likes of Britton, Rosen and Dixon, through LATE, in schools and the Institute of Education, provided templates for some young teachers to build upon. Here I concentrate chiefly on the teachers' developing attitudes, identities and working practices. They experienced a number of exciting yet challenging local contexts, but enjoyed broad support from ILEA and, later, the English Centre. Some of the teachers claim their early teaching was about 'survival'. But they all developed their careers in ambitious ways, sometimes initiating curricular change, sometimes trying to influence policy. In chapter four I explored how the teachers constructed identities and attitudes towards English. Here, I am interested in how these influenced their early practice.

BECOMING AN ENGLISH TEACHER

The teachers highlight the transition from trainee to qualified practitioner. Liz, Steve and David, through teacher training college, were familiar with classroom demands and suggest the transition was relatively easy. But Shaun, Ann and Michael, through PGCE courses, claim they were ill-prepared for the realities of teaching. Yet their postgraduate courses seem to allowed them to develop a particular sense of professional identity. By 'identity' here I mean the teachers' sense of the types of practitioners they are, shaped by professional and wider life experience. Ann suggests her PGCE was uninspiring, but enthuses about her first job,

> Yes, yes and it was very intensive. I would say that I've almost never worked that hard ever since as I had to then. But it was also very satisfying because it was always about innovation, and it was also always about utilising your own strengths, your own imagination and making full use of other people's at the same time. It was a fantastic learning experience. That's where I really learned teaching. (Ann)

CHAPTER 5

Ann highlights practical experience and teamwork as important factors in her development. Her experiences at the school evidently shaped her attitudes to the job, and she retains collaboration and teamwork as fundamental ingredients of practice. Michael started his PGCE in 1967 and suggests, 'things weren't opening up, you know, by sixty-seven in the way that they were subsequently in the seventies, you know *real* experimentation'. He claims 'the theoretical side was very weak', but seemed to change his mind when pushed,

> It was actually, when I think about it, it was quite an interesting course, because we had social sciences, they were interested in interdisciplinary work, you know, so we had quite a lot of contact with the social psychology department. Er, and, so it was a term teaching, you know, a term outside…you know the kind of things that we were doing I would call experimental *at that time*… You know, with kids writing about new settings, music and so on, they were collective class things that worked, you know, quite satisfying for teachers, I don't know what it's like for kids. Yeah, you know, we did quite imaginative things…one of our tasks was writing, er, compiling an anthology of poetry for, for students to read. (Michael)

Although theory and practice might not have been cohesive, Michael's course seems to have given him the confidence to experiment with different approaches. The 'spirit of the times' seems significant and nothing was off limits. Michael carried this spirit of experimentation into his first teaching post. He recalls being 'significantly influenced' by one PGCE session that explored using paintings in English,

> And, er, that took off for me, because one of the big projects I did, er, was looking at writing from visual stimulants, from modern paintings to classical paintings and so on. So I took that with me you know, into my subsequent career and still now actually. (Michael)

These early experiences cemented his commitment to creativity, to give students opportunities to explore their own experiences,

> I looked into ways of getting kids to engage with expressing themselves, and getting satisfaction from it. I mean, one thing that I was fond of doing was using films, slides and paintings, working in the dark, you know, and all the kind of things you would *parody* really, about a sixties teacher! (Michael)

He went on to 'do BBC programmes on painting and poetry' and devised a classroom tool called 'picture power' through his work at the English and Media Centre. But these ideas were developed earlier. In the late 1960s he showed films and encouraged students to write poetry as soundtracks to the action. Poetry 'was something to have fun with', which is the antithesis of the passive experiences the teachers claim they had themselves. Like Michael, Shaun is initially critical of his PGCE, claiming it was 'absolutely dire, a one-year PGCE course which was dull in the extreme!' Again, 'there was no relation between theory and practice'. Yet the course provided crucial learning experiences. Shaun was confronted with the social and educational realities of working-class children for the first time. This forced him to reflect seriously on his role and identity as a teacher,

> But, that year was very formative for me because it was the first time I'd lived away from home, but also, going into working-class comprehensives, er, informed my mind in areas and, er, confronting, er, school organisation for the first time, er, experiencing working-class kids learning, er, and er, the very stultifying experience that they had, and, er, in secondary school, especially at the lower end of the secondary school, er you know, brought me up with a kind of jolt and made me think very very hard about the kind of educational practice I wanted to engage in…I can remember vividly reading out loud to a class of thirty, bored working-class kids was er, a kind of social control really. And, er, I learned a lot about how *not* to teach! (Shaun)

This type of experience is common. The teachers all agree they had difficulty adapting to their roles. They also suggest their skills and abilities were developed 'on the job'. However they had opportunities to engage with theoretical ideas from different disciplines, especially in social sciences and humanities. Despite poor organisation on training courses, it seems practice was sometimes explored from sociological, psychological and historical perspectives, and the teachers were encouraged to be reflective and reflexive. These aspects of teacher education appear to have been common at the time. Brian Simon claimed in 1966 there was no need to campaign for studying history of education on 'the course offered to intending teachers' because 'it has long been established as such in most colleges and universities' (1966: 55, cited in McCulloch, 2000). Some trainee teachers were encouraged to locate their work into a number of contexts. There was also an expectation for practitioners to lead curriculum development. Education Secretary, Anthony Crosland, said of the time,

> I didn't regard myself or my officials as in the slightest regard competent to interfere with the curriculum. We're educational politicians and administrators, not professional educationists. (Cited in Francis, 2001: 14)

Conjunctural circumstances meant the teachers started when professional autonomy and trust were commonly assumed. This is a key factor in shaping their collective identities, and it is reflected in their commitment to reflexivity, creativity and innovation.

BUILDING POSITIVE RELATIONSHIPS

The teachers recall early struggles with the rigours of the job. But they developed clear ideas about the types of teachers they wanted to be. They suggest they were prepared to challenge the aims, practices and purposes of English. A strong feature to emerge is the teachers' motivation to 'do a better job' than the people who taught them. They emphasise a commitment to 'working-class' or 'ordinary' children, to give them a 'voice'. They argue English should provide children with the tools to critically assess their own life chances. There is a commitment to social justice. Some of the teachers describe themselves explicitly as 'socialists'. Michael suggests,

> So in small ways we tried to significate our teaching practice in the light of our, you know, socialist perspectives, you know about equality and justice and all those sorts of ideas. (Michael)

Steve has similar concerns, highlighting his commitment to students and others in the school community. He took 'great care' of his classroom, claiming he would arrive early 'to clean with the cleaners'. He wanted students to take pride in themselves and their local communities. This was important in the classroom too,

> There was never a mark on a desk, everything was precise and organised. So it was the brightest classroom and amazingly that's how they treated it. Next door was a shit-heap and they behaved accordingly! I was amazed the teacher never cottoned on you know. And so I would set the scene. For example I would be there before the children arrived…it transforms the possibilities of what you can do…I would be there every lunch-hour with my tutor group, in my room, not in the staff-room. So of course over the course of the year I'd build a totally different rapport with a cohort…it would set different expectations when they come into the classroom. (Steve)

Steve's commitment to the upkeep of the classroom might seem beyond the call of duty, and none of the other teachers make such claims. But his focus on positive relationships and high expectations is shared by them all. Steve suggests his methods were designed to offer students positive experiences: 'And it's things like that, that are all about being committed to the children, and the quality of their experience, that enables you to do things that formal pedagogies can't do'. The teachers are wary of 'labelling' children with deficits – issues discussed at the time by the likes of Hargreaves (1967), Keddie (1971) and *Teaching London Kids*. It appears there were close relationships between some theorists and practitioners in this conjuncture: what was happening in classrooms was being written about. The teachers share Steve's belief in building relationships and locating practice into wider contexts. Ann foregrounds the positive impact English can have on children's lives,

> There's my credo, there's my credo for what I found to be really valuable, and English teaching seemed to me to offer, I'm sure other subjects do the same and I don't, I'd not wish to denigrate other curricular areas at all, but English teaching…seemed to me to be intimately bound up with, with the development of the person, of the individual. And therefore of course with happiness, with a sense of purpose, a sense of fulfilment and not the least dimension here of course is relationships. (Ann)

The teachers identify strongly with the children they taught and their wider communities. English is presented as an arena where children might learn to be critical of issues affecting their lives. This is built on dialogic, mutually meaningful relationships. However the teachers draw on a range of sometimes competing speech genres here. Michael connects practice with 'socialist perspectives, equality and justice', drawing on radical discourses. Dixon's 'growth model' can be heard in Ann's insistence that English is 'intimately bound up with the development of the person'. Her focus on 'happiness' and 'fulfilment' seems a world away from current priorities in English teaching. They all agree positive relationships are a crucial, but they approach this idea from different perspectives. Ann draws on 'progressive' and 'child-centred' perspectives. Michael is more 'radical', linking practice with collectivist political perspectives.

Steve's comments occasionally appear inconsistent: sometimes strongly focussed on the collective, sometimes individualist. Here he presents himself as a lone teacher fighting the good fight, an individual in opposition to dominant discourses or expected behaviours. He constructs 'teacher-as-saviour' narratives (Trier, 2010) here and elsewhere, focussing on his willingness to go beyond the call of duty. By his own admission, his relationships with colleagues were sometimes problematic, and the teacher in the 'shit heap' next door is afforded little sympathy. Despite this, his commitment to students and to confronting the priorities and aims of English teaching remain consistent and undiminished.

DEVELOPING PRACTICE AND RESOURCES COLLABORATIVELY

The teachers claim they were committed to developing their own resources and methods. This was necessary because of a scarcity of high-quality materials. They had no interest in 'working through the course-book'. Resources were of course available, and three teachers refer to the same textbook, *The Art of English* (Newson & Mansfield, 1965). Michael actually worked with the authors but could not take to it,

> So I was, you know, in a very interesting department actually to be honest with you. They were the authors of a dire textbook, which again, I couldn't make work for me, called *The Art of English* by Newson and Mansfield. And they were my head and deputy in the department...it was a *very proactive* department. (Michael)

Michael, Ann and Liz claim they were fortunate to begin in departments that encouraged experimentation, with opportunities to develop materials, methods and curricula. The sense of collegiality and co-operation spread in London with the establishment of ILEA in 1965. Ten years on and this collegial spirit was fostered to a high degree by the English Centre. The teachers highlight the crucial role ILEA played in their development. They refer particularly to local English Centres and the possibilities for working with other teachers. David was quickly promoted,

CHAPTER 5

becoming head of department in two years. He explains how he encouraged a collegial approach,

> When I went in, when I took over the department there were things like, there were English textbooks and people worked their way through them and the first thing I did was bin most of those. There were some people who used to cling to them and would insist on having copies. *The Art of English* was the modern one at the time. But I started introducing themes, so you'd do something, science-fiction or something, it's old hat now…What we'd do, is as a department, somebody would take an idea and go and develop it. We had a box-file and if people came across anything from a magazine or something they'd put it in there. So if you were the next person to take it out there was stuff for you to work on. We'd work together in that way, pulling stuff together. (David)

David's approach was challenging for some colleagues who wanted to 'cling' to existing practices. But he was in the vanguard of promoting new methods. This approach was taken up more systematically by the English Centre,

> But I think the real sharing stuff came about when the *English Centre* opened. Before that there were networks, what were called local English Centres but they were really just, there'd be a meeting at a school and we'd all go up to Holloway school once a term or so for a meeting. But once the English Centre was established there were centralised courses and a resource base and like thinking people who you could get together and work with. (David)

At the Centre David developed ideas and co-wrote a number of books. Others worked in similar departments. Liz recalls working with 'some really very inspirational English teachers' at Holland Park, claiming 'it was a wacky place, and what was nice about Holland Park in the sixties is that everybody was doing experimental stuff…you could do what you wanted'. Colleagues in her department also produced books that circulated the schools. When explaining this, Liz reached into a bag and produced a selection of books she used when she started out: *Reflections* (1963), *English for Diversity* (Abbs, 1969), and both *English for Maturity* and *English for the Rejected* (Holbrook, 1961, 1964),

> I've found you this which is disgusting [the book was dirty], I'm very sorry. But this was the kind of English textbook that we used [picks up *Reflections*]. You'll see that it's incredibly experiential and experimental. This is the seminal book. It was the book that was sort of moving English teaching round when I started to teach. Nineteen-sixty-three you see. Reprinted sixty-four, and it's the Dixon and Stratta textbook. Which Peter Abbs would say it's taking away from the aesthetic, oh my god look! [finds piece of paper inside back cover] A piece of teaching material, aren't you lucky! Isn't that nice? And here, you are in luck. April twenty-third to May third revision, that's the fifth years,

comprehension, poetry, letter writing, poetry, listen to *Dragon slayer*...Ooh what treasure, I didn't realise. (Liz)

As Liz flicked through the book a piece of paper dropped out which turned out to be a scheme of work for the final weeks with her fifth-year class. She was excited to find it and she explained how her planning and teaching had been 'informed' by the books. She was also sensitive to the different traditions of the writers, suggesting disagreement between Abbs and Dixon. Liz suggests developing resources was expected at the time. Some of her colleagues became high profile names in English teaching,

> But it's all like that. It was right at the, you know, the timing was incredible to begin working in one of the best comprehensives in London at the right time with the right people was just amazing really. I can't say more about it. The next head of department turned out to be a guy called [a prominent figure] who, we've got lots of his textbooks in the English team, and then [another prominent name]. All these names! (Liz)

The teachers present themselves and their colleagues as energetic and creative. They claim they wanted to develop modern, relevant and exciting resources. This was done collaboratively and it seems anybody could get involved. In some cases this was an expectation. The teachers honed their skills and confidence in enabling circumstances, where practitioners could develop and publish resources. Michael eventually 'ran the English Centre for the whole of the ILEA, I mean two hundred schools.' He describes the possibilities for developing resources, and the Centre's potential to influence practice on a wider scale,

> So you were enabled to effect change by the kind of courses that you ran; and the way you treated teachers, and that's sort of empowerment. Because there was no established curriculum there was a heyday, in fact we [English and Media Centre] wouldn't exist now if *then* hadn't been then! Er, with its relative freedom and there was a different set of professional practices around the work you did. Obviously, er, the new contract that came in, I can't remember the name of it now, er, yeah, 1265 hours, and all this changed massively. So, you know, teachers come in the evening, a lot of the work was, a lot of the work we published was done by teachers in groups in workshops. So yeah, you were able to, to make changes...And, er, it's hard now, isn't it hard to identify how things change, because as a teacher I'd never experienced any of the national curriculum, or, or anything. So it was very open to us, which was why professional associations were relatively vibrant places, because that was the place where you, you know, shared your ideas about teaching and made new materials and used new texts. (Michael)

The Centre encouraged teachers to involve themselves in curriculum development, attend courses, share working practices and publish teaching ideas. The enforcement

CHAPTER 5

of more restrictive working practices in the 1980s curtailed this to an extent. But as Michael suggests teachers in the 'cauldron' were socialised into English teaching with a 'different set of professional practices around the work'. And, 'professional associations were relatively vibrant places' where new ideas emerged through collective endeavour. But some teachers had broader concerns than classroom practice alone. They were interested in defining and defending what it was to be an English teacher. Like other professions, Michael suggests English Associations such as LATE and NATE attempted to set the standards and practices of professional conduct.

The teachers view their work as a collective enterprise. They talk of 'working together', 'sharing' ideas and materials, and working 'with the right people'. Michael, Liz and David structure their narratives in similar ways, foregrounding collegiality and shared experience. This suggests a degree of 'trust' in colleagues. The teachers draw on speech genres generated in the 'cauldron' and there is a sophisticated level of 'addressivity' here. The teachers present themselves in particular ways, knowing they will be judged.

The collective and collegial picture presented contrasts with Steve's comments in the previous section. Far from enjoying working with the 'right people' or 'sharing' ideas, Steve talks of distrust and even animosity. It might be that Steve is the most honest? The emotional investment he gives his words seems based on negative personal experience. However, as Jones (1989) argues this type of collegial practice was not widespread. It appears some of the teachers were fortunate to start in departments that worked in progressive ways and promoted shared responsibility. For teachers who did not work in such departments it appears experiences were very different.

***

I want to focus on Ann's first department for a moment. She suggests it encapsulated the practices, beliefs and missions of progressive teachers working in the 'cauldron'. The department initiated a student-centred, language-across-the-curriculum policy that appears similar to the one described by Medway in *Finding a Language* (1980). I asked Ann if her early experience had been isolated,

> No, no. That's exactly what it *wasn't*...I joined a department of twelve to fifteen. It was team teaching in a block that was an English block. So we had a suite of rooms. There were doors, but they were never shut. So you never taught in your own little empire, you never took sole control. Nor in a sense did you ever take sole responsibility. And what was very nice on both those counts, it was a shared responsibility, shared planning enterprise, it was shared delivery. There were choices, there were options, both for the students and for the teachers, but it was bloody hard work.

The team worked closely. Planning meetings, every lunch-time, focussed on curriculum development for different year groups. Different team-members took responsibility each day. Ann oversaw the third-year,

I had to co-ordinate the meetings, do the planning, do the minutes, find resources, co-ordinate the whole thing and get the show on the road. We did units of work which we planned a half term ahead of what we were currently doing. It was very exciting. We had open door policy both for ourselves, you know so we could go in and out of lessons and kids had options to go, not with one *teacher* or another, but to go with one aspect of the work or another.

The work was 'very intensive' and, like David, Ann worked on projects and themes that students could develop as they wished. She claims she struggled having to lead teachers, 'many of whom had *many* more years of experience and much more confidence than I had in terms of teaching, but you got stuck in and you did it'. The collegial atmosphere provided support and shared responsibility. Even the head of department was 'just another teacher' in Ann's team. She claims having such responsibility so early meant she, 'very quickly climbed to a point of confidence, and had a thoroughly good time out of it'. She describes the working practices,

Er, so for example a topic you know, let's say the *supernatural* would, would be the enclosing title, and within that there would be opportunities for display work, drama work, writing, research work. And each of us, within each year group we had a class for whom we had a tutorial responsibility, so that you wanted to keep a little bit of a note of, of students actually changing between one way of working and another, so that there was a fairly, so that there was an even distribution of opportunity for them all. This is mixed-ability of course.

She describes the English block as 'a place where the walls were reverberating with activity'. Oral work in mixed-ability groups emerges as an important principle for all the teachers. Yet the flexible structure occasionally caused problems and students 'had to be retrieved from the grounds somewhere'. But Ann insists the system worked because it was 'tightly organised'. And despite the fact 'every lunch was a working lunch', Ann demonstrates a high level of commitment,

But *who cared*! Because it was so dynamic, interesting, it was, there was plenty of laughter, there were plenty of worries, er there were plenty of shared responsibilities. It was the absolute antithesis of that solitary experience that I'd had as a pupil.

The expectations and intended outcomes for students were high. Students were not instructed what to do, but were given templates and options. Ann insists the 'expectation was *clearly* them, for them to develop it, and they weren't just left to run wild!' Apparently others in the school criticised the English department's methods. But students were expected to give written accounts of what they had been doing. Ann explains there was plenty of opportunity for 'imaginative input', but students also had to 'account for that and to *reflect* on that'. Each student kept a journal with opportunities for self-assessment and self-reflection. Ann, 'had responsibility to oversee those journals and to *interact* with them, to read them and to comment'. The journals 'were the most important *written* thing that went on throughout each year'. The whole process, like Dixon's 'growth' model, was designed to encourage student reflection on their own learning and experience. The school was a working-class comprehensive and Ann suggests some students found the working practices difficult, especially in terms of oral work,

> Er, and I think for many of the students, you can imagine in general terms, the backgrounds of many of those students…many of them weren't encouraged to talk and to have social interaction of the sort that *we* were expecting from them. So I think to many of them it was very difficult, er, initially, but a sense of, er, a sense of *empowerment* er, I think was evident in many of them as time went on.

Ann claims students were encouraged to engage critically with different discourse types. It seems broadening horizons was more important than 'correctness' in language. I asked her how this related to formal assessments,

> But in a way [pause] in a way that didn't seem to be the point of what we were doing. I mean, I'm sure it was, but *how interesting* you see all these years later I can't remember anything about that. That doesn't seem to me to be the significant thing in what we were doing. We were actually, er, you know, we were developing a pupil's ability to er, to write, to read, to learn and to interact, to, to have a sense of team-work and co-operation. Er, and to question, and to above all be prepared to make a mess of something, to, to make mistakes and then discuss them, not to be condemned for them, but to discuss them and to build on them for further development later. So er, empowerment was, it was a high priority, absolute high priority!

The department's innovations in the late 1960s attracted attention from universities and professional associations. It was the focus of a number of articles and research papers. Ann suggests,

> We had loads of people visiting from America and from the continent. You know, it was obviously a bit of high-powered experimental work that was going on at that stage…it attracted attention in terms of NATE and international people as well.

Classroom observations were frequent and Ann recalls one incident when she had visitors. Students were engaged in different activities and Ann 'just got on with what I was doing, I was working with a couple of groups in various parts of the room'. The visitors stayed for 'about twenty minutes'. Subsequently one of them asked the head of department 'does it matter if you have groups working without teachers present in the room?' To which the head responded 'what do you mean there *was* a teacher present in the room!' Ann apparently fitted into the scene so well they had failed to notice her,

They never noticed me! And [laughing] and that was subsequently commented on, you know, departmentally, as an absolute accolade! Because the whole room was busy on its activities, purposefully engaged on their activities, and I was probably hidden, you know, among four or five kids in the corner saying "well how about trying this?" But I was completely inconspicuous, but of course, yes *I was* in charge and I was in control, but students had a magnified, in terms of what I'd experienced, they had a magnified opportunity to engage with the topic in whatever way they determined. And they were busy doing it! So we were in complete control, but it convincingly did not *look* like it! So, you know, some people outside the department in the school, particularly the head-teacher, were extremely worried, because it looked as if, you know, revolution had broken out!

Ann left the school after three years, but took with her systematic, tightly-organised ways of working that have influenced her professional life. In fact all the teachers suggest their early experiences enabled them to develop clear identities and ideas about practice. Ann's first school, Churchfields, opened in 1956 and has been written about by ex-student Sandra Meredith (2011), who provides a personal history of one of the earliest comprehensives, and a 'well loved, amazing school'.

BRINGING POPULAR CULTURE INTO THE CLASSROOM

The teachers exploited popular cultural developments in the 'cauldron' and experimented with contemporary material. They followed Dixon's advice that lessons should focus on the 'learning processes and the meaning to the individual' (1967: 1–2) in content and structure. Liz, Michael and Ann started in departments with a culture of experimentation. This was not the case for all the teachers. Steve claims he was often the only teacher to try out new ideas. David's attempts to make changes met with resistance. But they all drew on the wealth of cultural resources available. Michael used a variety of media to make lessons more interesting and relevant – watching and making films, developing drama activities. Liz used drama in English lessons, often inspired by contemporary texts. She was excited by English teaching at Holland Park, which was caught up in the wider 'spirit of the times',

> But it was the flavour of the time don't forget because it suddenly all happ, I mean I sort of, you know, it all happened…you couldn't *escape* it, does that make sense? Because that was the mood of the time, and I was young enough, I didn't, I didn't have preconceptions or say "rubbish, I can't do this, this is rubbish", because this was "*wow* we'll do this"! Nothing was off limits. That was, that was what was so good about being there, you could play, you could take some risks, you could have a go. And people let you. (Liz)

Liz developed drama in the English department,

CHAPTER 5

> Drama wasn't actually a curriculum subject…people weren't timetabled for drama. You were part of the English department. Er, and I mean, I very quickly *got* to get it on the timetable, you know I was allowed. (Liz)

This was 'very risky', she claims, because most teachers were concerned 'to keep them *down*'. So 'to *wilfully* expose yourself to taking kids to the hall…then invite them to go *mad* was a big risk when you're twenty-one!' But the benefits outweighed the risks. She learned how to teach 'without texts, it was you and them'. Liz used pop songs to stimulate ideas in drama and claims this often helped students produce better writing,

> One of my pieces de resistance was She's Leaving Home from Sgt Pepper. So you would, er, they *loved* it, because somebody *leaving home,* leaving their mum and dad was exactly what it was all about, so it is pretty chall, I mean it's boring, it's obvious *now*, I think, but in nineteen sixty-seven, er, it was actually quite amazing to get kids to sit down and write the note that *should have said more*. (Liz)

The teachers generally suggest their methods are 'old hat' or 'boring' today. But Liz claims there was resistance to using contemporary material then: 'in nineteen sixty-*seven*, when it was first *released*…the Beatles hadn't acquired their academic credibility [laughs]'. But working in these ways challenged and broadened the boundaries of 'English'. Such material might be common in English lessons today, but it was controversial in the 'cauldron'. Liz says she used 'chunks of that John Lennon book' (holding up *A Spaniard in the Works*, 1965) and relates this back to her own school experience of English,

> I'd use bits of that. Er and always bringing, and bringing pop culture into the classroom all the time. Now that was something that, in the Wimbledon convent, [Laughs] you know, you didn't do it, you know what I mean! Because it wasn't *education* and it wasn't *English*! (Liz)

At the start of their careers the teachers confronted dominant conceptions of English in order to transform it. They used drama, role-play, film, music and creative writing. They are reluctant to claim any credit for initiating change in English however. They suggest change was organic and couldn't be avoided. But this appears not to have been the case for all teachers. Cunningham foregrounds teacher reactions to the 1967 Plowden Report,

> It might be a starting point, a turning point or an endpoint; the launch-pad to a career of idealism or commitment, or the symbol of the decadence in which one was trained; the point at which primary teaching found its feet, or the point at which it all started to go wrong; the culmination of what had been anticipated and worked for for years, or the nail in the coffin that terminated a career. (2007: 21–22)

It seems only certain *types* of teachers were attracted to working in these ways: maybe those committed to challenging dominant conceptions of English? The teachers all used 'pop' culture in their lessons. Michael used contemporary film. Ann did project work, with students pursuing their own popular interests. Steve recalls using Jimi Hendrix songs, Coronation Street or The Goon Show. His intentions for doing so are clear. He claims Hoggart's *The Uses of Literacy* (1957) was a catalyst for some forms of change: 'there became a greater recognition and the use of dialect and regionalism and different kinds of English'. He argues,

> And when the explosion of things like Kathy Come Home and Coronation Street started to appear, they were so self-evidently high art in a way. The early episodes of Coronation Street, if you look at those and they're as good as Samuel Beckett, I mean, they are astonishing in their linguistic structure and what's being done. But it beggared the question, "why aren't we using this contemporary material as the raw material for English?" (Steve)

Confronting social issues, explored alongside students' social realities, emerges as a driving motivation. The teachers claim they chose material to encourage this. In certain instances there is a deliberate 'oppositional' tone in the accounts that seems to have led to confrontation. Steve claims he 'faced explicit opposition' and would be 'literally brought into the headmaster's office' and 'not given resources'. He claims that when video machines emerged he 'bought the machine myself' so he could show Coronation Street. Steve is explicit about the political implications of his approach and the opposition he faced,

> And there was total opposition from some sources, you know? My experience was always of deep suspicion because there were some of us who saw it as fundamentally challenging the way English was taught, as a way of shifting the entire political agenda in education, because it was a core subject. *Core* subject! And people hated us because of our politics. (Steve)

Again, Steve refers to being 'hated' and foregrounds his struggle to challenge dominant discourses. This contrasts with Michael, Ann and Liz, who worked in departments that fostered collegiality which, in Liz's terms, could not be 'escaped'. They suggest teacher-led curriculum development was a collaborative endeavour. Steve highlights these processes as sites of conflict, locating them specifically into radical discourses. He claims he and his colleagues asked new and challenging questions of English that demanded new answers,

> Yes, the idea of a canon, that schools were there to enculturate and people brought from their lives deficits, and if you can inculcate elements of the canon, er, they were *educated*. We just thought this was rubbish...And when people like me started to say, "hang on, some of this advertising linguistically is fantastic. Some of this TV is brilliant, or The Goon Show on the radio,

CHAPTER 5

> these are amazing uses of English." We'd bring them into the classroom and suddenly the kids were with us. They loved English. It was *their subject*. And so then we made English into a really *pop* subject, you know? I'd bring in the lyrics of The Doors for example ok? And then I'd do Rimbaud, French impressionism, poetry of the late-nineteenth century and show how popular music was drawing on the French literary tradition for example. Do The Doors, and then show them a TS Eliot poem, and hey, it all makes sense! (Steve)

Steve claims 'it is almost beyond belief that we did things like that', but bringing media and film 'in alignment with English' gave the subject 'a whole new meaning and significance'. These changes, he claims, were significant and lasting. It does appear some practitioners in the 'cauldron' developed practice in ways that left an indelible mark. Introducing new methods alone was not enough for some of these teachers however. They foreground a more overt political agenda. Like Postman and Weingartner (1971) they suggest they engaged in 'crap detection' to confront and re-imagine dominant discourses.

DEVELOPING ORAL WORK

The teachers place great importance of developing oral skills. They insist on giving children a 'voice'. Oral work was important from the beginning of their careers, partly as a reaction to their own school experiences. They argue well-designed oral activities are crucial in English; they should be integral to planning, not 'tagged on'. Michael and his colleagues 'were always on the lookout' for resources to provoke meaningful discussion,

> And yes we had a high value on that, and on talk, we, our group, you know, group projects, we had a recording room, and we'd send kids out to you know, go and develop their projects and things…They had a choice…we did a group project, and an individual presentation, so it was good. Because we talked to other kids in other classes, and we'd look through these students' work…I just sent them off. We had this room, it was cut off in the English room you know, and so you just booked it and sent your five kids off, or out into the corridor to work. (Michael)

Giving students 'choice' and trusting them to work 'unsupervised' is a common element in the teachers' practice. Underpinning this is general awareness of contemporary theory and they argue the need to contextualise student talk. They understand, like Douglas Barnes for example, that many oral activities make 'meretricious gestures towards the real world' (1988: 52). Shaun is aware of Barnes' work and he understands the limitations of decontextualised talk. He explains how he generated student autobiographies by using taped conversations as starting points with reluctant writers,

And, er, but I also encouraged group work, oral work and tried to relate all of them together, you can't, I don't think you can focus on any one in particular, I think you *have* to focus on literature, language, oral and written work and make sure that they relate to each other in er, you know a fairly interactional way. I did, er, the project...transcribing students' *oral* autobiographies into *written* autobiographies and showing how students speaking their story, could be turned into a written version of that story, and that was really, really enlightening, and worked very, very well. It was very, very time consuming, not the sort of thing you could do every day as a teacher, but you could take some bits of that technique and, er, you know, use oral contributions to develop written confidence, if you like. So I would say that once I was in a position to influence how things were, I would say there was the right kind of balance between speech, er, speech, writing, er, and language, literature you know. (Shaun)

Shaun's autobiography project sounds simple enough, but he highlights the benefits for some students in developing confidence, writing, re-drafting and developing a sense of identity. Shaun suggests he worked hard to make the curriculum both coherent and cohesive. Writing, reading, speaking and listening were integrated into a whole process, with each element influencing and informing the other. But the teachers insist oral activity is the fundamental starting point.

Steve also foregrounds the importance of talk, again drawing on radical discourses. He claims his approach aimed to challenge dominant orthodoxies, intending, as Freire says, 'to expose the mythification of reality' as part of 'conscientization' (1970: 226). Steve contextualises children's school experiences, suggesting 'the school is organised around a containment theory, and it's structured'. He refers to the physical layout, corridors and rooms with rules for entering and exiting. Along with spatial limitations, he highlights temporal ones, with days 'sub-divided further by lessons, with different subjects and different grades'. These levels of structuring bring about an 'artificiality of a child's experience and the teacher's. You're a little sub-unit at a certain level and there are expectations'. He claims he tried to counter these restrictions,

But I just abandoned all of this completely and would just talk to the kids, believing that language starts with listening. And we are developing as high a level as possible the ability to listen, and when you have that you can speak. So colleagues would be totally bemused at what was supposed to be a *classroom*! The word itself tells you everything. But there I am, I've got rid of the furniture, got rid of the blackboard, and had circles of chairs, or would sit on the tables in the corridors and just *talk*. Because most of the teachers found it hard to control the kids, and because I said to the kids, "look I just want you to come in and we're gonna enjoy ourselves, we're gonna listen to each other, we're gonna talk", and get them used to listening and exchanging. (Steve)

Once more, Steve foregrounds his oppositional stance by abandoning established practices. He claims this caused 'major problems' throughout his career. Other teachers, 'were very suspicious of, very confused by, didn't understand what was going on.' Steve's methods invited suspicion that he was letting students down. But he claims his approach had positive effects on achievement – 'when the exam results came out, every year of my twenty-three years' teaching, my classes got the best results'. All of this, 'despite the fact that, throughout all the twenty-three years, in six or seven schools, I had a sustained barrage of criticism about the way I went about things'. He insists speaking and listening are the foundation for more sophisticated literacy skills,

> And it started with this idea that you listened to each other, you learn to speak, you enjoy speech, then you can start to be interested in language and at that point you use literature as an example of effective communication, or interesting communication or relevant or whatever. And at that point the kids are with you, they're *with* you. So we might spend six weeks talking about psychotic behaviour and losing it and anger and violent speech, and when we've kind of got really into the subject, we'll throw in a bit of *Macbeth*. Then the kids say, "well, should we read the whole play?"...And then when it came to the exam, because of the way that Macbeth had been introduced into the context, it was that it was common sense because they'd spent weeks talking about psychosis, about the effectiveness of violence in language and all that stuff. So when they started to read all this weird stuff it made total sense to them. (Steve)

Whether or not Steve's methods gained widespread acceptance, he maintains they were effective. Indeed, all the teachers foreground oral work as the essential base from which to develop broader skills in English. Foregrounding these concerns is, of course, radically different to the experiences they claim to have had at school themselves.

A FOCUS ON CHILDREN'S AGENCY

All the teachers believe English can help students develop a clearer sense of personal identity, generate meaningful relationships and communicative competence. English can provide linguistic, cultural and critical tools to help students reflect upon and improve their life chances. Challenging static conceptions of language and literature are important in relation to this. They are aware of, even anticipate, criticisms that could be levelled at this, but they remain insistent and committed to these principles. All the teachers worked in schools with mostly working-class students. Michael suggests,

> We were looking at the radical potential of what children learned, and *how they learned it*...and what they learned and in what ways it resourced kids to make changes. What kinds of ways to help kids to be critical, to analyse and actually

> to *act!* It's kind of romantic now really but...well, it's partly the rhetoric now, and the words social justice, the words social justice used to be part of Labour Party rhetoric in the seventies. And I think, when I'm looking at standards and the curriculum to see if there's any mention of that, 'cause it seems such a kind of utilitarian world that we live in, er, they just seem to see children as maintaining the status quo. (Michael)

Locating practice into wider contexts, Michael laments a perceived loss, or re-interpretation, of 'social justice'. The 'spirit of the times' seems influential. Social justice was a major concern for *Teaching London Kids*, which aimed to 'present positive strategies for action'. Michael connects practice with student agency, encouraging children to 'analyse' and 'act' on their life chances. David is equally concerned with giving students the cultural tools to critique social realities. He encouraged critical engagement with different discourses,

> I think there was the opportunity to er, to encourage kids to debate issues of importance to *them*, and I think there was a definite move to use English as er, to empower kids, I mean you can't...this notion of, unless you've got a grasp of the sort of language that you use in that context then you haven't got any power, so the argument was, you know, we need to empower kids in standard English so that they could take part in these debates. Discourse, that's the word...you can't take part in this discourse unless you've got the tools to do it. (David)

Developing language skills, especially among working-class students, is a consistent aim. Michael suggests this was done on a significant scale,

> Well, I think, er, quite a lot of us at that time as English teachers were interested in, er, giving voice to our mainly working-class students....we were publishing children's work, children publishing their own work. So that actually we used to have, I mean, I remember thinking "well what can we do to make this work real, to really make kids have real audiences?" and so on....all the lessons were really thinking about ways of making them active and giving them a voice. (Michael)

Giving 'voice' is a major priority in theory and practice. This, it seems, was a broader concern at the time: remember Worpole's Centerprise project. Shaun also links practice to wider contexts,

> Er, the good things were always to encourage debate, always seek to, er... always seek to encourage students to say what they think, to gain confidence through discussion, er, to respect other people's views...But also that, er, while I went into teaching very deliberately because I wanted to work with working-class kids, er, I wanted to become involved in a union and in working-class struggle, if that doesn't sound too grandiose! (Shaun)

CHAPTER 5

There is a collective commitment to developing children's confidence in their own languages, cultures and backgrounds. The teachers' approach is in deliberate opposition to 'deficit' models of language, culture and intelligence. Remember Steve's claims about the link between children's agency and curriculum content,

> Well we thought obviously that children have rights. And that's based on an idea that a person grows and develops and they're *free*! And that it was wrong for schools to imprison and to structure and to limit people, and schools needed to be liberative! So that means that when we chose a piece of literature it was because we thought that it had some potential for that. (Steve)

Steve's use of 'we' evokes a sense of shared identity, responsibility and practice, a joint enterprise. He highlights deliberate attempts to develop 'liberative' models of practice, encouraging students' critical consciousness. Liz recalls similar motivations, claiming contemporary ideas motivated her to work with 'lower bands',

> I was incredibly powerfully influenced…there was a bloke writing called David Holbrook who fired me up a lot to teach English. And I definitely wanted to work with the lower bands; I was very interested in getting, yes, the *rejected* writing. And I had plenty of those…I liked that, it worked well for me. But that was because I was using drama a lot of the time to teach the English. We were in role, we would improvise, you know, everything came out of the drama. (Liz)

I asked Liz to explain her desire to work with 'lower-bands'. She admitted to feeling intimidated by illustrious colleagues. Liz's department included Jane Miller, Anne Barnes and Terry Furlong, who became leading figures nationally, internationally in Jane Miller's case. As a new teacher Liz decided to 'go down the other end' (not that her colleagues were averse to working with less-able students). However it seems the prestigious team significantly influenced her practice,

> I think it came from the fact that everybody could write something, and what everybody had to say was worth saying and hearing, do you know? You know all that autobiography stuff, the Jane Miller stuff? Yes, it all came out of that. And I think teaching at Holland Park, where don't forget you might have had the Wedgewood-Benns and the glitterati, but most of the kids came from Ladbroke Grove and Notting Hill. So you had this opportunity I think to unlock a few voices. And that is forty years ago! (Liz)

Liz claims she and her colleagues were especially motivated by 'celebrating ordinary lives'. Shaun echoes this, and questions the purposes of education: 'is education about being *told* things or is it about *learning* things?' He claims a teacher's 'very powerful' role can 'encourage various forms of learning'. However, 'the emphasis *has* to be with the students themselves' to consider their own life chances, with teachers 'giving them opportunity to do that, facilitating that'. There is a strong sense of convergence in the narratives. The teachers foreground similar concerns and missions. For example they talk of children's 'rights', of finding ways to develop critical skills to be able to 'act', to 'unlock voices'. There is a collective sense they tried to engender dialogic relationships. They do this in different ways, but Shaun sums it up,

> Also I think to have respect for them, I think that's a very important thing. I taught at a very, very tough school in north Islington, er, and you know, you were dealing with kids who were at a superficial level creating you an awful lot of problems, er, but they were also kids with tremendous potential. And I got a great deal of satisfaction out of dealing with them, and you know, er, seeing them progress and develop... I really love the idea that every kid had the op, er, every kid had the potential to develop. (Shaun)

DEVELOPING CURRICULA AND ASSESSMENT

The teachers had opportunities to influence a range of educational processes. In this period the curriculum emerged through negotiation and experimentation, and the teachers claim they were involved in all aspects, from design to delivery and assessment. They had opportunities to work with exam boards to develop courses. Dixon argues the 'great educational project of the sixties was participant led' (2013: 24). New models of curriculum and assessment emerged organically and,

> What's more, this curriculum, and the changes in assessment patterns that accompanied it, depended on many thousands of teachers willing to learn, to invest their time in study and experiment, and to respond to opportunities offered. (2013: 24)

The teachers specifically recall developing 'mode three' Certificate of Secondary Education (CSE) programmes. David wrote a syllabus early on. Like Michael, he enjoyed using film and his head of department said if he was 'serious' about doing it 'why don't you write a mode three CSE?' He reflects,

> But you could actually, er, so I went and wrote er, a sort of basic CSE course, and then you have to submit it and validate it and so on. Erm, and that's how I got started [PT – And could anybody do that?] Yeah yeah. Oh, yes, I mean, well the school had to agree and to sponsor it. But you submitted it to the board, and if they agreed then that was it. You examined it every year and er, they're externally moderated, obviously externally marked and moderated and so on. (David)

The teachers highlight various changes in English at the time, claiming teacher-designed courses like the 'mode three' fostered higher expectations of students than previous incarnations. Michael refers to the freedom some teachers had in writing 'mode three' courses, which were controlled locally with up to 100% coursework,

CHAPTER 5

> You know, it's quite hard to tell you, but what is interesting is that at Wandsworth, the freedom that we had, you know, we had our own mode three…so you know extraordinary freedom really. We did our, obviously our syllabus had to be passed, but nevertheless, we did what *we* wanted for *our* boys. We wrote it and we marked it and, you know, obviously it was moderated. And what is surprising looking back on it now, and I realise it was quite *tough*, we wanted classes…to read *five novels* in a two-year period! Now, you know, you can get away with much less now, but our value, er, we placed on literature was very high. (Michael)

Michael foregrounds 'mode three' several times, insisting that it demanded higher standards than today's specifications. He compares expectations for his 'mode three' students with his daughters' experiences of GCSE,

> We had a very ambitious CSE curriculum which, you can't believe it now, my daughters have been through the local comprehensive and got by without having to read a novel! But actually our thought was that every child ought to read *five* novels! But do you think we set the standards too high to get these kids to write? (Michael)

The school's 'mode three' syllabus had significant expectations of supposed 'lower ability' students. And whether Michael's daughters 'got by without having to read a novel' or not, there is no current expectation that students read five novels. Shaun highlights similar 'mode three' demands,

> Well, the first thing to say is that it was dead easy! In those days if you had a group of teachers who were interested in, er, we set up a curriculum group, we looked a different ways of teaching, we collaborated between subjects, er, setting up all sorts of different models of teaching…It was nothing like today, I mean I, for example the mode, er, mode three CSE, er, where it was a hundred percent coursework, it's interesting because people think "oh, that must have been a doddle"! But the students produced folders of *ten* units of coursework! I mean they were *phenomenal* portfolios, an *achievement*, you know. (Shaun)

The 'mode three' was introduced initially for lower-ability students. A key feature was the amount of coursework it allowed and the teachers agree about its substantial academic demands. However, the ways in which they talk about it reveal how they represent themselves as particular kinds of practitioner. Thus, in connection with 'mode three', Michael describes himself as 'radical', whereas Shaun balks at the term. These disagreements demonstrate the teachers' sensitivity to competing traditions in the 'cauldron'. But their comments represent a view of themselves as teachers committed to curriculum development aimed at giving so-called weaker students a chance to succeed in an ungenerous system. They are also keen to show their concern for academic rigour, by insisting that the 'mode three' was not, in Shaun's words, a 'doddle'. The teachers' accounts contain a marked awareness of language and social class. Steve also wrote his own courses, which he links with wider contexts,

We very much believed that you took people's speech and communicative, communicative culture, brought them into the classrooms and developed and sustained it. So language is always there. (Steve)

He presents his approach in deliberate opposition to 'traditional' versions of English. He describes how he challenged what he took to be prevailing attitudes towards 'language' study,

And the underlying message was that we're going to teach you why it's the best language in the world! So it was essential that we learned the structure, and then you learned the *correct* forms! And so a lot of English teaching was corrective and remedial, *attacking* the native and localised speech forms! And then we came in and said that we wanted those forms sustained and brought into the centre of the classroom! So you're hitting the ideology. (Steve)

Steve describes himself as an 'ideological Marxist', but not in a dogmatic way. This is an instance of genuinely reflective practice. Steve understands the historical configurations of earlier versions of English, punitive teaching methods, and the social and cultural implications of the way he was taught. His insistence on changing practice highlights his effort to democratise English, to give legitimacy to his students' experience. Steve suggests that even if teachers have opportunities to design courses, it is of little value if they are not connected in the broadest sense to wider communities,

What I wanted to do, what lots of us wanted to do, was to connect children's learning with the learning of their parents. And to use life histories, and life experiences and community language as a main source for what you might call classroom products. And to produce our own literature, and we did develop this and community organisations initiatives. (Steve)

The teachers recall high levels of reflexivity to improve practice and resources. Their comments represent an act of speaking back, consciously and deliberately, to the relentless attacks on teacher-designed curricula and assessment that have featured in the English teaching landscape in recent decades. And their individual recollections reveal a PM of ideas, values and commitments held in common.

INSISTENCE ON MIXED-ABILITY

The teachers all insist on mixed-ability teaching. They claim they organised classrooms to benefit children of different abilities and backgrounds, to acknowledge diversity. The insistence on mixed-ability is motivated by social as well as educational concerns. Arguments for mixed-ability have been strong in English, but the teachers' early schools did set and stream most subjects. David explains how he rejected established practices,

CHAPTER 5

> And talking about groupings, well I, the first school I was in, I mean I inherited a situation where it was, there was some streaming and there was certainly separation of O' level and CSE sets. And I, er, I always preferred mixed-ability in English because it *worked better* if you did it well. (David)

Like the Bullock Report, David argues that 'even in streamed groups there is a wide variety of abilities'. He claims this is problematic because children inevitably end up in sets they should not be in, and 'hardly anybody ever moved between groups'. David initiated mixed-ability groups, arguing they demand better practice from teachers, who have to ensure effective differentiation. There was serious discussion about classroom organisation and its effects in the 'cauldron' (Hargreaves, 1967; Bullock, 1975). While David struggled to establish mixed-ability in his department, Ann suggests teaching in ability sets was ridiculed in her first department. Curriculum organisation demanded mixed-ability,

> And the framework for almost all that was going on…was initially oral expertise and oral confidence. That was the basis for any work that would arise and develop from it. Reading was obviously quite well integrated, both fiction and non-fiction in different aspects of the projects that we did. But the important thing was group discussion, interactive questioning and answers, interviewing, you know, a whole panoply of oral activities that were extremely buzzy. So I mean no classroom was ever quiet, in that sense. I mean there were quiet classrooms where only reading was going on, but that was specific to that particular room at that particular time. The expected basis for work was oral exchange…and writing came out of that, and presentations came out of that, and all of the exam coursework came out of that. (Ann)

Ann claims this made mixed-ability teaching appear natural. I asked if this was an example of 'progressive' practice,

> Yes, it was in every way a demonstration of those principles. It was mixed-ability because no-one ever thought of doing anything else! Other departments did, the school did stream, but if anyone said "why doesn't English stream?" You just laughed! (Ann)

Not all the teachers worked in such departments and some highlight a struggle for mixed-ability. Shaun's first school had rigid streams and the teaching was hard-going. Looking back, he criticises structures that affected staff and student expectations. I asked if he had opportunities to organise early classrooms in preferred ways,

> Absolutely not! Absolutely not! Absolutely not! And if you tried to undermine the existing structures, the kids would feel uncomfortable and they would resist it because they expected teachers to be bastards, they expected the teachers to behave in particular ways, and if you tried to react in a different way they saw it as a sign of weakness. (Shaun)

The social organisation of learning shapes possibilities, and Shaun highlights the difficulty of challenging existing orthodoxies. Hierarchical teacher-student interaction was ingrained in the school. But Shaun moved schools and had 'a total transformation'. He became more active in the NUT and local politics, which he suggests gave him the confidence to challenge existing structures. He and his new colleagues set about implementing mixed-ability teaching in the English department,

> Absolutely, and when you talk about possibility, the, the school was not run on mixed-ability lines, but we very quickly established mixed-ability teaching in the English department. (Shaun)

Shaun claims 'teacher shortages' in London at the time might have been influential here. Apparently management were so relieved to get capable people they took a 'light touch' approach,

> But in terms of the managerial structure at the school, I think that they thought that if you wanted to come and teach in these schools and were committed to it, then you could get on with it and do your own thing. (Shaun)

Shaun started at Holloway in 1974. But *Teaching London Kids* ran a piece on the school in the Autumn Term 1973, claiming 'the school lacked, at that moment, the equivalent of 13 full-time staff. County Hall implored the staff to "cope"' (no 2: 1). David also refers to 'a big staff shortage in London when and I started in sixty-nine'. He was quickly promoted and claims 'it sounds good you know, he must have been a whiz-kid, in two years he's head of department, but I think it really just reflected the situation at the time. I mean if you could stand upright and speak English, you were probably gonna end up as head of department very quickly'.

Problems with teacher retention meant some young teachers were quickly promoted, changing the demographic in some schools. High staff turnover meant sometimes young, relatively inexperienced teachers were running departments. I suggested in chapter two that ILEA recruited young teachers from training programmes and schools around the country. Remember Jones' (2003) claims that some of these entered the profession with a sense of militancy,

> Especially between 1968 and 1974, universities and colleges of teacher training were affected by, and themselves generated, movements of protest and attempts to develop new kinds of knowledge and new sorts of social identity. The teachers who graduated from these institutions formed a generation which sought to translate these experiences into an educational practice that could transform the ways in which schooling related to the majority of its students. From the perspective of many of them, comprehensive reform was important, but on its own it was not enough. (2003: 87–88)

And while this kind of 'radicalism' was only ever 'a minority commitment' (2003: 88), some teachers did initiate alternative, counter-hegemonic practices. Other

CHAPTER 5

factors also influenced arguments for mixed-ability. Michael refers to a wider theoretical movement,

> Well, er, sociologists had a big impact, you know. I mean people like David Hargreaves, er, looking at the effects of banding in secondary schools, er, which was a huge influence in thinking about, er, agitating for mixed-ability and stuff. Nell Keddie and Michael Young and those people in the new sort of sociology were helping us understand the relation between knowledge and how different classes took on that, er, er, knowledge. (Michael)

All the teachers recall building theory into practice. Michael claims Hargreaves's *Social Relations in a Secondary School* (1967) helped him 'make sense' of the school he worked at. Hargreaves, he claims, helped him to understand that in 'segmenting kids by supposed ability you were creating...an alienated group of boys'. He jokes that boys in different streams supported different football teams – 'I mean it was [laughing] that divided, that clear where you stood!' He recalls the struggle he and his colleagues faced in insisting on mixed-ability,

> Well, er, going mixed-ability was, I mean I, er, trying to take a school to play a part in moving from a stream, effectively a streamed school, well, banded, but streamed, to mixed-ability was a big battle that, er, I and few other colleagues waged. (Michael)

The teachers' commitment to mixed-ability is connected to wider concerns around social justice and equality. The climate of experimentation allowed them to make their arguments, and their claims were backed up with academic research that underpinned practice.

THE INFLUENCE OF ILEA AND THE ENGLISH CENTRE

The 'cauldron effect' of this conjuncture extends well beyond 1975. Attitudes, values and practices formed in this period have remained with the teachers throughout their careers. These effects are particularly evident in their stories about ILEA and the English Centre (which was not established until 1975). They agree that ILEA offered opportunities for professional development in and beyond the classroom that simply do not exist today. They foreground collegiality and co-operation between ILEA, schools and some English teachers. Developing new materials, methods and curricula, enabled and encouraged by ILEA, feature strongly in the narratives. The teachers highlight the possibilities local English centres provided for meeting colleagues, sharing and developing new ideas. ILEA ran many courses. Liz recalls a memorable one in the late 1960s, run by film director Mike Leigh at the Royal Court Theatre. She enthuses about the support given to teachers at the time,

> One of the things that was incredibly powerful at the time was that if you were teaching in the ILEA, you had a very strong inspectorate, you had advisory teachers, you belonged to the professional association of each subject, yes? And the drama, *London Drama* [magazine] was huge. And so there was, we, er, you'd go for weekends and courses. (Liz)

As well as this support, ILEA offered some teachers the chance to gain experience as advisers or consultants. David was seconded as an English adviser,

> So yeah, so that was a two year secondment...you were lined managed by one of the inspectors...but there was a lot of freedom within it. You used to meet once a fortnight and you know he'd come around and there'd be things he'd want me to do or pursue in some of the schools, but equally I could come up and say "I would like to do this, how about it?" and nine times out of ten he would say "yes". You know, so there was a lot of going round, working with individual English departments, you know supporting them, producing materials, er, helping people implementing ideas and so on, so it was really good. I think it was the best two years that I had really because I had freedom within a sort of really good structure, so you felt supported as well. (David)

David recalls building networks of teachers from different schools who designed courses they might run for colleagues – 'when I was an advisory teacher ILEA had a course support unit, so there was a lot of freedom to put on courses you know. If you come up with a really good idea the chances are you'd be supported and you could put something on'. Opportunities for collaboration and co-operation were common and these expanded rapidly with the establishment of the English Centre. Successful projects could be published. David co-produced a number of books and claims this provided professional satisfaction and greater agency for some teachers,

> I mean in terms of practical stuff, just look at the materials that came out of the English Centre, I mean a lot of that stuff is still around. And that, I mean, *that* sort of empowered people to sort of, to contribute and write stuff. I mean I was involved in several things there, you know, you got together with a tremendously exciting and really good group of people, you know with lots of ideas and you were just empowered to do it. (David)

All the teachers hold the English Centre in high regard. David locates it alongside the Institute of Education as the most powerful influences in London English teaching at that time. There was broad agreement between ILEA, LATE and the Institute, despite differences in perspective. There was a concentration on children's agency and writing largely coming from LATE and supported by ILEA. But it seems there were tensions between ILEA and the Institute about how theoretical ideas, particularly on issues of 'diversity', were implemented. The combined influence of the Institute and English Centre provided high-level support for the teachers. David claims this helped teachers connect theory with practice. But it seems only certain *types* of teachers were attracted to working in these kinds of ways,

> I mean the two centres for English teaching are the, well you've got the Institute and the ILEA English Centre. And they were really important because you know they were places that you could go to and you met, er, teachers you know, I don't know how you categorise it, but left-leaning or liberal people you know and, so for those who did feel isolated in their schools, it was the opportunity to network with other people of, er, of a like mind and sort of throw ideas around, work on stuff, collaborate, you know so you didn't re-invent the wheel in every school, sharing stuff. (David)

These circumstances offered some teachers the possibility of collaborating to explore alternative practices. Teacher-led development was achievable, which Dixon claims 'derived its creative energies from the democratic aspirations that followed WW2' (2013: 24). Those with 'democratic aspirations', maybe 'left-leaning' teachers, understood the conditions demarcating practice and generated more equitable alternatives. The structures and opportunities offered by the English Centre and the Institute made a significant contribution to the teachers' professional identities.

Professional development was not the only motivation for some teachers. Shaun and Steve claim they tried to influence policy. When Shaun moved to Holloway in 1974 he found colleagues who were 'more sympathetic politically and in terms of trade unions'. As a result, 'there was scope to develop, er, your own structures in the school'. He recalls how he and his colleagues located their work into wider social and political contexts to develop radical new initiatives,

> One of the first things we did, very early on, was develop a curriculum group, which met voluntarily after school, and we would discuss ways in which we wanted to reshape the curriculum, especially in English and Humanities. And that was a precursor to, probably our finest achievement, which was we were the first school to establish a non-racist policy, er, in seventy-seven, which was years before the ILEA adopted similar policies, er, in the early eighties. So, you know, we were able to develop those practices, and those practices were developed in, er, with developments in the outside world. (Shaun)

Shaun was involved with anti-racist and anti-fascist movements at the time (he knew Blair Peach and attended the 1979 Anti-Nazi League Southall demonstration). And despite ILEA being slow to take up some of these issues, he also acknowledges its support and encouragement for practitioners,

> So the anti-racist policy was developed in response to the growth of the National Front and other fascist groups and, er, their electoral success. And so, er it was a completely different atmosphere. And the other thing that has to be

said as well, is that the inspectorate and the advisory system in London, in the old ILEA, whilst not necessarily being particularly progressive, was incredibly supportive of teachers in schools. You always had people you could talk to… the atmosphere was one that encouraged what I would call good practice, you know, collaborative learning, teachers treating the kids with respect, using their own cultures and their own language, their own conditions to partner the learning process. (Shaun)

All the teachers claim to have understood how wider social, cultural and political circumstances influenced their working lives, and they were prepared to confront these. Steve locates his work into wider contexts, but suggests he was 'routinely victimised' for his approach. Looking back, he says he was conscious of how he tried to fulfil his professional roles and responsibilities through his political perspective,

So it was quite interesting and there are definite links between how I saw myself as a teacher and the kind of priorities I had in my political life, definite links. (Steve)

Steve wanted to influence policy and claims he and his colleagues 'took over the ILEA', demanding wider systemic and social change. Steve and Shaun were committed to their jobs, their students and working in ILEA. However, they were dubious about the ability of English teachers, even politically motivated ones, to 'change the world'. Their perspectives differ however, and they draw on different traditions and discourses. Shaun claims he 'never joined the Labour Party', whereas Steve was an active Labour member. Even among 'radical' teachers there were competing and contested ideological traditions. Nonetheless, they both suggest English teaching was only a small part of a broader militancy they wanted to engender,

It was cross-borough, people from all different perspectives, er, you know, not everybody was from the same political background or political perspective. In fact, I would have said mine was in slight minority in the sense that many people, er, when I first came into English teaching in the early seventies, thought that English teachers could change the world. It was a kind of messianic zeal about English teaching, which I never, it was something I never shared [Laughs]. Er, the idea of being a twenty-four hour a day English teacher, well I just thought well I'm sorry, you know, there's a bit more to life than that! (Shaun)

And we decided at a certain point that we, we realised we couldn't change the world as teachers so we thought well let's take over the education authorities, and we went about it systematically. (Steve)

Steve explains how he and his colleagues stood as candidates for election to the board of ILEA. He was a member from 1982–1990, and argues his presence was a 'cuckoo in the nest' for the Greater London Council and Labour Party at that time. He and his colleagues tried to initiate change internally,

CHAPTER 5

> I ended up being an elected member and running the ILEA. And because it became obvious to me and lots of people that you couldn't change from the classroom, it had to be structural. And so we went into the political and public sphere, took over the Labour Party, took over the ILEA and institutionalised a number of quite radical changes and it was a period from 1982 to 1990 when we did that. So I spent seven and a half year as an elected member of the ILEA. (Steve)

Steve claims some of the structural changes he and his colleagues initiated made the workforce more 'representative' by 'shifting the gender balance'. He claims they took responsibility for appointments 'from senior officers and gave it to elected members'. They wanted to 'get to a state where equal opportunities questions were coming from within school leaderships and the administrative leaderships, rather than politicians'. His approach to classroom practice influenced his desire to see equal opportunities policies adopted more broadly,

> Well we wrote those landmark documents, I was actually involved in the drafting of those. And we wrote them and published them, they caused a furore! The very fact that we'd published them, it was a waste of public money and all this. What now, what now has happened of course, and it's people like myself, English teachers and teachers who did all that, er, it's the common sense of the times thirty years on. There's *no* organisation in Britain that doesn't have those policies in place. And so we were doing that in the classroom, and we sort of expanded on that elsewhere. (Steve)

Differences emerged in how the teachers view ILEA. There is some consensus: they all agree it offered excellent opportunities, support and promoted good practice. They also suggest they were involved with many initiatives through the English Centre. But some of the teachers wanted to have influence that went beyond English teaching and they draw on different ideological traditions. It should be noted that these differences emerged with reference to events after the 'cauldron', in the 1980s, in a different conjuncture with a different type of educational politics – in what Ball (2008) calls the 'neoliberal state'. But the 'cauldron effect' of 1965–1975 is striking. The teachers maintain and promote values, practices and ideologies developed in this period. Their formative experiences in the 'cauldron' have had a lasting effect on their professional identities and actions.

Some of the teachers had the confidence and commitment to agitate for equality across a range of contexts. They view teaching from an 'activist' perspective – an approach Judyth Sachs (2003) advocates. She argues that the erosion of professional trust in recent decades has seen teachers lose 'social capital'. To regain professional integrity and autonomy requires a sustained, coherent and collective strategy,

> An activist teaching profession is an educated and politically astute one. The will to achieve this is lying dormant in many of us, and now is the time to work towards its development and realization in systematic and collective

ways...Teacher educators, bureaucrats, unionists and others interested in education also need to join together in order to make public and to celebrate the achievements of teachers. They also need strategies to inform those in positions of power and influence of the importance and necessity of a strong teaching profession. It is this kind of profession that can educate our children to be socially active and responsible citizens. There is no time to lose, we can frame the future agendas for schooling and education, we just need to harness the various intellectual, social and political resources available to us in order to achieve it. (2003: 154)

The teachers in this book share some of Sachs's motivations. And PM studies can help 'make public and celebrate the achievements of teachers'. But this was 2003, and Sachs's concerns remain as urgent today. PM studies have the potential to locate teachers' collective voices more prominently into educational debates.

PROFESSIONAL DEVELOPMENT IN OTHER AREAS

The teachers refer to their professional development in various ways. They all took on extra responsibilities early in their careers, sometimes through promotion or expected departmental duties. Some of them suggest they deliberately set up 'oppositional practices', as Shaun puts it. They were prepared to assume extra responsibility if it offered greater autonomy or improved student experiences. Their careers developed in a number of ways in the 'cauldron'. Liz set up and headed a drama department; Ann was second in English before becoming head of department; Michael moved out of the classroom to run the English Centre. Sometimes they claim they were in the right-place-at-the-right-time. David was promoted quickly at his first school,

> There were a load of us who were new teachers. After the first year everyone in the English department, except for me and the head of department left. So I applied to be second in department and I got it. The next year the head of department left and I thought [makes 'light bulb' facial expression] so I applied and I got it so I was twenty-three when I got the head of English job. Obviously it was too soon you know. I could do it, I could relate to the kids and do the paperwork and stuff, but I didn't have the experience. But I was nine years then the head of English, and I needed to develop in the job. I ended up as acting deputy in that school. There was a lot of good camaraderie there. (David)

David tells this story a number of times, suggesting it is a memory that has been 'worked on'. He appears to underplay his role in his promotion, highlighting his inexperience. However, it seems he was allowed time to develop, and the 'camaraderie' suggests a collegial atmosphere. He also suggests there was almost nothing else he could do, that 'teacher shortages' forced him to take the job because of desperation on the school's part. Sometimes the teachers appear reluctant to claim

CHAPTER 5

personal credit, preferring instead to connect their own success with collective responsibility. Shaun also refers to teacher shortages when he got a second in department job,

> I applied for, er, second in charge of the English department at Holloway in Islington. I was very surprised when I got the job. Little did I realise that there was a massive teacher shortage in London, having to teach in, in certain schools was regarded as exceptionally difficult. (Shaun)

Like David, Shaun suggests desperate circumstances, rather than his ability or commitment landed him the job. He became head of English at Holloway and worked there for over twenty years. Despite promotions and responsibilities, there is a reluctance to make claims about personal achievements. They suggest circumstance or luck allowed them to develop into these roles, almost as if anybody could do it. This might be true. But these teachers have worked in English in one guise or another for forty years, suggesting they were capable, adaptable and committed. Opportunities they had early on gave them professional satisfaction, and the skills and knowledge they developed in the 'cauldron' have been sustained through successful careers.

The teachers used their experience to develop into areas beyond the classroom. Steve and Shaun were involved in political activism. Both have written and published work on topics as varied as history of education, language and power or professional football clubs. David has had a varied career, moving from teaching, to advisory work, teacher education and consultancy. Ann stayed in the classroom as head of English and eventually became English adviser for a Local Education Authority. After leaving Holland Park, Liz taught English in a Further Education college. She did this while editing *London Drama Magazine*. She has edited and published a number of books, one of which collates drama practitioner Dorothy Heathcoate's writing into one volume.

Of all the teachers, Michael's career is probably the most unusual, in that he has been out of the classroom the longest. Yet he has probably had the most significant influence through his work at the English Centre. His role at the Centre was not a chance move. He had been attending ILEA and LATE courses and meetings in the 'cauldron'. He recalls one meeting with some illustrious colleagues,

> Yeah, ok, er, but they obviously recognised me as teacher with some energy, so I was invited to a committee meeting, extremely daunting, Tony Burgess, Nancy Martin, Jimmy Britton, Harold Rosen were all there and they were saying "well what should we do? Should we plan a programme?" So I said "well, you know, should we focus on teaching in the inner-city?" in the association, you know. So they said, "well go and organise it then". So I got a group I knew and we organised this series of conferences called Teaching London kids at Holland Park School. And I would say that on average, there were three to four hundred people came to each day, I can't remember. And

they were, as the result of, you know, all the kind of workshops and the interest in new writing and new thinking about education we started a journal called *Teaching London Kids*. (Michael)

Michael presents himself with characteristic understatement. Like the others, he highlights the collective first, suggesting the successful TLK conferences came about because he was 'recognised' as having 'some energy'. The TLK sessions ran during 1971–1972 and having hundreds in attendance is remarkable. Michael had been inspired after he was invited to speak at the 1971 International Teaching and Learning English conference in York. He explains the motivations behind the TLK magazine, of which he was one of the 'founder editors',

And at that conference a group of people passed a resolution, and you know we have all these aspirations as English teachers for the kind of world that we want our children to create and live in, but that actually the world that they are going into, er, in many ways negates all the values that we are proposing, er, you know to engender in the lessons, you know our English lessons. And so that in a way was a, you know, a request to think bigger really, rather than just developing your expertise out of writings about language and learning, and think in a much wider sense about how schools and English teachers were located. So we weren't content to be exclusively political animals doing endless resolutions and everything like the SWP and IMG, nor were they prepared to apply, er, or link their political ideology with anything that went on in the classroom. (Michael)

Michael acknowledges disagreements between different factions. But he suggests there were attempts to create a theoretical base for English teaching that emphasised collectivist and humane values, to understand the conditions and structures that practice is framed within. He seems to echo Shayer's argument that,

Out of the present soul-searching will at least come a body of theory for future decades which will be distinguished by its positive rather than by its conservatively negative qualities. (1972: 185)

The TLK sessions and the magazine promoted 'positive strategies for action' and had broader concerns than English teaching – they attempted to locate practice into a range of social, cultural and political contexts. Michael was involved in setting up the magazine 'from about seventy-two, seventy-three'. He served as an editor for a short time, leaving 'after about eleven issues'. And TLK was not unique at the time; he refers to other publications sharing similar concerns: *Rank and File, Libertarian Education, Socialist Teacher*. Circumstances in the 'cauldron' meant some teachers constructed professional identities in a period of ideological conflict and overt activism. Michael had worked as 'local leader' for ILEA, arranging fortnightly meetings, which he describes as 'built in' and 'not like today', where 'heads of department meet for the day...but it's to get the latest from the Strategy!' Instead he claims there were 'institutional arrangements' for 'creating partnerships between different schools'. This encouraged him to try and bring different elements together in one place and he approached ILEA with an idea that evolved into the English Centre. He explains how contemporary debates in English teaching were influential,

> Well it was endless talk wasn't it about how you could get ideas that would be shared by everybody, that was the level of discussion, you know. Politically, when it came to it, the politics of NATE and English teaching was, how can we share this stuff on a wider basis? You know, what would it take? And obviously that brought to the front questions about the nature of schools, the nature of teaching, who teachers were, what class they belong to. (Michael)

Through the Centre Michael became an influential figure in London English teaching. The Centre became a conduit between new theoretical ideas from the Institute and inner London schools. It also offered opportunities for teachers to develop theory, practice and resources. All the teachers talk positively about its influence.

WHAT DO THESE MEMORIES TELL US?

Circumstances in the 'cauldron' provided opportunities for the teachers to work in collectivist ways. They represent themselves as collegial and relational agents, with a strong co-operative ethos. When located alongside other developments (comprehensivism, establishment of ILEA, English Centre), the teachers' memories indicate the potent effect this period had on different aspects of their lives. This 'cauldron effect' has remained strong through subsequent conjunctures. It is important to stress however, that the teachers' narratives, even in the 'cauldron', are oppositional positions.

They foreground reflexivity, creativity and experimentation. They highlight collective concerns for social justice and equality. One way they claim to have advanced this was by bringing popular culture into the classroom. They argue this made lessons relevant and exciting, but also meant dominant discourses could be challenged. They insist on developing oral confidence and children's agency, with mixed-ability teaching a major collective concern. Learning is presented as a socially distributed, interactive process. They produced curricula and exam syllabuses locally, working collaboratively through teachers' centres, associations and the Institute. This had wider institutional support from ILEA, which seems to have encouraged professional development in a range of areas. Some of the teachers worked in 'activist' ways and sought to locate practice in broader political arenas. The evidence presented in this chapter suggests the teachers' work was underpinned by a set of shared practices, beliefs and concerns. Practice was theoretically underpinned and responsive to new developments. Equipping students with critical skills was a priority and 'measurable outcomes' seem secondary considerations. Yet they insist their methods still produced excellent results. The memories go beyond individual recollection and the teachers highlight similar concerns and priorities in their work – many of which are absent in current conceptions of the subject.

John Dixon argues recent changes in English 'squeeze the joy and pain out of any imaginative responses to literature, and crib, cabin and confine any language for life into the unreal world of test questions' (2013: 28). In present circumstances, he suggests it is difficult for practitioners to recognise the limitations placed upon them, and the relative lack of structured support they have,

> But how do teachers under this system learn to improve teaching and learning in their classes? Typically they lack LEA advisers, a teachers' centre, and any national project. (2013: 28)

Current models of English teaching restrict possibilities for teachers and students. PM studies have the potential to contribute practical, theoretical and ideological alternatives to current debates. As well as highlighting alternative models of practice, the teachers' PM foregrounds attitudes, identities and outlooks that can make valuable contributions to discussions about the future of English teaching.

ACKNOWLEDGEMENT

Sections of this chapter have appeared, in other forms, in Tarpey, P. (2009). Professional memory and English teaching. *English Teaching: Practice and Critique,* 8(1), 52–63; Tarpey, P. (2015). Professional memory in context: Can it help counter the "counter-revolution". *Changing English,* 22(4), 382–392; Tarpey, P. (2016). "Fire Burn and Cauldron Bubble": What are the conjunctural effects on English teacher professional memories, identities and narratives? *Changing English,* 23(1), 77–93; and Tarpey, P. (2017a). 'We not I' not 'I me mine': Learning from professional memory about collectivist English teaching. *Changing English,* 24(1), 103–117.

CHAPTER 6

FROM 'CAULDRON' TO CURRENT CONTEXTS

INTRODUCTION

In this chapter I explore the teachers' current outlook on English. Their experiences in the 'cauldron' influenced attitudes and beliefs that still resonate strongly in their narratives. A number of concerns and interests emerge in relation to current English teaching contexts. And, after full careers, the teachers' PM provides a critical resource from which to critique present circumstances.

ATTITUDES TO REGULATION AND PRESCRIPTION

Despite what they consider to be detrimental changes to English in recent decades, the teachers share a general optimism about the future, remaining confident in practitioners' resourcefulness and adaptability. But they understand conjunctural circumstances mean newer teachers construct different identities and expectations. They identify perceived constraints placed upon current practitioners. Shaun argues,

> And now the constraints, er, they're not constraints in the sense that they're stopping you doing, it's much worse than that, er, they are *pro-active* constraints, if that's not a contradiction in terms, where they tell you "this is what you have to do". The three-part lesson and all that nonsense. Er, so and er, downloading lesson plans from the internet you know, things like that, it's anathema to me. (Shaun)

Shaun criticises external expectations that inevitably influence professional identities. The teachers view curriculum development as a collaborative, negotiated aspect of practice. And despite claiming 'teachers are now primarily a conduit for the National Curriculum', where 'you download your worksheet from the bloody DfE website', Shaun remains optimistic. He suggests many practitioners 'are sustaining oppositional practices', and 'are still able to relate to the kids and work with kids in ways that are very progressive and very collaborative'. However, he suggests there might be less of the collective identity that his generation enjoyed, claiming, 'I think that in some ways we were much more sophisticated then in how we operated'. A stronger collective identity might encourage practitioners to confront present circumstances more systematically. The other teachers share similar concerns about statutory regulation. Ann claims,

CHAPTER 6

> You see once you make something statutory, you've in a sense restricted the field of opportunity. Unless you get people who are determined to carry on with their own creative ways; and there will always be those in English teaching won't there? Well there always seems to be. (Ann)

Again, despite external constraints, Ann remains optimistic that English attracts people who are prepared to question and challenge dominant orthodoxies. This might be because successful English teaching depends heavily on strong relationships? Dixon makes a similar point,

> I doubt if the resistance will cease. After all, the central factor is the teacher/student relationship. If this isn't cooperative, mutually encouraging, and stimulating on both sides, what hope can there be? (2013: 28)

Relationships are important. But the teachers suggest it is difficult to foster meaningful ones when working within some current constraints. Michael criticises the expectation for teachers to share whole-class 'objectives',

> Well in one sense it's a weird notion that you write all the objectives up, as though all the objectives were the *same* for everybody! [Laughing] You know, actually in a class, and we're discovering this more and more now, because we go into classrooms and look at these objectives, and you realise that, you know, that for half the class these objectives are actually irrelevant. You know, it's nice to know what, what your *hopes* are for the lesson, but they'll be *so different* for different kids and their interests and their abilities and so on. So yes, once you set up a series of objectives, you yourself are less open to surprises, and the more you're likely to plan your lesson to constrain the possibilities. (Michael)

Michael acknowledges the importance of developing children's meta-cognitive abilities, but current models restrict opportunities for this. He seems less optimistic than the others, suggesting English teachers are beleaguered by current regulations, which he compares with very different circumstances when he started out,

> And now of course, where you have a curriculum enshrined in statute…and all the drawbacks associated with that…but at that time nobody would have dared to er, institute that level of state control. You know the times just wouldn't have, people would start talking about Nazis and repression and state control, at that time, *respectable* education officers…as soon as any power was taken away from the local authority…so happy, chaotic days! (Michael)

Michael understands different circumstances produce different expectations. 'Repression' and 'state control' indicate the reaction some teachers might have had when professional autonomy was threatened. He seems to suggest current circumstances might produce more conformist attitudes, with a focus on 'accountability' or 'standards'. When the teachers began they were entrusted with curriculum development and Michael argues these concessions were hard-won. He perceives a disconnection between current attitudes to practice and a critical appraisal of the circumstances in which it occurs. Prescription, he suggests is now an accepted part of professional practice, 'enshrined in statute', and current practitioners might allow themselves to work in ways that are against their own best interests. He argues for a re-invigorated, overtly political approach to English teaching, claiming: 'English, it's sort of limp now. I mean if you look at the politics… people wouldn't march anymore'. He laments a perceived lack of militancy among current practitioners who have been socialised into English in different times. The 'spirit of the times', reflected by the likes Freire and Postman and Weingartner, has been replaced with more conformity. Ann agrees,

> A good teacher professionally now is someone who is delivering what is statutorily there to be delivered. Whereas a professional on earlier experience, and really my *preferred* definition, is someone who is prepared to innovate and try things out, and document evidence for the success, or indeed *lack of success*, for a particular enterprise. (Ann)

Ann's 'preferred' model is the collegial approach she experienced at her first school. Early experiences in the 'cauldron' inevitably influence the narratives. There are disagreements however. David argues there are plenty of opportunities for English teachers to develop good practice in present circumstances,

> There's nothing that stops you being creative. If you're not inspiring kids then you're using it as an excuse. (David)

David echoes Shaun's suggestion that many practitioners are innovative and creative. However 'inspiring kids' is not enough for some of the teachers. They argue practitioners should be more fully involved in defining professional practices and identities – practice should extend beyond 'delivery'. Experimentation, curriculum design, building and reflecting on evidence are important aspects of practice. Current practitioners are seen as doing a very good, committed job. But the teachers suggest a critical understanding the circumstances framing practice might help teachers develop greater agency. Shaun, typically optimistic, suggests different generations of teachers can learn much from each other,

> I think a lot of people are very dismissive of young teachers coming through, they think young teachers don't have the same tradition and ideas that we had. Well they don't have the *same* tradition and ideas but they still have that intellectual capacity for inquiry and challenging, er, prevailing ideas…I'm very optimistic about the future, I'm not actually someone who's hankering after that past…I look forward to a few more years and engaging with students and colleagues who are much younger than me, in a way that I hope is enlightening for both of us. (Shaun)

CHAPTER 6

IS THERE A CONTINUING RELEVANCE OF THE TEACHERS' PRACTICE?

There is a reluctance to claim personal credit, but the teachers suggest their work in the 'cauldron' had a lasting effect. Compared with their own school experiences, they argue English classrooms are dramatically different. Some of their methods are now embedded in 'common-sense' approaches. They claim to have broadened the curriculum, making English more relevant for students. They locate their work into wider social, cultural and political contexts, focussing on children's agency and critical consciousness. Steve foregrounds different realities in content and practice before and after he started,

> If you look at a picture of an English classroom in nineteen-seventy-nine and you look a picture of and English classroom in nineteen-fifty-nine, you're on a totally different planet. If you look at course materials that are typically being used by English teachers from fifty-nine to seventy-nine, it's a totally different world. The content has changed radically…there's been a *dramatic* shift, I would argue. (Steve)

All the teachers agree practice in English changed dramatically in the 'cauldron'. Steve argues there was greater emphasis on 'speech as a medium for teaching and learning', referring to the Bullock Report as key to these developments. There was significant emphasis on the role of classroom talk in learning at the time (see Barnes, Britton & Rosen, 1969; Britton, 1970, 1982, 1993; Barnes, 1976; Barnes & Todd, 1977). Barnes and Britton famously claimed learning 'floats on a sea of talk', and this influenced the teachers to develop oral tasks in different ways. Steve claims he is 'not one of these pessimists that think that what we were doing got crushed by the 1988 Act…a lot of what we were doing has in fact become institutionalised and universally recognised'. He suggests many developments are,

> Part of the *common-sense* of our times, that for people to understand the way their language works, they have to have a sophisticated appreciation of how, er, the newspapers, television, advertising and so on all works. When we were saying this in the nineteen-seventies people were aghast, saying "what's this got to do with *English*?" Now it's conceded to be absolutely central to survival…So what we started is still there in a very strong way. (Steve)

Steve claims this is, 'not as free and open as it needs to be but it's definitely embedded'. He argues that opportunities for broadening language work in the curriculum have been significantly enriched,

> We've succeeded in broadening the focus on language in the curriculum. And it's permanent, so no-one would think twice of, er, using advertisements, using recorded speech, using television. There has been a change. (Steve)

None of the teachers experienced being taught English in the ways Steve describes and he is right that the content of English has been broadened. But some of the

FROM 'CAULDRON' TO CURRENT CONTEXTS

teachers are reluctant to make claims about leaving a 'legacy'. Shaun cautions against nostalgia for an imagined past: 'I'm more interested in engaging at the moment with exposing the internal contradictions of the system you know'. He claims it is 'very hard to say' if his generation contributed to developments in English. But he insists important aspects of their work must be maintained,

> I mean being politically engaged...being unionised, being unionised of course is a phenomenally important part of the development of progressive education. Er, anti-racist education, er, the issue of gender, class, mixed-ability, er, all those issues, er, they're a part of our legacy. Er, engaging with the students' experience, er, not regarding kids as deficit models...but you have to be careful you know, I think modesty is a good thing when you're reflecting back. (Shaun)

Shaun recommends prudence. But being politically engaged and actively unionised feature strongly in the teachers' narratives. They suggest practitioners must be able to critique existing power relations and cultural practices. Ann is optimistic about this. She argues 'the spirit of enquiry doesn't seem to have died a death'. However, she suggests current practitioners might be more overtly politicised,

> I have a feeling that most English teachers need to feel more militant, if they want to pursue that approach to their job, they have to have a degree of militancy and a degree of determination. For example, to fight head-teachers who aren't always sympathetic with, who are preoccupied with league tables and all the other extraneous rubbish. (Ann)

Ann acknowledges younger English teachers are committed and capable, but recent circumstances have produced different expectations about the job. She suggests dominant discourses often go unchallenged, with professional identities shaped by 'extraneous rubbish'. The teachers claim they engaged in 'oppositional practices' to define professional standards. They argue teachers need to be 'politically engaged', 'militant' or prepared to 'march'. They draw on discourses in the 'cauldron' that foreground collectivism and activism. They perceive these as less prominent in current conceptions of the job. Steve explains why he thinks a more critically alert approach to practice is important,

> What we did is that we made English relevant for hundreds of thousands of kids and families...They learned a lot and they became people who could adapt in very different circumstances. Can I give you an example of that? When Thatcher destroyed the economic base of traditional industrial communities, those communities survived. And the only way that they survived is because there were some resources, social and educational resources within those communities that enabled them to do that. And when you look at the history of local writing groups, local publishing groups, local self-help groups, local political activism and all that sort of stuff, it came out of those demolished communities. They had to get it from somewhere, and one of the places they

CHAPTER 6

> got it from was the positive things that they got in the sixties and seventies in their schools, with teachers like myself...I'd argue there's a direct link between the way they were taught...we gave them the ability to survive, you know. And I want that story, that's the story I want told. (Steve)

It is difficult to discover the truth of these claims. But Steve presents an ambitious project for English, which initiates skills and sensibilities that extend well beyond measurable outcomes and subject boundaries. English is about 'survival' – the story Steve 'wants told'. Evidence suggests practice changed with this generation, but important aspects of their work have been overlooked.

WHAT DEFINES THIS GENERATION OF ENGLISH TEACHERS?

I asked the teachers how they might define their 'generation'. Their responses indicated remarkable similarities in how they represent their professional lives. The answers bring together the historical, the collective and narrative representations in ways that constitute PM. To highlight this convergence, here are testimonies from all the teachers:

> I was in the classroom from sixty-nine to eighty-four...I think there were more opportunities then, there was more flexibility. We weren't so answerable...I think we got wrong-footed, if we were a generation, when sort of Thatcher and the National Curriculum came along...We'd been left alone for so long we hadn't bothered to structure our theoretical arguments. We didn't have the arguments, we were caught out. (David)

> I think I come from a generation of English teachers who had certain precepts, who stood for certain values and had certain priorities. And they would make trouble, in the context of work, if they couldn't have what they wanted – for example, mixed ability, that was a *very* strong suit indeed...we defined ourselves as, well a *movement* sounds preposterous, you know, but as part of a *movement in English teaching*, I think we did identify ourselves. (Ann)

> Yes I do! The late sixties and early seventies was a time when a lot of socialists got together and decided to do something positive. We were inspired by revolutionists like Che Guevara, the Cuban example...we didn't just have a bit of politics and then our job, we thought we'd lead a life that's useful. And we played Jimi Hendrix, we politicked hard and we talked hard. And it was all one thing, and the word we used for our music and politics and our teaching was *progressive*...And so there's definitely a sense of belonging to a distinct generation, and we need to find a way of getting that history back on the agenda again. (Steve)

> Yes I do! Well I'm very glad to have come from the second half of the sixties. Because it was, because we really tried to make English *fun*, and de-acad,

oh, what's the right word? Make it non-academic? Get away from traditional, get away from the canon. Celebrate *ordinary lives* I think. Doesn't that sound cheesy, but yes...That's where it was, and it's all gone! (Liz)

Well, funnily enough, I found this question strange in a sense, because obviously I am from a particular generation because of my age. I started teaching in seventy-two, so, by definition, I'm from a different generation... the way I would sum it up is this – it's that I'm working with colleagues now, the most experienced and the best of them embody and have retained the best traditions of the ILEA, which don't forget [laughing] was abolished in eighty-nine, and...have sustained the best practices that we developed in those years of experimentation. (Shaun)

There was the rise of the comprehensive school, and radical teachers coming together...The sixties generation is a very, very important generation that enriched public life and still does because all these people are now working in the system, you know, they're all there...But other messages are so strong that they're being drowned out...all the [Education] secretaries are recognising that you can't force...the coercive model of change which they adopted and which has proved to be wrongheaded, is not working, and they're floundering around, looking for ways to revive things that modify it, so now *creativity* is back on the agenda but what does it mean? What does it mean if it's drowned out, if you have to spend your time coaching kids for SATs? It's marginal rhetoric. (Michael)

There is a strong sense of collective identity here and convergence on a number of themes. The teachers mostly refer to themselves using the collective pronoun 'we'. They evoke a clear sense of professional freedom and autonomy. They highlight a struggle to establish what it is to be deemed 'professional' – the standards and values of English teachers. They express various levels of opposition to present circumstances, where professional standards are imposed externally. There is sense that something has been lost over the years and that their earlier concerns need to be maintained. They suggest their work was of lasting value and that it can provide templates for future professional practice.

The narratives contribute to a collective picture of what was achieved. These achievements are expressed in specific terms. For example, Shaun suggests the 'best' of them 'embody and have retained the best traditions of the ILEA'. David laments the loss of 'opportunities' and 'flexibility'. Ann suggests they were a 'movement' who would fight on issues that affected practice, 'for example, mixed ability, that was a very strong suit indeed'. Liz strikes a characteristic note when she claims her generation tried to 'celebrate ordinary lives'. Initiating curriculum change to give 'ordinary' children opportunities to confront social realities is a motivating concern. Steve goes further, suggesting they, 'decided to do something positive', and 'lead a life that's useful'. Above all, they seem to recall the past in order to provide a

CHAPTER 6

vantage-point from which to reflect critically on current arrangements. So Michael criticises current appropriations of progressive ideas: 'but what does that mean… if you have to spend your time coaching kids for SATs?' There is a suggestion that current practitioners, and policy-makers, might learn lessons from this generation: their motivations and concerns need to be put 'back on the agenda again'.

CHANGES IN ATTITUDE

Attitudes inevitably change over time. Reflecting, discussing and thinking about the past changes how events are remembered because experience intervenes. Despite claims about 'counter-hegemonic' and 'oppositional practices', the teachers' perceptions of some events have altered. Shaun claims it is not useful having teachers 'reminiscing' about the past. There are cautionary tales and re-assessments of some aspects of their work. David recalls initiating language work in the late 1960s with 'very little advice' about teaching it. His approach 'certainly wasn't the formal focus on grammar that I had at school'. He worries about this now,

> So I mean I think, er, in some ways I do feel guilty about the teaching that we did, because we probably didn't give kids enough, er, of the sort the secretarial skills. Looking back on it, you know you can either look back and think, you know everything was rosy, or you can look back and feel terrible guilt you know. And I think probably the truth lies somewhere in-between. (David)

David has re-evaluated his approach. Despite claiming he rejected 'old-fashioned' practices he now feels 'guilt' about letting students down. Perspectives inevitably alter over time. There are many examples of establishment figures ridiculed for being 'radical' youngsters. Some academics alter their perspectives – see Michael Young (1971, 2008). But do dominant discourses in different conjunctures influence how we remember? Conceptions of 'accountability', 'standardised testing' or 'targets' undoubtedly find their way into practitioner understandings of the job. David makes these comments many years after he started teaching, in very different political, social and professional circumstances. Liz makes a similar point,

> Again it was a lot more free expression actually in those days. And in a way I think we did, we threw grammar out of the window and we didn't do it. We didn't pay any attention to it and I think I still have a residual suspicion about that. I worry about it now, because I don't know enough, I don't think, it was all just being your own person. (Liz)

Liz too has altered her position. But different conjunctural circumstances in the 1980s/1990s put a very different emphasis on events in the 'cauldron'. Conservative attacks on progressivism and comprehensivism and been consistent since the first *Black Papers* in 1969 (Jones, 2013, 2014). But to take a recent example, when former Ofsted chief Michael Wilshaw removed the word 'satisfactory' from school inspection processes he justified the decision with a personal account of the supposed excesses of 'progressive' teachers:

> Our education system is much better because of greater accountability in the system. Those who think we haven't made progress need to remember what it was like before Ofsted. I certainly do. In the seventies and eighties, when I worked in places like Peckham, Bermondsey, Hackney and West Ham, whole generations of children and young people were failed.
>
> The school where I was head before moving to Ofsted, Mossbourne Academy in Hackney, stands on the site of Hackney Downs School, which in its day represented the worst excesses of that period. But there would have been many others just as bad that never hit the headlines and got away with blue murder. (2012: 2)

These comments highlight the power of recollection in colouring how the past is remembered and shaping future action. Wilshaw draws on, and contributes to, a particular collective memory of these periods that is hostile to progressivism. This particular collective memory has a long history and it reproduces 'fairly stable types of utterance' to characterise this period – one of Bakhtin's 'speech genres' (1986). These narratives have proven to be politically expedient for initiating various kinds of systemic and ideological change. Former Education Secretary Michael Gove holds similarly negative views on progressivism. In a 2008 speech Gove ventured the thought that 'pupil centred learning' had 'dethroned' the teacher, suggesting this 'misplaced ideology has let down generations of children. It is an approach to education that has been called progressive but in fact it is anything but' (cited in Howlett, 2013: 1). Gove presents these ideas as though they were commonly agreed facts requiring no further discussion. Both men present the past as objective reality. Yet they make no reference to specificities, wider historical contexts or social and cultural circumstances. They choose not to recognise empirical evidence or written histories that gainsay these claims. The teachers in this book tell a much more nuanced and positive story about the period. Their practice and motivations were organised and theoretically underpinned. But as McCulloch (2000) argues, official versions of the educational past have been re-imagined to tell a different story. But even supporters of progressivism are critical of its limitations. Remember Jones' (1989) argument,

> But progressivism, though it correctly stated the importance of building educational development upon the interests and motivation of the individual, did not sufficiently consider issues of curriculum content. Stressing 'discovery', 'relevance' and 'expression', it downplayed the enormity of the task of equipping non-privileged students with the knowledge and conceptual equipment they would need to improve their life-chances, still less to understand and change their world. (1989: 131)

Jones, like Liz, suggests encouraging children to 'be their own person' is insufficient. But some of the teachers claim they developed children's critical skills and encouraged them to act to 'change their world'. They identify with the kind of 'critical pedagogy' Kellner (2000) defines,

> Critical pedagogy considers how education can provide individuals with the tools to better themselves and strengthen democracy, to create a more egalitarian and just society…to become sensitive to the politics of representations of race, ethnicity, gender, sexuality, class and other cultural differences in order to foster critical thinking and enhance democratization. (2000: 197)

Steve, Michael and Shaun mostly adopt this outlook. But even those advocating more militancy accept some aspects of external regulation. Ann considers the development of the National Curriculum,

> Because of the environment in which I worked and the team that I joined, it didn't take long before I realised that I was actually the lucky exception…many teachers had been trained in the same era as me but had found themselves jobs in schools which weren't that different to the one that I'd been taught in myself… where I think kids had a very meagre experience of English…It wasn't as if all schools were being innovative and being exciting and developing at all. Many schools didn't even think about developing along those lines…So in a way I think the National Curriculum was a valid event. (Ann)

However she claims the Curriculum, 'would have been welcomed with a much greater support from English teachers than it actually was' if it had been presented as 'guidelines' rather than 'imposed'. Her comments embody a number of competing speech genres. She acknowledges her first school was exceptional while most offered a 'meagre experience'. And despite consistently calling for more 'militancy', she accepts centralised prescription as a 'valid event'. Ann's use of different discourses highlights the complicated struggles practitioners must engage in to maintain professional identities. Different conjunctures, discourses and the passing of time have influenced the teachers' perspectives. Nonetheless, Shaun remains optimistic about current possibilities,

> But even with the constraints of national curriculum tests, you know a prescribed national curriculum, er, inside the classroom and if you've got a group of good, coherent colleagues working together you've got all sorts of different ways that you can, you know, provide opportunities for, er, children developing their ideas, introducing materials, generating discussion and debate. So all of those things are still possible, and they always have been. (Shaun)

HAS SOMETHING BEEN 'LOST'?

The teachers suggest important aspects of practice the 'cauldron' have been lost. These 'lost' elements include: loss of overt political engagement; loss of support from advisers/inspectors; loss of autonomy; loss of involvement in curriculum development; loss of commitment to English associations (LATE/NATE); loss of opportunity to develop exam syllabuses; loss of wider professional development opportunities.

Ann claims professional expectations have changed: 'those opportunities to use the professionals *at their very best* was evident, I don't think it is now'. Again she laments a loss of 'militancy': 'there seems to be a passivity, er, which I don't remember feeling'. Ann's 'militancy' is located into wider educational debates,

> Er, militant is such a simplistic term, I think what I really mean by that is that we were, we were imbued with the ideas of a truly *comprehensive* education. That was our militancy. And, er, you know, hence one's commitment, and even under duress, to mixed-ability teaching. (Ann)

The commitment to comprehensive principles meant children's social and cultural backgrounds were fundamental considerations in planning, classroom practice and assessment. Ann suggests teachers locating practice into broader contexts is 'evident less and less'. But in the 'cauldron' the teachers engaged with theoretical explorations of these issues (for example Grace, 1978; Postman & Weingartner, 1971; Freire, 1970; Hargreaves, 1969; Lawton, 1975). Michael claims English suffers if teachers are disengaged from critical debate. Existing arrangements influence not only practice, but expectations of the job,

> And why NATE now, you know…is having a struggle to hold on to its membership and run national conferences. You know, it's a different generation of teachers in place. Very good! I mean, you know, but, but just, er, you know, professionalised into a different world. So, so where you had a curriculum that is open, then the opportunities for professional development, and *full* professional development, in terms of what's best for *my* kids, what might work, what can *I do* about it, how can I make it happen? Er, you know it's open to, er, that the change, that was the change, and then the big change was, you know, now you'll do, er, this is the, this is the recommended recipe! You know your starters etc. (Michael)

The teachers argue 'full' professional development, using teachers 'at their very best', is difficult in current circumstances. Preferred conceptions of practice allow teachers to make professional judgements about 'what is best for my kids'. 'Full' professional development involves teachers having control of all aspects of the job. Michael laments the declining influence of English associations, with newer practitioners 'professionalised into a different world'. He suggests current practitioners are not encouraged to engage in professional discussions about the nature, identity and aims of English. Instead, the focus is on delivering a pre-determined curriculum to meet external accountability measures.

Central to the teachers' development was support from ILEA. Liz claims, 'the death of ILEA…it was Thatcher again of course, but I mean it was one of the most wanton bits of destruction *ever*'. She deplores the diminished power of

CHAPTER 6

LEAs to provide the support she enjoyed. She is critical of current conceptions of 'inspection',

> We didn't have to contend with the Daily Mail, yes? And that mind-set, and people like Chris Woodhead, and Ofsted, that wasn't there. And if anybody came in who was an inspector or an adviser, they were *there to help you!* (Liz)

Liz foregrounds a professional support network. Her insistence that inspectors were there 'to help' is a world away from current inspection regimes. Shaun makes a similar point,

> So yes constraints were gradually beginning to be imposed and when the inspectors began to *be* inspectors and ask for schemes of work and things like this, and they'd have you in and tell you what a [laughing] scheme of work was. (Shaun)

Shaun's laughter is funny. But it reveals his attitude to changing circumstances. New working practices were imposed without acknowledging practitioner experience. Shaun's laughter indicates confidence in his own abilities, but also exasperation at developments that insulted his professional integrity – external inspectors with narrow agendas passing judgement on committed and critically alert teachers. There is a collective view that new inspection and accountability regimes ironically had the opposite effect for which they were implemented. The teachers suggest these developments have eroded trust in English teachers. Steve confronts discourses that perpetuate damaging myths about supposed teacher autonomy in the 'cauldron',

> So the idea we had complete, or individual, autonomy is ridiculous because to start with there's a team...so there was an intense relationship between English staff in a way that possibly was unusual in other departments. There was a sub-culture that was strong socially, creatively...there was a strong teachers' association...so the idea of work and autonomy needs to be unpicked a little and historicised. It's one of the right wing's, the reactionary gang's mythologies. (Steve)

Steve foregrounds the importance of the collective. His point about 'reactionary mythologies' echoes Whitty's (2002) argument that myths about teachers 'abusing power' and 'betraying' students influence social attitudes. Teachers who worked in the period are evidently frustrated by dominant, negative accounts. Remember Tony Burgess's claim,

> Today, I find it puzzling to read about the trendy theorists of the sixties who are supposed at that point to have been corrupting literature into relevance and turning writing into creativity. They do not figure in my memory. Revolution was not on offer, but there were lines of work and new interests. (1996: 57)

Steve argues there were layers of accountability and respect for group and individual identities. This of course presents a very different account of events to the likes of Wilshaw and Gove. Steve insists present circumstances erode any sense of professional autonomy and collective endeavour,

> So you're having to succeed, and having to be energetic and committed and convincing. So we worked in that kind of very powerful, accountable, contextualised system…actually the best way to describe it is that there was still a powerful sense of professional respect and recognition for individual teachers. *That's* what's gone. (Steve)

And it is not only respect and professional autonomy that have gone. The teachers suggest critical, professional development opportunities are also lost. Shaun recalls opportunities to confront social realities through the English Centre,

> I mean it was an explosion of collaboration at the English Centre in the old days, I think it's changed dramatically now…But in the old days it was brilliant you know, the English Centre was fantastic at running courses…I remember in particular one of the advisers set up a group studying, there had been English teachers studying the issue of gender, and we did one on class…we had feminist speakers and they debated with us as teachers, how can we ideologically relate these issues in the classroom. It was fantastic, schools from the local areas, teachers from local areas, and it was fantastically supportive and very, very helpful. (Shaun)

Critical and collaborative ways of working were supported by official institutions. English was about more than developing skills or subject knowledge. The teachers suggest students must be encouraged and helped to explore how discourse has the potential to divide communities in terms of race, class, gender and so on. They refer to the Bullock Report's insistence that children's social and cultural backgrounds are central to learning. Steve perceives a lack of critical engagement in present circumstances,

> Well at the time of the Bullock Report I think most teachers actually sat down and read it. That's why you'll see it so frequently occurring in Oxfam charity shops now, because it was a really quite commonly owned book by English teachers. Nowadays I would be *astonished* if any English teacher had ever read anything produced by the government…that's a major memory of mine anyway and it seems to be important. (Steve)

Current English teachers navigate their way around curricula, standards, strategies and the like. They do read documents 'produced by the government'. But Steve's point is that current policy constructs practitioners like Shaun's 'conduit' for 'delivering' somebody else's curriculum. This contrasts significantly with the collaborative spirit in which the theoretical ideas in Bullock were presented. Steve's comments are also interesting because he consciously selects a 'major memory'. Remember Shotter's argument that stories about our experiences are designed 'to represent them in such a way as to constitute and sustain one or other kind of social order' (1990: 122–123). The teachers locate professional autonomy, social justice and critical agency at the

CHAPTER 6

top of the 'social order' of English teaching. They suggest wider support networks and professional associations have been replaced with accountability mechanisms that de-professionalise teachers. They argue much has been 'lost'.

PERCEPTIONS OF PROFESSIONALISM AND ACCOUNTABILITY

The teachers suggest current models of professionalism and accountability have a negative impact. Before specified 'directed time' the suggest teachers 'did what the job needed'. But reformers in the 1980s sought to make teachers more accountable for their time. Education Secretary Kenneth Baker imposed a minimum teaching contract of 1265 hours (Jones, 1989). This eroded goodwill. David argues his preferred flexible ways of working were curtailed,

> The whole sort of assessment regime got tightened and I think the thing what killed a lot of that stuff was 1265 hours. Because up until that you had to put in the hours the job needed. But it was recognised and you were treated like a professional, no-one was checking up on you the whole time. You know PE teachers would run things after school and go on Saturdays and so on. But once you say "you will do a minimum of 1265 hours", once you start doing that sort of stuff and you don't trust people professionally, well they just said "stuff it". (David)

Professional autonomy is fundamental to David's identity. Michael is equally critical. These changes limited professional development opportunities through the English Centre. Teachers stopped attending evening courses,

> Er, with its relative freedom there was a different set of professional practices around the work you did obviously. Er, the new contract came in, I can't remember the name of it now, er, yeah 1265 hours, and all this changed dramatically. (Michael)

Michael suggests Baker's policy backfired. He claims teacher unions, who resisted its imposition, now defend 1265 hours to keep workloads down. The term 'professionalism' is also contentious. Shaun is ideologically opposed to it. He creates an interesting dialectic, foregrounding his suspicions of 'professionalism' and its changing connotations,

> I always used to argue against it, I used to say that professionals were *workers*... But I always rejected the idea of the professional because of the connotation. The connotation was that you didn't behave like a worker. And that's to say that you didn't behave like a trade unionist, you didn't go on strike. I spent most of my life going out on strikes! [Laughing] Why? Because I thought it was an important way of collectively resisting things that were happening, pursuing objectives you wanted to pursue. So I always argued very strongly against the notion of professionalism. (Shaun)

In the 1970s Shaun focussed on union activity and defining teachers' identities as 'workers'. But he is sensitive to the evolving connotations of 'professionalism' and the ways teachers are currently positioned. He argues critical engagement is crucial for current practitioners,

> Interestingly, and I suppose this is where it is, er, where, er, the dialectic comes in. In some ways now you want to *affirm* the professionalism, you know of the, er, the English teacher, and of teachers in general; *because* professionalism then embodies a certain degree of independence, a certain degree of, er, of thinking about the subject that you teach in the way that you want to teach it. (Shaun)

The teachers challenge the theoretical bases that underpin practice. Shaun, once insistent on teachers as 'workers', now recognises the need to demand a reconceptualisation of 'professionalism' so current practitioners might agitate for the relative freedom, status and agency he had. This is not an about-turn. His ideals and values are consistent. But Shaun promotes oppositional practices by challenging definitions of professionalism and their 'internal contradictions', encouraging practitioners to turn these to their 'own advantage'. Steve also challenges myths about teachers being unaccountable and irresponsible,

> What we used to have were self-referencing professional groups, like our own English teachers' association, our trade unions, our local drama groups, links with parents. I mean there were *intense* layers of accountability, it was massive. There were local inspectorates for example. You had your own departmental structures in schools, you were constantly being looked at and examined, but it was all internal. And we've shifted and so what's happened is that people like me have gone. (Steve)

These 'layers of accountability' forced practitioners to take responsibility for their work individually and collectively. Steve criticises existing models that 'de-professionalise' English teachers,

> There is no professionalism. What's happened is that professionalism has been systematically demolished and obliterated. Professionalism, if you take the concept, the key idea is the concept of authority through self-regulation. And you self-regulate, individually and collectively, to set a standard that is unimpeachable...And that idea has been demolished by external accountability. And because it then has to be assessed you are assessed on things that are then extremely low-level. So it's quantities, systems and thing like that that are explicitly unintellectual and unprofessional...so people like me are gone... because it's not possible to survive in this system and have a brain! And when I hear, I don't want to be critical of colleagues, but when I hear gaggles of younger teachers talking, I'll be frank, I haven't got a clue what they're on about. There's nothing there. (Steve)

CHAPTER 6

'Professionalism' is defined in different ways. David and Michael suggest professional trust has been eroded. Shaun claims he opposed conceptions of 'professionalism' in the 'cauldron', but demonstrates a critical ability to recognise its changing connotations. He suggests current practitioners might fight to defend 'professionalism' as a way of establishing greater autonomy. Steve highlights different layers of accountability in the period and offers an interesting response to myths about teachers' abuse of power. He argues the erosion of professional autonomy has resulted in an exodus of people 'like him', to be replaced by younger teachers who sometimes have 'nothing there'. There are different perspectives here. David, Steve and Michael appear nostalgic for earlier times. Shaun seems typically optimistic. He is equally critically of the changing connotations of professionalism. But he problematises the issue to find ways of improving teacher agency, encouraging a critical praxis. The changing nature of teacher professionalism is explored by Andy Hargreaves, who identifies four distinct 'ages' of the concept since WW2. Most recently we occupy a 'postmodern' or 'post' professional age. Hargreaves argues professional status is 'by no means fixed, but is being and will be argued about, struggled over and pulled in different directions in different places and times' (2000: 167). The teachers understand this fluid conception of professionalism. Hargreaves insists it is crucial for practitioners confront and re-define professionalism as more 'democratically inclusive'. This,

> ...should not be left to 'fate', but should be shaped by the active intervention of all educators and others in a social movement for educational change which really understands the principle that, if we want better classroom learning for students, we have to create superb professional learning and working conditions for those teaching them. (2000: 175)

CAN LESSONS BE LEARNED FROM THIS GENERATION?

I asked if the teachers thought other practitioners might find their stories interesting. I was surprised by their intensity. They all suggest practitioner accounts of English are helpful for building a sense of identity and tradition. They are wary of over-sentimentalising however, and argue accounts of events must be problematised. By contextualising practice, the teachers suggest it is possible for practitioners to locate themselves into broader narratives, potentially giving them greater agency through the weight of tradition and precedent. Ben-Peretz (2002) argues 'learning from experience' is essential,

> The accumulation of experiences leads to growth. Sensitivity to failures plays a cardinal role in this process. Awareness that something is missing, a sense of dissonance between expectations and reality, seem to be prerequisites for conscious and explicit learning from experience in order to improve one's practice. (2002: 318)

PM studies can generate accounts of English to highlight valuable collective experiences. These accounts might provoke critical reflection on current practices and circumstances. And while it is important 'to improve one's practice' as English teachers, it is equally important to locate it into conjunctural circumstances and deal critically with any 'dissonance between expectations and reality'. The teachers recall ways of working that seem to achieve this. David offers very practical reasons for younger teachers to learn from experienced colleagues,

> But yes, I mean it does help to know where things have come from, because occasionally [laughing] you come across a teacher and they come up and say "have you seen this?" and you say "yes, about thirty years ago!" (David)

Younger teachers might find knowledge of curriculum development useful so as not to 'reinvent the wheel'. But David suggests there are more important lessons to learn. He encourages practitioners to engage critically with theory,

> I think it's, well I hope it's a willingness to engage with theory, er, with new theory and seeing how, you know, does this have anything to say to us? Does this, er, is this actually going to influence what we do with kids in the classroom? And, er, you know if it does, a willingness to change not only your own ideas but your practice. And I think, you know, it's the openness to those sorts of ideas that's the key thing for being an English teacher, that's it there. (David)

Theoretically underpinned practice is a strong and recurring theme. David's advice seems important. But how easy is it for current teachers to work in these ways? How do new theoretical ideas find their way into schools? The kinds of links that existed between the Institute and English Centre have gone. Membership of English associations has fallen. Circumstances are different. Again, Shaun cautions against having experienced teachers 'reminiscing' about the past. He argues young teachers 'are crying out for that experience but in a different historical period'. Yet he recalls being influenced by the likes of Rosen, Britton and Dixon and their attempts to theorise practice,

> The thing about all of those people then, they encouraged teachers to become their own theoreticians, they had some grasp of the organic intellectual, er, intellectual development arising *out of working practice*. (Shaun)

Shaun refers to Richmond and Eyre's *Becoming Our Own Experts* (1982) as an example of this. Being 'their own theoreticians' is an ingredient of the 'full' professionalism Michael depicts. The teachers began in circumstances when theoretical engagement was encouraged. Hardcastle and Medway (2013) suggest the Institute was particularly influential in defining English from the 1950s. Five of the teachers studied there while this influence remained and they developed the confidence to put theory into practice. Recognition is due to teachers who theorise. But this was facilitated by work from academics like Britton, Rosen and Barnes, who produced research into children's learning and cultures that helped teachers in classrooms. This generation of academics, comprising mostly former teachers, pioneered theoretical perspectives that had not existed previously. Collaboration between practitioners and researchers is important and the teachers understand the agency it gave them. Hardcastle and Medway (2013) argue this collaborative approach energised some teachers,

> Far from being handed their marching orders from above, the most committed teachers felt themselves to be empowered agents in an enterprise to build a better, fairer society. (2013: 40)

Michael studied at the Institute with Britton and Rosen and their work has survived in his interactions with teachers at the English Centre. But he recognises a different sense of theoretical engagement currently, which is less critical and discriminating. He recalls an encounter with a recently qualified teacher,

> But to talk to teachers now, who have been recently trained in the last two or three years, it would be really, really interesting to try and sort out exactly, because they are *not* joining associations, they're *not* going to meetings, and er, we've been working with a group of teachers, I've been working with a group of teachers, and a really *good* teacher, or she seems to be, and in her report of the thing we've been looking at, boys and writing, she said "I don't know whether I dare, er, not have a writing frame if an inspector came into my classroom." (Michael)

Far from encouraging good practice, Michael argues curriculum demands, inspection regimes and expected outcomes limit possibilities and opportunities. He suggests practitioners should be more critical in confronting the theoretical bases that underpin practice,

> So somehow or other it's intelligent teachers who have got this idea that, if you are seen, er, you know, if you get that, er, when we've tried to wean them away from objectives, you look through these exercise books of some of these kids, and they're really *nice* teachers, and you can't work out what the task was! I haven't a clue what it was they were meant to be doing…So somewhere or another the messages, er, what they call the unintended consequences, er, is strong. But it's a really interesting area for someone to explore, is the training and making of a new generation of teachers. (Michael)

Through his work at the Centre, Michael knows recently qualified teachers are committed and capable. But he claims the 'recommended recipe' is so integral that some teachers struggle to adapt if the template is removed. He argues training programmes focus too heavily on 'delivery'. Steve suggests something similar: 'I have a major criticism of teacher training institutions at the moment, is that there simply is not enough *real* history of education'. He argues historical contextualisation can help practitioners adopt more critical perspectives,

FROM 'CAULDRON' TO CURRENT CONTEXTS

> There's simply just not enough history of education, it's unbelievable. It's also, the decline of history of education, it's one of the necessary elements of the reactionary shift, which is why now, I'm situating myself in the history of education because it's the, *the*, discipline focus that can unlock a lot, you know, recover the past. *Very* important. (Steve)

Understanding educational history is important, but Steve also stresses the value of younger teachers learning from experienced ones. He argues an institutionalised system might:

> ...structure reflective interaction for younger would-be English teachers with people in their thirties, fifties, seventies. And actually expose them to reflective things like we're doing here to get them to think. What we would find now, most interesting...is that a lot of the intuitive feelings of younger teachers... will closely reflect on what my generation was doing because of course they are now wanting to react against the prison that's been put in place since 1988. So there'd be a real purpose in institutionalising the sort of things that we're doing here. (Steve)

Steve might be right that teachers want to 'react against the prison' of the Education Reform Act. Encouraging new and experienced colleagues to reflect critically on developments in English would be positive. This can foreground alternative ways of working, missions and ideological perspectives from different periods to be re-imagined for new times. Liz and Ann argue that if practitioners understand historical narratives in English teaching they might be more critical in the present. Ann foregrounds the potential agentive effects of this,

> Because I think historical narrative is what it's all about really isn't it? I think it's all a narrative isn't it in a sort of key basic way. You, we, are all part of our own narrative, our own specific individual narrative, but also a narrative of what our job is like today and where it's come from. And I think to understand where it is today, you know the story of how it developed is not just satisfying, but I think it's essential. I mean if I were in the business of training teachers now...I would find that really pertinent to what I was doing. (Ann)

Practitioners can develop stronger professional identities by locating themselves securely into the historical trajectory of the subject. This can foreground the ways individual experience is mediated by various discourses, narratives and ideologies. Ann claims this is 'essential'. Like Steve, she suggests this should be institutionalised. Liz makes similar claims about the importance of identity and tradition,

> I think the history of English teaching would be...it's quite a nice feeling to belong to a tradition...And I think that as it's not provided by advisers and it's not provided by continuous professional development very much, I think that would be a *very* nice thing for people to feel part of something. Who were the

135

CHAPTER 6

> greats, what were the changes? It could offer...an opportunity to reflect on their practice, where does it come from, why did I do that, er, how can I push the *boundaries*, how can I transfer a good sixties idea into a current idea? (Liz)

The teachers have different priorities. David and Shaun highlight the importance of theoretically underpinned practice, the 'organic intellectual' and teacher-led development. Michael laments the erosion of collective and collegial approaches. He suggests that because teachers do not 'join associations' or 'go to meetings' they are disempowered in discussions around their own professional status. Steve, Liz and Ann stress the importance of having a clear sense of 'history', strong 'narratives' and 'belonging' in English teaching. Steve argues life history and professional memory work should be 'institutionalised' in teacher development programmes. There are differences of opinion. But collectively the teachers highlight lessons that can be learned. The combination of priorities can be traced back to the 'cauldron' when they began their careers. They suggest newer practitioners would benefit from a critical understanding of the subject's history. PM studies have the potential to create a sense of collective identity and tradition by provoking critical examination of practice and conjunctural circumstances. Histories of English should include teachers' voices.

SUGGESTIONS FOR FUTURE DEVELOPMENTS

I asked the teachers how they thought English might develop. They all demand greater emphasis on oral work. They suggest a comprehensive language strategy is required, with more relevance to students' own lives and interests. They suggest teachers should make it their business to involve themselves in critical debates around the subject. There should be wider opportunities for reflection and professional development. Shaun suggests he would 'like to see the exam syllabus much more flexible and much less rigid'. Liz 'can see as an English teacher there may be more challenges because of technology, because of the intervention of technology'. David and Ann worked as English advisers and are concerned about the status of speaking and listening. Ann argues 'speaking and listening is actually the basis for nearly all really good work in English'. Despite this, she claims oral work is often a 'post script' to lessons and not 'fully integrated', which 'is an absolute shame, I think it's a scandal'. I asked why this was so important,

> I think there should be a revolution on the issue of speaking and listening. I can't think of anything that would be more likely to create a new era of success for pupils...It's most unfortunate that it got pushed out in the way that it did, and in a sense you can identify the generation that did it can't you? Because they came in large measure I suspect from the same type of education that I received...So it's come full circle hasn't it? Because I came from that type of experience, and lo and behold, people of that era have written it now as a very sort of tough framework to impose to teachers now. (Ann)

Like Lowe (2007), Ann criticises a generation of 'meritocratic elitists' who have imposed what she sees as regressive practices. Her sense of 'militancy' is evident again when she calls for a 'revolution'. David has similar concerns,

> I think I'd like to see a greater emphasis on speaking and listening…I think more work needs to be done there. I don't object to looking at Standard English, language study stuff, looking at the differences between speech and writing. But I'd like to see a greater emphasis on discussion. It's better in schools than it has been, but I still see an *awful lot* of teacher-led discussion. (David)

Nonetheless, David insists many current English departments demonstrate good practice: 'I suppose I shouldn't say this because it sort of implies criticism of other subjects, but er, generally if you want to see good, imaginative teaching in a school… go to the English department'. The other teachers have similar concerns. Michael wants a stronger emphasis on children's own interests. He criticises conceptions of 'personalisation', arguing this really means 'target setting'. He imagines an alternative approach,

> What you have to do is to re-introduce engagement and enjoyment, you know, you have to look at, er, if personalisation means anything, it *must* mean re-introducing the idea of, er, you know, groups of kids with passions and needs and everything and starting with that. And that is the way forward. (Michael)

Practitioner voices are largely ignored in present circumstances and recent interventions have seen the downgrading of classroom talk, the re-introduction of grammar testing and an elitist curriculum (Coultas, 2013). Michael has spent a career thinking of creative ways to improve English teaching. Policy makers mostly ignore this experience. He highlights the contradiction of promoting 'personalised' learning when teachers are restricted externally in the types of 'personal' programmes they can initiate. He criticises policy makers who do not understand (or ignore) these contradictions,

> But you know the strategists seem to come up with a range of, you know, debatable collective strategies in the classroom…And when you look at them in use, I don't know how useful this is but I've always felt that, in a way, governments if they don't provide sufficient feedback loops are destined to reproduce the very ills they are trying to address…and they're pursuing educational policies that apparently make no difference to truancy rates, make marginal difference to the literacy rates, produce the unhappiest children, the least interested readers, you know, and you could go on. (Michael)

There are big ideological differences between the teachers and current policy-makers. Shaun argues practitioners should be alert to different ideological and

CHAPTER 6

political perspectives. He concedes this can cause difficulties for teachers trying to work in 'counter-hegemonic' ways,

> And if anybody said to me "oh well you shouldn't be overtly political", er, I would say what you're really saying to me is I shouldn't be overtly political *with my politics*. It's perfectly alright to be political so long as it reflects the prevailing ideology. (Shaun)

The teachers insist on locating English into wider political contexts. Steve echoes Shaun. He visualises a reconfiguration of the political landscape in English teaching. He wants a 'holistic approach to the nurturing and development of the child'. This, he claims, requires a coherent language-across-the-curriculum strategy and 'breaking the boundaries' between discreet curriculum subjects. He refers to the 'cauldron', claiming: 'there was a critical shift that occurred really, the shift from language as an object that can be analysed, to the idea of, er, an endless network of communicative practices'. Dixon's echoes can be heard here. Steve wants to move away from 'reified' conceptions of language to studying the effects of 'signs in use'. Current models of English are monological, elitist, and ultimately ignore the heteroglossial realities of language in use – they are 'cut off from the fundamentally social modes in which discourse lives' (Bakhtin, 1981: 259). Steve argues for a new conceptualisation of English teaching that is collectivist and heteroglossial:

> Well one of the things that I think is important is that at the core of all English teaching there needs to be an explicit study about the growth and development of language. Not as an add-on, as a kind of small topic-based thing, but it needs to be actually the underpinning and unifying agent of the whole English teaching. So that we can see language as something in flux, that's multi-national, that's dangerous, that's controlling, that is a social and historical construct. So that when we look at the way we speak and write and communicate, it's seen as part of the flow of time. Now, that would be a radically different way of organising the curriculum content in English than that which is sanctioned and legitimised now. (Steve)

This is a big ambition. It would require immense collective effort from practitioners to re-imagine the subject in these ways – politically, theoretically, practically. Current circumstances make it hard for teachers to maintain any sort of commitment to a co-operative ethos. The teachers suggest they were 'fortunate' to begin when they did. They acknowledge the support and opportunities they had. But the circumstances they started in did not emerge by accident. They were the organic culmination of deliberate attempts to democratise English throughout the 1940s and 1950s. Practitioners did it for themselves. And they can do again. If English teachers can communicate and collaborate more freely, initiate dialogue through their writing, through meetings, conferences and the like, then it might be that a new, organic, conceptualisation of the subject can emerge through this collective endeavour? Steve claims he 'doesn't think there should be English teaching at all', but a 'social and historical based curriculum'. Focussing the subject in these ways would be 'very different from the skills-based rubbish that exists at the moment'. This approach would of course demand a clear theoretical underpinning and sense of purpose. A stronger emphasis on theory and critical reflection is common theme. I will leave the last word to Liz. She had opportunities in her career to write and edit a number of publications. She argues current teachers would benefit from similar opportunities,

> I think there's a need probably for more teachers to be encouraged to contribute to things like the English Magazine, er, and if English teachers are teaching reading and writing they should be encouraged to write about their work a little bit more so that you've got an archive, a national archive. And that would help people leave good stuff behind…I mean in some ways that demonstrates some of the things that seem natural to sixties teachers isn't there anymore. That *now matters*. (Liz)

ARE THEY 'PROGRESSIVE' TEACHERS?

I asked if the teachers regarded themselves as 'progressive' practitioners. I was surprised to find a general distrust of the concept. The term 'progressive' itself is complicated. Howlett (2013) shows how it can be a blanket-term for a range of approaches or indeed broken into 'experimental' or 'radical' versions. The teachers hold conflicting views about it. Some of them view it suspiciously. Yet despite their reservations they agree some aspects of progressivism are valuable and need preserving. They highlight significant disparities between the realities of progressive practice and myths generated about it. Indeed Gove's claim that progressivism is a 'misplaced ideology' that 'privileges temporary relevance over permanent knowledge' (in Howlett, 2013: 1), seems ridiculously ignorant when located alongside the PM presented here. David claims,

> I don't know whether I'd describe myself as progressive or whether that was a term of abuse by others to react against…I mean I think the stereotype means that there were no standards, it's just slapdash and you can do what you like…I think it was always characterised as touchy-feely, kids could do what they liked and stuff like that. But that's not how I remember it. And it was also characterised by some early training stuff that, but where, you know, a stimulus for writing, the teacher would bring in a snake in a box, or set fire to the waste-bin, you know, that's sort of the cliché of the time, then write about it…And, er, no I mean I never saw any of that silly stuff. (David)

David is wary of how dominant discourses can undermine serious, well-organised work. Socially constructed myths about practice in the 1960s/1970s make the teachers recoil from the term. David is not alone in his suspicion. Shaun suggests, 'it's a word that is much maligned…progressive education has always been associated with woolly-mindedness. Well you know I was never woolly-minded!' Michael elaborates, making a distinction between 'progressive' and 'radical',

> Well you know, it was, er, it's how *left* people were insulted really. We, *we* thought of ourselves as *radical,* not progressive. Progressive people were simply people who thought of enlightened ways that teaching and learning could happen...progressive is co, er, terminus with child-centred and those things. So I think we used the term progressive because there are different ways you can use it. You know, you can make progressive sound quite sharp and, er, and political, but, er, you can make it sound a bit, er, you know *liberal* [laughs]. So at the time when we were, this group were writing and talking, we would call ourselves, er, radical. (Michael)

The teachers' comments foreground the difficulties of defining ways of working. They define 'progressivism' on their own terms – a very different definition from the 'liberal, woolly-minded stereotype'. They all reject claims their work held only 'temporary relevance' for students. Michael's insistence on the term 'radical' suggests a professional identity aimed at actively seeking to provoke social change. Howlett (2013) argues 'radical' and 'progressive' perspectives have been reconciled in the past and are 'far from mutually exclusive'. However he suggests,

> ...few progressives have sought to incorporate their theories of child development into any larger scale analysis of society or, even further, to agitate directly for social change while dreaming of a distant utopia. (2013: 212)

Howlett might be right that, historically, progressive teachers have shown little concern for implications beyond the classroom. But the teachers suggest that in the 'cauldron' progressivism was defined in broad terms and they did seek social change. David claims it means being 'accepting' and 'never resting on your laurels'. Ann suggests progressivism goes beyond the classroom, it is linked with wider ideological debates around education: 'I think it would have to be seen in the context of *comprehensive* education because I can't, I can't really conceive of it as being, er, as existing in a selective system'. I asked why,

> I think being open to all opportunities and values that are wider in origin than one's own upbringing and one's own experience so that, implicit in progressive is a sense of never standing still, you know there is, at no point in time can you think "oh we've been progressive, now we're where we wanted to be!" Er, so there should be a continuing flexibility and continuing accommodation of educational possibilities, of social facts, I mean for example racial mixtures in classrooms. Progressive I think to me means always open to opportunities and being prepared to acknowledge that mistakes can be, or *mis-directions* can be useful and they help to determine a more positive future...And as I say, I can't really see that progressive could be, could have meaning within a *selective* framework. (Ann)

Ann links progressivism with personal development. She highlights a commitment to social justice, equality and a continual re-assessment of 'social facts' to 'determine a more positive future'. Shaun echoes this,

> It is an educational philosophy which was rooted in the experience of the child but which sought to develop that experience intellectually, academically in such a way that the child was able to communicate orally and in writing, in standard English I might add because that's essential to survive in contemporary society, in such a way that the student was able to flourish, able to develop, able to make choices, able to have aspirations to be something they wanted to be. *That's* what progressive education's about. It is about valuing the experience of the child, it's about valuing colleagues as colleagues, er, not as competitors, er, it's about creating a collective atmosphere in which children can learn, and that's what I think it is and I think it still exists. (Shaun)

The teachers' definitions highlight the social implications of practice. They argue progressivism demands serious consideration of how contextual circumstances mediate the construction of knowledge, ideology, values, beliefs and so on. Progressivism stands alongside radicalism. The teachers worked in radical ways – re-imagining the curriculum; challenging existing orthodoxies; promoting children's agency. But they claim innovative or radical ideas are now re-presented in 'sanitised' forms. Michael claims 'what goes around comes around...what we called child-centred, or whatever, and which were our primary imperatives, now re-emerge as personalised learning, so it's lost some of its guts, but it's embedded more deeply in the curriculum'. Losing some of the 'guts' means that practices incorporated into dominant cultural perspectives lose their effectiveness. Theoretical ideas seem to be appropriated in similar ways. Shaun recalls an article he read on Vygotsky, 'by an Ofsted inspector, produced *in* the Ofsted journal'. It was a 'very good article' and Shaun is happy these ideas have 'become part of the mainstream'. However, he argues 'they do take out the bits they think are helpful, like ZPD and stuff like that, they like the idea of scaffolding and all the rest of it'. But it appears important aspects of Vygotsky's ideas were overlooked,

> It was a very good article actually, very progressive. Now, you know, you cannot, er, you *cannot* sort of get away with [laughing] introducing Vygotsky and putting him at the centre stage of educational studies, and developmental studies on language with young students and young teachers, and *not* expect them to avoid coming into contact with his whole philosophy of life! He was a revolutionary socialist and, you know, you can't insulate them from that experience that he had that was vital to his theories. (Shaun)

Shaun argues that attempts to assuage teachers by offering selected aspects of theory results in inconsistencies and contradictions. Teachers need to grapple with theory, and broader contextual circumstances, if they are to use it meaningfully. Shaun argues that presenting ideas in these ways subordinates teachers,

CHAPTER 6

> I think there is an awful lot of good practice that is officially sanctioned…but the ruling class are much more sophisticated than that, they don't just try and impose a rigid curriculum on schools, full stop. They incorporate a lot of very, very good pedagogical practices in the course of doing that, so it's very double edged. It's, er, it's important that we recognise the internal contradiction in that process, you know, that's what I've always said education, it's a contradictory process, therefore you play with the contradictions and turn them to your advantage. (Shaun)

Confronting and manipulating 'internal contradictions' is important for the teachers. Steve makes similar claims, encouraging practitioners to confront myths about progressive or radical practice,

> And it's part of the mythology of the right and reactionaries that somehow it was a hippy free for all! It's a *complete* and utter mythology. It's *totally* wrong. It was *highly* professionalised. And you've only got to read the Bullock Report and you've got a, er, a sort of a *massive* definitive, descriptive account of what was going on. (Steve)

Steve's oppositional stance emerges again, arguing 'this myth about us lowering standards is a total reverse of the truth'. He and his colleagues were 'committed, progressive and wouldn't do a bad lesson because we didn't believe in it…we got the best results and we *raised* standards'. He defends his generation from 'this huge *myth* that has to be challenged and countered. A whole historical lie is being perpetuated'. Steve was animated and angry when he spoke. The teachers view the term 'progressive' suspiciously. There are tensions in their accounts, and they come from sometimes competing traditions. But they are critical of stereotypical myths about progressivism. They draw on different speech genres to do this. Ann makes connections with comprehensivism. Michael distinguishes between 'progressive' and 'radical' approaches. Steve challenges the 'mythology of the right' by claiming he was highly organised and professional. Shaun again draws on radical approaches. He defends 'progressivism' as 'much maligned', stressing the importance of 'creating a collective atmosphere in which children can learn'. But he links progressivism with praxis and encourages teachers to recognise and challenge 'internal contradictions' by turning them to their 'own advantage'. The 'touchy-feely', 'woolly-minded', 'liberal' stereotype causes resentment because it perpetuates a 'whole historical lie'.

WHAT DO THESE MEMORIES TELL US?

The teachers recall their collective past to reflect critically on present circumstances. They suggest current practitioners do an excellent, committed job. However they argue that a more 'politically engaged' or 'militant' approach might help them to critique the conjunctural circumstances in which they work. They argue for a re-invigorated sense of collective professional identity, to agitate for greater agency and autonomy. There are moments of suspicion or doubt about their own working practices. They offer cautionary tales and re-assessments of some aspects of their work in the 'cauldron': teaching grammar for example. But they remain critical about the demise of wider support networks and professional organisations. They are equally critical of current accountability mechanisms. They remain committed to collaborative, practitioner-led, theoretically underpinned practice. Their work seems to have been underpinned by a complicated mix of progressive and radical ideals and commitments. They locate speaking and listening as the central component in a curriculum that relates to students' experiences. They argue that collaboratively learning from experience is crucial for practitioners to understand how identity, practice and agency are mediated by various contextual factors.

ACKNOWLEDGEMENT

Sections of this chapter have appeared, in other forms, in Tarpey, P. (2009). Professional memory and English teaching. *English Teaching: Practice and Critique, 8*(1), 52–63; Tarpey, P. (2016). "Fire Burn and Cauldron Bubble": What are the conjunctural effects on English teacher professional memories, identities and narratives? *Changing English, 23*(1), 77–93; and Tarpey, P. (2017a). 'We not I' not 'I me mine': Learning from professional memory about collectivist English teaching. *Changing English, 24*(1), 103–117.

CHAPTER 7

MAKING SENSE OF THE MEMORIES

INTRODUCTION

The teachers' PM highlights their commitment to particular types of practice, their relationships with students, their conceptions of learning and, sometimes, 'socialist' principles. A strong collective identity emerges, shaped through various conjunctures. The teachers' foreground 'counter-hegemonic', or 'oppositional' practices. They suggest current practitioners might benefit from narratives that offer alternative approaches. The teachers construct a PM of ideas, values and commitments shared in common. These commonalities include:

- A strong collective identity as progressive/radical, oppositional (or 'militant'), politically engaged teachers
- A vibrant, participatory professional culture based on strong collective organisation, critical engagement with wider organisations (ILEA, IOE, LATE, NATE) and theoretically underpinned practice
- A commitment to building positive working relationships with colleagues and students
- A commitment to locating professional practice into various contexts
- A commitment to developing children's agency, giving 'voice', and a desire to equip children with critical skills useful beyond the classroom
- An insistence that new generations of English teachers should understand the history and development of the subject
- A willingness to adapt, engage with theory and generate new teaching ideas, materials and curricula
- A commitment to developing student talk and dialogic approaches to practice
- A commitment to mixed-ability teaching and comprehensive education
- A commitment to reflective practice, reflexivity and 'full' professional development

In this chapter I will discuss these issues from a number of perspectives.

IDENTITIES AND WORKING CULTURES IN ENGLISH TEACHING

The teachers' identities have been constructed within and through particular material circumstances: for example the time they were born; their own schooling; when they began teaching; early professional experiences; working in ILEA; through different conjunctures. These circumstances and experiences influence claims about the types of teachers they have become. They display a collective commitment to reflection, adaptability and a willingness to develop professional skills in and beyond the classroom. They foreground a commitment to social justice, equality, and a determination to defend important ways of working. Militancy is presented as a valid ingredient of professional practice. This is sometimes described in a strategic, organised (even 'entryist') way. Sometimes it is used in a more general 'oppositional' sense. At the same time there is modesty about their developments and innovations in practice. They appear wary of the label 'progressive' but seem to promote practice that could be described as such. But what needs to be stressed is that the PM presented represents an oppositional stance in relation to dominant discourses and practices in the 'cauldron' and ever since. This oppositional character is strongly reflected in what the teachers say.

These aspects contribute to the teachers' collective identity and working culture, by which I mean how they act and the practices they generate. Identities and cultures inform and influence each other, and they generate attitudes and motivate social action. The teachers' working culture is one in which they are critically alert and politically engaged. They claim they wanted to re-orientate English away from dominant cultural perspectives, to engage with children's own realities, agency, cultures and experiences. This is also a 'collectivist' culture – evidenced in the teachers' commitment to curriculum groups, collaborations with advisers, wider institutions, teachers' centres, union activity and political activism. These factors influence their professional expectations and practices. But what kind of working culture is it?

It is useful to consider how the oppositional stances in the teachers' PM are located into different kinds of cultural activity. Raymond Williams (1977, 1981) suggests the ongoing processes of cultural production occur in three distinct, yet inseparably related ways: 'dominant', 'residual' and 'emergent'. The 'dominant' perspective is characterised by clear, deeply integrated social forms and institutions. Dominant perspectives are often seen as 'natural and necessary' to those dominated by them. Those who promote particular dominant perspectives 'may be quite unevenly aware' of why and how they are produced. This 'unevenness' can range from dominant groups having 'conscious control' of cultural production, or a 'presumed' acceptance of the 'autonomy of professional and aesthetic values' (1981: 204). However, Williams claims,

> But then it is also the case that in cultural production both the *residual* – work made in earlier and often different societies and times, yet still significant – and the *emergent* – work of various new kinds – are often equally available as *practices*. Certainly the dominant can absorb or attempt to absorb both. But there is always older work kept alive by certain groups as an extension of or alternative to dominant contemporary cultural production. And there is almost always new work which tries to move (and at times succeeds in moving) beyond the dominant forms and their socio-formal relations. (1981: 204)

These different perspectives locate cultural practices into space and time and they emphasise the inescapable inter-connectedness of history (the 'residual'), current circumstances (the 'dominant') and potential future developments (the 'emergent'). Williams's categories represent powerful dialectical processes that produce different kinds of conflict and tension. 'Dominant' forms are consistently challenged by 'residual' and 'emergent' perspectives which compete for legitimacy and identity. These dialectical processes help define the character of 'emergent' and 'residual' forms whilst at the same time illuminating contradictions and flaws in the 'dominant' perspective. If applied to the context of English teaching Williams's categories help shed light on the intense struggle practitioners must engage in to maintain identities and working cultures. These identities and cultures can never be fixed or immutable because of the constant pushing and pulling of the different perspectives. In short, English teacher identities, cultures, beliefs and agency are continuously negotiated through a complex and unstable set of ideological and historical tensions. Considering how these processes work is useful for understanding English teachers and their working lives. But if English teachers themselves understand these processes then they would be in a stronger position from which to challenge 'dominant' perspectives that might work against their own best interests – to push back in 'oppositional' ways. The teachers represented in this book are sensitive to these processes and seem to have consciously constructed identities and working cultures in opposition to 'dominant' perspectives.

Conjunctural circumstances in the 'cauldron' meant different cultural perspectives clashed in ways that allowed various types of change to occur: socially, theoretically, practically. These circumstances seem to have had a lasting effect on the teachers' collective identity as progressive/radical practitioners. The PM presented offers a residual account of practice in the 'cauldron', which can be drawn on by English teachers, and which might provoke them to locate their own practices critically into existing contexts. But Williams argues contemporary analysis is difficult. Historical analysis makes categorisation easier because the 'emergent' becomes the 'emerged'. He argues 'in contemporary analysis, just because of the complex relations between innovation and reproduction, the problem is at a different level' (1981: 205). Understanding the immediate contexts we live in is difficult. But PM studies have the potential to sensitise different generations of English teachers to their own cultural, professional and social contexts. By tracing various genealogies and trajectories, teachers might be able to foreground and confront different cultural perspectives. Current 'dominant' perspectives in English teaching limit professional autonomy and agency. Practitioner voices are largely ignored. So how might PM studies be useful? Individuals are born into material circumstances that influence consciousness, as Marx insists,

> In the social production of their life, men enter into definite relations that are indispensable and independent of their will...The mode of production in material life determines the general character of the social, the political and

spiritual processes of life. It is not the consciousness of men that determines their existence, but, on the contrary, their social existence determines their consciousness. (1972: 4)

A complicated range of factors influence identity construction. And understanding the 'general character' of life at a given moment is crucial for critical engagement with present circumstances. But how do current 'dominant' perspectives in English teaching (the 'social existence') determine the 'consciousness' of practitioners? Tracing the genealogy is important for understanding how 'dominant' cultural perspectives emerge and evolve. Williams (1993) criticises 'dominant' perspectives which assume that by promoting particular ideals and values it is somehow possible to generate a common culture,

If you get into the habit of thinking that a bourgeois society produces, in a simple and direct way, a bourgeois culture, then you are likely to think that a socialist society will produce, also simply and directly, a socialist culture.' (1993: 282)

This kind of thinking produces pre-determined cultural norms, or 'acceptable' types of social behaviour. Indeed, some aspects of life (and English teaching) will have been 'commonly defined in advance, as an authoritative prescription' (1993: 283). Yet this can never create universality in social and cultural practices. 'Residual' and 'emergent' cultures inevitably generate a diversity of competing and clashing perspectives. But this does not mean those in dominant positions do not try. To take one example, I want to return to concept of 'growth' in English teaching, which appears to have had a significant influence on the teachers. In 2013, former Education Secretary Michael Gove used a speech to argue for a more traditional curriculum in English. He made several assumptions about what the subject should be aiming to do. He also implied that by promoting certain values, certain aesthetics and certain discourses, English classrooms might 'grow' children to become 'cultured'. Gove argued children should read *Middlemarch* rather than *Breaking Dawn*, because 'there is a Great Tradition of English Literature – a canon of transcendent works – and Breaking Dawn is not part of it' (Gove, 2013). Gove's confidence in these 'transcendent works' foregrounds a common belief that they contain 'universal truths' about human existence that are easily and equally applicable to all people. So, much more was at stake than simply getting children to read George Eliot: Gove was evidently in the business of promoting particular types of knowledge and a homogenised conception of culture as natural. This 'growth' through English literature discourse enjoys an enduring continuity in dominant narratives around the subject (Goodwyn, 2012).

Gove's elitist curriculum concerns reinforce a teacher-focussed, knowledge-based model of practice – the literature over the learner, as it were. And since Gove's speech English has been re-defined through the language of cultural elitism (Coultas, 2013). The curriculum has been re-orientated to focus closely on the 'canon', on 'correctness' in Standard English grammar and spelling, with speaking and listening almost eliminated. Other recent policy initiatives also explicitly promote this elitist approach (changes to GCSEs, grammar testing). But where is the room for students and teachers to 'grow' in current models? Where is the room to engage critically with a diversity of cultures and backgrounds? Gove's model is divisive, as Valerie Coultas points out,

> These elitist themes in the New English curriculum are linked to a wider philosophy that views working-class culture, linguistic practices and knowledge as a deficit. This philosophy is also sceptical about educational theory and dismissive of ideas that link educational practices to child development. By caricaturing progressive educational ideas in headline grabbing and simplistic ways Gove seeks to re-establish meritocratic values that preserve elitism. (2013: 53)

So the current curriculum will no doubt make it harder for some children to succeed. Yandell claims this is precisely the intention. He argues recent developments are designed to 'ration educational opportunity', and indicates broad evidence for this – 'the scrapping of EMA (education maintenance allowance)...the rise in university tuition fees...the closure of Sure Start centres' (2013: 12). Punishing changes to assessment arrangements, the return of 'norm-referencing' and an even narrower curriculum will ensure 'that there are failures' (2013: 13). This is clearly unsatisfactory. But how does the 'growth through literature' discourse go down with practitioners? Kate Findlay researched English teacher identities and found that the dominant discourses they draw on 'remain firmly rooted in the study of literature' and that 'the cultural heritage model is still dominant' (2010: 13). She adopted Williams's framework and concluded that the 'dominant' perspective 'could be applied to the personal growth through literature discourse which research suggests has had a powerful and tenacious grip on the profession' (2010: 12). This 'dominant' model 'has absorbed the once emergent discourse of personal growth', with writers studied for their ability to raise issues and promote discussion (2010: 13). But 'personal growth' needs to be defined. The teachers in this book understand it on Dixon's terms, who suggests 'growth' in English should focus critically on 'culture as the pupil knows it' (1967: 3).

Findlay is right that in England cultural-heritage perspectives continue to dominate English policy discourse, with some elements of 'personal growth' absorbed. However, current conceptions of 'growth' eschew any serious consideration of children's social and cultural backgrounds in learning contexts, or the kinds of practices and relationships that Dixon argues for. Findlay suggests the teachers in her study 'have coupled the heritage model with reader response theory' (2010: 13). This coupling, she argues, allows teachers to value individual students' views about their reading experiences without having to look necessarily for 'right or wrong' answers. Dixon's growth model is more radical and presupposes a dialectic: that social existence shapes consciousness, which in turn acts back on the material conditions of that social existence. This conception of 'growth' does not feature in 'dominant' definitions of English teaching in present circumstances. Yes, the language of 'growth' remains prominent in English teacher narratives, but despite its continued presence, the potency and radical potential of Dixon's model is largely absent.

Of course, for Williams (1958) culture is 'ordinary', a 'whole way of life', and Dixon alludes to this by insisting on the need 'to redirect our attention to life as it really is' (1967: 114). The point is not to fill 'cultural gaps' in children's lives through literature, but to start with an exploration of their own social realities and consider how language might be oppressive or liberating. By adopting this approach practitioners can help students to consider how the narratives, discourses and cultures they exist within have a significant influence on how they view themselves and their life trajectories. The working culture of the teachers in this book is underpinned by these principles. For example, Michael claims his lessons were targeted at 'looking at the radical potential of what children learned, and how they learned it...what ways it resourced kids to make changes. What kinds of ways to help kids to be critical, to analyse and actually to *act!*'. Steve claims 'we thought obviously that children have rights...And that it was wrong for schools to imprison and to structure and to limit people, and schools needed to be liberative! So that means that when we chose a piece of literature, it was because we thought that it had some potential for that.' The other teachers say similar things. Liz talks of 'unlocking voices', David wants students to engage critically with 'discourse', Ann put great emphasis on 'empowerment', and Shaun insists 'every kid has tremendous potential'.

This working culture is oppositional in current contexts. It is difficult for current practitioners to generate 'counter-hegemonic' practices like the teachers did in the 'cauldron'. Dominant discourses and structures focus attention on other concerns. However, there is something more here. The teachers suggest that cultural undercurrents in English teaching are passed from one generation to another. These undercurrents differ temporally and spatially but they seem to provoke particular kinds of practitioner attitudes, values and sensibilities. For instance Ann suggests the 'spirit of enquiry doesn't seem to have died a death', and Shaun claims some younger teachers indeed try to keep that 'residual spirit alive'. The teachers make positive comments about new recruits, but are aware they are professionalised into different circumstances. PM studies have the potential to offer different generations of English teachers a way of engaging critically with their own cultural contexts as well as inherited ones – to connect the present with the past. In doing this, might there be potential to locate discussions around teacher cultures and identities into more prominent, and 'dominant', positions? Many of the enduring continuities, the dominant discourses in English teaching, might be disrupted and re-imagined to generate alternative narratives and possibilities.

ARE THERE ALTERNATIVE SPEECH GENRES IN ENGLISH TEACHING?

Do dominant discourses in English promote particular kinds of teacher identity that are out of tune with the current realities of the job? This is obviously not a simple case of cause and effect, and there are inevitably various levels of 'refraction' – different critical responses (Goodson & Rudd, 2012, 2016) – in how practitioners respond to dominant models. Goodson and Rudd (2012: 5) argue that, in present circumstances, the 'prevailing hegemonic orthodoxy' constrains any debate around education through a 'truncated discourse'. Dominant orthodoxies are presented as the sole bases for solutions to educational, social and economic problems. The effects of this process render possible alternatives as 'ineffectual or fanciful against the harsh "realities" facing the existing dominant order' (2012: 5). Goodson and Rudd propose the concept of 'refraction' as a way of investigating and uncovering the relationship between 'actor and structure', by placing 'context and history as central to explorations' (2012: 8). Exploring structural circumstances, cultures, discourses, policy initiatives and social action can foreground the struggle practitioners must engage in when confronted by the various 'power relations within them'. Are there contradictions between English teachers' personal and professional narratives, and the material circumstances they operate within? As suggested, the 'cultural heritage/personal growth through literature' discourse proves to be resilient in English teacher narratives, having survived through various incarnations of the subject. Indeed, Findlay found this perspective 'as apposite for new entrants to the profession as for those nearing the end of their careers' (2010: 14). But there appear to be critical differences between what teachers *say* they have been doing, and the realities and expectations created by policy initiatives. The teachers in this book present a model of English in which practitioners have influence over both classroom practice and the wider aims and intentions of the subject.

So how do dominant discourses influence English teacher identities, attitudes and ultimately practice? What alternative narratives might encourage practitioners to assess critically their professional identities and actions? At this point I want to return to Bakhtin's concepts of speech genre, dialogism and heteroglossia. The teachers generate alternative narratives to speak about English. For example they do not emphasise the 'growth through literature' discourse like Findlay's informants. Rather, they draw on 'oppositional' discourses around the subject. Bakhtin argues that because 'all the diverse areas of human activity involve the use of language', then the 'nature and forms' of that language must inevitably be as diverse (1986: 60). So any subject can be spoken about in a multitude of ways. By their very nature speech genres are 'heterogeneous'. But for Bakhtin each 'sphere of human activity' develops its own 'relatively stable types' of utterance, or speech genres, which tend to dominate ways of talking about a subject. Different types of genres exist: primary (or simple) ones equate to everyday dialogue, they are located in immediate social contexts and relate to the 'direct utterances of others'. Secondary (or complex) genres are intensely ideological and tend to be 'highly developed and organised cultural communication...that is artistic, scientific, socio-political and so on' (1986: 62).

It is these secondary genres that might be particularly influential in the construction of inner speech, identity and ideological perspectives. When secondary genres emerge 'they absorb and digest various primary genres' (1986: 62) which can give the impression that dominant ideological perspectives represent social

CHAPTER 7

reality. Bakhtin insists this is far from the case, and that, once absorbed, primary genres 'assume a special kind of character', which orientates them towards the dominant perspective. This 'special character' might mean some groups talk supportively about subjects that are ironically against their own best interests. By examining the connections between primary and secondary genres it is possible to interrogate the 'interrelations among language, ideology, and world view' (1986: 62). For example the once emergent 'growth through literature' discourse has been absorbed into dominant secondary genres in English teaching. Within these genres is a diversity of sometimes conflicting primary genres around 'growth', which over time have clashed, amalgamated and morphed in 'acceptable' contemporary models. 'Growth's' current 'special character' does not incorporate Dixon's radical dialectic, making it less potent. This means practitioners can use the language of 'growth' without necessarily seeing an ideological conflict in promoting this approach and working within existing policy constraints.

Contemporary conceptions of 'growth' are not considered threatening to the dominant orthodoxy in English teaching, and thus they remain a prominent, yet effete part of the broader discourse. But just recall the reaction to Dixon's ideas in the 1960s, the *Black Papers*, and Allen's (1980) criticisms. Dixon's model re-imagined the priorities of English and generated new speech genres around the subject. Over time, the digestion of Dixon's model into dominant secondary genres has neutralised some, but by no means all, of its radical potential: in Michael's terms it has 'lost some of its guts'. 'Growth' has been absorbed into broader secondary genres that promote functionality and uniformity in practice. However, the speech genres that Dixon's work generated still exist residually, and the teachers reproduce them. But how do various speech genres influence English teacher identities?

Individuals acquire genres as they learn their native language and we learn to use them long before we master abstract aspects of grammar. Genres enter both our experiences and consciousness simultaneously through social, dialectical processes. All utterances, and speech genres, are coloured by our evaluative perspective of the subject at hand; this determines syntactic, lexical and structural decisions. Meaning, intention and expression are not inherent in the linguistic properties themselves, but are generated through the complex processes of 'addressivity' (utterances directed at somebody with intention and expected outcomes) and 'active response' (on the part of the listener/reader, linked to whole sequences of utterances, also with intention and expectation) (1986: 69). Some genres provoke an immediate response in social action, for example orders or commands. Others though, evoke 'a silent responsive understanding…with a delayed reaction' (1986: 69). Bakhtin argues that sooner or later what is heard and understood will 'find its response in the subsequent speech or behaviour of the listener' (1986: 69). He argues in most cases,

> …genres of complex cultural communication are intended precisely for this kind of actively responsive understanding with delayed action. (1986: 69)

Dominant secondary genres influence English teacher identities and practices. An utterance's ultimate purpose is 'determining the active responsive position of the other participants in the communication' (1986: 82). Think back to Gove's insistence on the 'canon of transcendent works' in English, which is patently aimed at this 'responsive understanding with delayed action'. This process is exemplified in Michael's story about the young teacher worried about 'not having a writing frame' if an Ofsted inspector was present. In that case it is important to consider how 'any utterance is a link in a very complexly organised chain of other utterances' (1986: 69). All utterances, teacher identities, discourses, inner speech and actions must be analysed within this contextual chain. Bakhtin argues,

> When one analyses an individual sentence apart from its context, the traces of addressivity and the influence of the anticipated response, dialogical echoes from others' preceding utterances, faint traces of changes of speech subjects that have furrowed the utterance from within – all of these are lost, erased, because they are all foreign to the sentence as a unit of language. All these phenomena are connected with the whole of the utterance, and when this whole escapes the field of vision of the analyst they cease to exist for him. (1986: 99–100)

When English teachers talk about their practice, attitudes or beliefs, what does it mean in different contextual circumstances? How do audience, setting, previous utterances, dominant secondary genres and 'echoes' of others' voices influence what they say? What are the specific effects of 'the fundamentally social modes in which discourse lives' (Bakhtin, 1981: 259)? Exploring these issues can shed light on how dominant secondary genres in English have changed and developed over time. Bakhtin argues the 'history of speech genres...reflects changes taking place in social life' (1986: 65). Ways of talking about English should no doubt change along with other social, political and cultural developments. Yet despite wider social and cultural change, dominant discourses in English consistently present the subject in elitist terms. If it is possible to identify and define the 'dialogical echoes' in practitioner narratives (where do our ideas come from?), then it is feasible that contradictions will emerge between what teachers say their intentions are and the realities of practice. If teachers can locate their utterances into these wider contexts it might be possible to generate alternative discourses and definitions: much like Shaun's critical assessment of the changing discourses around 'professionalism'.

But which speech genres have influenced the teachers here? These are combinations of primary and secondary types. The teachers discuss English critically and many of their utterances deliberately oppose dominant discourses. As 'focussed elaborators' (Goodson, 2013), the teachers are highly skilled users of language, capable of moving quite freely between different genres. Bakhtin argues the better our command of speech genres the more we are able to represent our individuality through them: 'in a word, the more perfectly we implement our free speech plan' (1986: 80). However, there are contradictions in what ostensibly appear to be individual, independent utterances. Individuals are given 'mandatory forms of the national language' (grammar, syntax, lexis); but they are also given mandatory forms of speech genre which are more crucial for mutual understanding than the language forms themselves,

> Speech genres are much more changeable, flexible, and plastic than the language forms are, but they have a normative significance for the speaking individuum, and they are not created by him but are given to him. Therefore, the single utterance, with all its individuality and creativity, can in no way be regarded as a *completely free combination* of forms of language. (1986: 80–81)

Utterances are shaped by, and dependent upon, pre-existing narrative templates. So which inherited genres have influenced the teachers' narratives? Several are interconnected, including powerful secondary genres around the aims of English teaching, professional practice and theoretical perspectives. They also include primary and secondary genres around the purposes of school, 'favourite teachers', 'rebelliousness', attitudes to classroom practice, relationships and so on. They argue they were largely self-taught, or they could 'do a better job' than their own teachers. They all describe an influential teacher who inspired them. Despite coming from diverse backgrounds and experiences, the teachers' utterances are remarkably similar, suggesting 'mandatory' forms of genre have been incorporated into their personal narratives. They deliberately select utterances that are, in Williams's terms, 'oppositional'. They consciously use phrases like 'counter-hegemonic', 'radical', 'revolutionary' or 'militant'. They reject the arguments of the *Black Paper* authors, Allen (1980) or Marenbon (1994). They appear sensitive to McCulloch's (2000) argument that dominant educational discourses have been manipulated to distort perceptions of the 'cauldron'. There is evidently some anger about this. Steve claims a 'historical lie' has been perpetuated. Several of the teachers call for more 'militancy' among practitioners. Bakhtin argues that in each 'epoch' and in every social circle (family, friends, colleagues), there are always 'authoritative utterances that set the tone – artistic, scientific, journalistic works on which one relies, to which one refers, which are cited, imitated and followed' (1986: 88). Because of this, particular traditions are retained and promoted that form the ideas of the 'masters of thought' in a given period. The teachers' PM puts a spotlight on practitioners themselves attempting to define the 'authoritative utterances' in the 'cauldron'.

There are conflicting speech genres in English teaching. The teachers draw on residual discourses to represent themselves. They seem attracted to particular ideas that might not always correspond with the reality of lived experience. Nonetheless, they represent 'agentive' narrators who have managed to re-position themselves successfully through various periods of social, cultural and political change. Their narratives offer alternative perspectives on English teaching. These perspectives might encourage critical discussion about what English is, its past and its future. Practitioner-led dialogue can generate powerful secondary genres to challenge dominant discourses around the subject.

THE IMPORTANCE OF CONFRONTING CONJUNCTURAL CIRCUMSTANCES

Different conjunctural circumstances influenced the teachers' identities and practices. Some of their attitudes have been influenced by circumstances when they were born. Big structural changes when they were young seem to have encouraged particular values and ideals – the development of the welfare state, social housing, NHS, expansion of education and so on. But wider social attitudes at the time also seem to have been influential – post war 'euphoria', camaraderie, 'make do and mend', optimism for a better future. For some, there was a ferment of ideas and political activity. These circumstances inspired film-maker Ken Loach to document them in the *Spirit of '45* (2013). Loach is a well-known left-wing commentator and his interpretation of events has been disputed. But he claims,

> The achievements of the '45 Labour government have largely been written out of our history. From near economic collapse we took leading industries into public ownership and established the Welfare State. Generosity, mutual support and co-operation were the watch words of the age. It is time to remember those who were intent on building a better world. (2013, DVD sleeve notes)

Whether these were widespread attitudes at the time is open to debate. But Loach captures something that resonates with the teachers in this book. They put great emphasis on 'co-operation', 'mutual support' and collectivity in all aspects of their lives: solidarity over individualism. These ideas influenced their attitudes to learning and practice. They emphasise the crucial importance of literacy when growing up, which undoubtedly influenced their development as English teachers. These wider influences are now manifested in particular ways – a commitment to social justice, collective consciousness, egalitarianism, equality, democracy, learning as a social activity. They claim these principles underpin their personal and professional lives.

These same conjunctural circumstances also seem to have influenced those pioneering English teachers and LATE members throughout the 1940s, 1950s and 1960s – the likes of Britton, Barnes, Rosen, Martin, Dixon. The teachers were at school themselves during this period, but as the evidence indicates, the types of English lessons they experienced were a world away from the ones they claim they went on to teach. But templates had been established by earlier practitioners that offered alternative models for practice. When the teachers started their careers in their early twenties another influential conjuncture was unfolding. The enabling circumstances that came together between 1965 and 1975 offered opportunities to instigate different types of (sometimes radical) change. Various structural, theoretical and social movements coincided, which saw the development of comprehensive schools, scrapping the 11 plus, the establishment of ILEA, the Plowden and Bullock reports, new theories about language and learning, setting up the English Centre. Circumstances also influenced new social and cultural movements – counterculture,

CHAPTER 7

'youth' culture, 'swinging' sixties, film, art and music among them. These circumstances provided fertile ground for some critically alert teachers to imagine a new landscape for English.

The teachers lived through two distinctive and influential conjunctures. Since then of course, they have lived through 'counter-revolutionary' (Jones, 2013) changes in education since the 1980s, which present developments in the 'cauldron' negatively. But their early experiences have provided them with a resilient sense of professional identity. They are consciously aware of this too. They refer to their 'generation' in particular ways. They reject current conceptions of professionalism and dominant models of practice. This does not mean their identities and attitudes are static: it highlights their adaptability in encountering new circumstances and realities. They foreground their agency, suggesting they actively sought to change the theoretical, political and structural circumstances they operated within. Goodson argues the 1960s/1970s was a 'distinctive conjuncture of change':

> The conjuncture of the 1960s and 1970s aligns with the economic long wave upswing, which ended with the oil crisis in 1973…In Hobsbawm's words, this was in general a 'golden age' of social progress, although one littered with contradictions and contestations. (2005b: 127)

Throughout the 1970s various circumstances and events laid the foundations for a new conjuncture – the period of 'neo-liberalism'. Goodson examined eight schools affected by 'long waves' of educational reform and found that by the 1990s the period had produced 'cohorts of teachers who are disenfranchised politically, alienated intellectually, depressed emotionally and drained physically' (2005: 127). In a remarkably short period any sense of teachers as autonomous professionals able to affect change was eroded. Instead, a new set of practices and responsibilities have been normalised by discourses aimed at eradicating alternative models of practice. As Goodson and Rudd (2012: 5) argue, the 'prevailing hegemonic orthodoxy' in the present conjuncture constrains economic, educational and social debate through its 'truncated discourse'. So, in order to generate alternative, emancipatory narratives it is even more important to critically examine conjunctural circumstances, discourses, policy initiatives and power relations. Goodson and Rudd argue,

> In seeking to uncover the ideological orientation and its broader influence on action and practice, and implications for equality and social justice, we must seek to develop conceptual understandings that enable us to make visible that which is masked or concealed within predominant language, rhetoric and narratives, map the origins of its social construction, and develop alternative language, discourse and narrative capital to diffuse the symbolic violence and power being exerted and construct viable alternatives. (2012: 5)

PM studies can provide a vehicle for English teachers to engage in this kind of analysis, and thus to have a greater agency in defining their work. Practitioners must find a way of critiquing the conjunctural circumstances, policy initiatives, structures and discourses that constrain their professional lives. But this alone is insufficient. There is also an urgent need to examine teachers' personal and professional narratives, to consider how they 'act back' on the material conditions they are forced to operate within. Understanding these processes would mean that alternative narratives can be generated to challenge dominant perspectives and 'diffuse' their power.

IS THE TEACHERS' WORK STILL RELEVANT?

Dominant discourses in English currently focus on the 'canon', grammar testing, Standard English, with speaking and listening all but wiped-out. Yet language variety, media work, advertising, song lyrics, modern novels and poems, soap operas, drama and so on can all be found in contemporary English classrooms. It seems that some curricular and pedagogical changes developed in the 'cauldron' have had a lasting effect. As we have seen, the teachers are nervous about claiming to have left a 'legacy'. But is their work in the 'cauldron' still relevant? Steve is the only one to overtly claim his generation made radical and lasting change. He is correct in terms of curriculum, which was undeniably broadened. And, despite their reticence, the teachers also succeeded in moving English lessons away from the silent, restrictive experiences they had as students, and instead made 'the walls reverberate with activity'; oral work is more firmly embedded in classroom practice. However, it is no longer 'assessed'. So despite improvements, many of these developments have been absorbed, and limited, by dominant orthodoxies.

Current models of English omit important aspects of the teachers' working practices. Fundamental questions about the nature and aims of the subject were being asked in the 'cauldron', and some of the problems posed have yet to be resolved. For example Dixon's proposed 'new model' to reflect 'life as it really is' means practice in English must constantly adapt to changing contexts and realities. The current English curriculum presents static conceptions of language and meaning. The teachers suggest there should be greater focus on semiotic analysis, sign and utterance, rather than abstract conceptions of 'correctness'. They also suggest practice should be underpinned by a commitment to social justice. Remember Shayer's claim that in the 'cauldron' there was,

> ...no disputing the fact that English teaching priorities are now (theoretically) more thoughtful, humane, far-sighted, imaginative and worth while than they have ever been before. (1972: 185–186)

Shayer's focus on 'humanity' reflects the work the teachers claim they did. But as conjunctures change so do attitudes, values and intentions. Political, economic and social change in subsequent periods meant discourses around English became more hostile. Arguments in the 'cauldron' for education as a means of achieving a fairer society were challenged. Dominant discourses were not concerned with 'humanity' or 'equality', but with 'meritocracy' and 'social mobility' – that is the opportunity to 'compete' in a fundamentally unfair society. English was caught up in this ideological battleground. Remember Cameron's (1995) claims that in the 1980s/1990s,

> The unfolding debate about English teaching was presented to the public liberally garnished with scare stories about falling standards among pupils and ideological subversion among teachers. (1995: 89)

Such was the panic, Cameron claims right-wing pressure groups 'sought access to teacher training institutions and wrote scathing reports on the "permissive" methods of English teaching being advocated to trainee teachers' (1995: 89). These discourses helped lay the foundations for the radical systemic changes implemented in the wake of the 1988 Education Reform Act. In terms of English teaching there were a number of concerns from those on the right. One concern, Cameron suggests, was evident in attempts to 'de-politicise' English, to thwart practitioners from engaging in 'oppositional' practices. There were struggles, particularly over the *content* of English. This came to a head with the first version of the National Curriculum, which was boycotted by some practitioners. Jones argues the first curriculum 'reflected the traditionalist, ethnocentric preferences of ministers and pressure groups' (2003: 132). Similarly, Poulson (1998) suggests the boycott, initially led by LATE members, became hostile because of 'a deliberate attempt to rewrite the English curriculum to reflect the views of a small number of right-wing individuals in the government and ministerial advisers' (1998: 46). She claims,

> Four issues were central to the dispute: the teaching of Standard English; grammar; the place of Shakespeare in the English curriculum; and assessment arrangements. (1998: 46)

These issues remain central to the present English Curriculum. Yet it is not that these aspects were ignored by the teachers here. Far from it, they were integral to their working practices and they stress their importance. Yes, they have some reservations about how they dealt with 'grammar'. But they talk of teaching 'standard English' as a way of empowering students with greater agency and critical awareness (remember Shaun and David). Shakespeare is used to explore issues relevant to students' lives (think about Steve's descriptions). Assessment was designed 'for our boys' to succeed (Michael). The teachers have no issue with teaching the 'canon' or Standard English. But they object to these being used to maintain dominant orthodoxies at the expense of children exploring their own cultures and experiences. Many practices the teachers developed have found their way into current models of mainstream English teaching. However, there are fundamental aspects of their practice missing – such as locating learning into its social, historical and political contexts. English remains an ideological battleground, and efforts have been made to silence radical and alternative voices. Indeed, Dixon (2013: 28) condemns the recent 'ramshackle interventions in English' of which 'the central goal is political power'. It is important that practitioners find ways of exposing and confronting existing power-relations.

COMPETING AND CONTESTED CURRENTS IN THE TEACHERS' STORIES

There are tensions and occasional disagreements in the teachers' narratives. There are differences of opinion, and after several decades their attitudes to some events have changed. In the evidence presented however, differences among them appear to be relatively few. The teachers claim to have been politically active in different ways. Sometimes this is focussed on classroom practice: Liz and Ann for example use terms like 'militant', 'movement' and 'giving voice' in relation to their work. Some of the teachers refer to broader political engagement. David claims he and his colleagues were 'all fairly active' Labour Party members and trade unionists. Steve was an elected member of ILEA, representing the Labour Party for seven years. He was also 'secretary of two [local constituency] Labour Parties'. Shaun was active in revolutionary politics with the Socialist Workers' Party, as well as being active in the NUT. Michael sought radical educational change through his involvement with LATE, TLK and the English Centre, alongside trade union activity. These circumstances represent a shared commitment to activism, to try to effect change. However, the ideological commitment of each of them stems from different roots and traditions.

Shaun, Steve and Michael are the most likely to be described as 'radical' practitioners. But their political commitments highlight different priorities. Michael explicitly calls himself a 'radical teacher', demonstrating a commitment to developing student-centred, agentive practice through the English Centre. He was also committed to locating practice into wider social, cultural, historical and political contexts through TLK. Steve foregrounds his 'entryist' tactics in 'taking over the ILEA and Labour Party'. He also claims to have cleaned his own classroom and spent most lunch-times with his students. This sits in stark contrast to Shaun's ideologically tinted summary dismissal of the 'twenty-four hour a day English teacher'. These claims foreground contrasting views of professionalism, motivations and social action arrived at through differences in outlook, experience and political conviction. Some of the teachers are explicit, like Jones (1989), in seeking 'socialist alternatives'. Whatever their perspective however, they all view teaching in the way that Grace describes it, which is not exclusively about the 'advancement of learning', but also about 'socialisation, community regeneration and political consciousness' (1978: 86).

Other differences emerged between the teachers. There are different attitudes towards colleagues for example. They mostly refer positively to colleagues, foregrounding the vibrancy and productivity of the collegiality they enjoyed. As Shaun suggests, they treated 'colleagues as colleagues, not as competitors'. Steve on the other hand foregrounds constant criticism, struggles with authority and victimisation. He recalls a battle against the odds to work in preferred ways. He sometimes presents himself as engaged in an individual struggle to confront and challenge dominant discourses, practices and ideologies. But in the 'cauldron' Steve's memories might represent a more typical kind of experience for many practitioners. There was significant variation in London schools and many did not promote practice in the ways described by the teachers. But Steve's confrontational approach is also evident in his attitude to younger colleagues when he occasionally dismisses them for not having a 'clue'. Similarly, Michael is critical of how 'intelligent' young teachers appear to lack critical consciousness.

All the teachers suggest aspects of English they would like to see improved. But again they have different priorities and do not always offer solutions to perceived problems. Shaun probably maintains the most consistent narrative, drawing on radical discourses to critique existing circumstances, and to find ways of engaging in praxis, or 'counter-hegemonic practices'. He claims to enjoy working with younger colleagues and exploring how 'oppositional practices' might be provoked in present circumstances. So the evidence presented might under-represent differences among teachers, and further PM studies are needed to explore these.

TEACHER MEMORY AND TEACHER NOSTALGIA

It is important to consider the connections between teacher 'memory' and 'nostalgia'. Does generational experience influence teacher attitudes to different kinds of 'change'? Some critics argue that teacher memories, situated in particular historical periods, become increasingly compelling for older practitioners as they near the end of their careers. Hargreaves and Moore (2005: 132) suggest memories 'are as much about *generation* as *degeneration*' because they allow practitioners to preserve a sense of themselves as energetic, committed professionals, but also to protect against a sense of decay and finality. These circumstances, they suggest, mean older generations of teachers are sometimes resistant to change. This resistance is not necessarily negative because it represents a 'process of fulfilling, preserving and protecting the missions and memories of one's generation [and] draws attention to a positive sense of what teachers are fighting for over time' (2005: 132). Hargreaves and Moore foreground the 1960s/1970s generation as having a particularly strong sense of identity, purpose and mission.

But how are memory and nostalgia distinguished in teacher narratives? Hargreaves and Moore suggest similarities and differences between the two. However they argue all nostalgia is 'sentimental' because it 'comprises particular selective, even false, distorted and idealised memories of the past that are invoked by embittered experiences of the present' (2005: 133). In a follow-up piece with Goodson (2006), the writers examine long-serving teacher testimonials from three schools, each with its own distinct identity and ethos. The schools went through various processes of change and reform – socially and politically. The writers found that teacher 'narratives in all schools reflected a pervasive and intense nostalgia for the past' (2006: 55), which was closely connected to change in the respective schools. There was considerable resistance to systemic reform where it ignored professional experience and re-configured teacher roles and responsibilities. The writers also discovered a lament for earlier social realities where strong relationships with students and colleagues generated a supposed 'family' atmosphere of committed teachers working collegially. They conclude that 'change initiatives' will unavoidably meet resistance if they fail to engage seriously with teacher memories:

> Only when change initiatives achieve more meaningful engagement with teachers' missions and memory might we expect change to move from transient government rhetoric to sustainable school reality. (2006: 56–57)

For structural and cultural change to be effective in schools it must be negotiated and agreed. This sense of 'government rhetoric' is also picked up by Hartley (2009), who suggests the recent focus on 'personalisation' in learning is an attempt to appease older practitioners through the 'nostalgic revival of child-centred education'. Hartley argues 'personalisation' in its current guise appeals to modern individualist and consumerist attitudes, at the same time as providing a 'safe association with a "progressive" past, which, although no Golden Age, conjures up a nostalgic appeal to those better times whose day is done' (2009: 431). He argues,

> In sum, the semantic similarity between child-centred education and personalisation may serve to appeal especially to that generation of older teachers whose professional ideology was formed and firmly sedimented within the early 1970s. Of course, that ideology may find little accord with the centralising reforms of education which have occurred since. But re-labelling these reforms as 'personalisation' may give the *impression* that something of the progressive era is being resurrected. (2009: 431)

Curiously, the teachers in this book, whose 'professional ideology was formed in the early 1970s', seem explicitly aware of how dominant discourses influence social realities. Michael is clearly not influenced by this 'impression' of progressivism when he recognises 'personalisation' is 'back on the agenda but what does it mean? What does it mean if it's drowned out, if you have to spend your time coaching kids for SATS?' Shaun claims it is necessary to exercise caution when having teachers 'reminiscing' about the past, suggesting 'modesty is a good thing when you're looking back'. Ann points to a sense of 'never standing still…at no point can you think "oh we've been progressive, now we're where we wanted to be"'. Steve is alert to how such 'impressions' of progressivism might be generated: 'So the idea that we had complete, or individual, autonomy is ridiculous…it needs to be unpicked a little and historicised. It's one of the right wing's, the reactionary gang's mythologies'.

These reactions do not immediately point to 'nostalgia' in that they are 'sentimental' or 'idealised'. The teachers' memories provide the basis from which to critique current contexts. Also, some of the circumstances they refer to were actual

CHAPTER 7

realties – remember Liz's claim that, 'if anybody came in who was an inspector or an adviser, they were *there to help you*'. Yes, there may be elements of nostalgia in the teachers' memories – for the early days of practice, for colleagues, ILEA, the English Centre. But this is not the same thing as PM. Where there is no systematic record of teacher experience, PM serves to hold representations of practice for future generations: a resource for evaluating demands in current circumstances. Teacher accounts may be tinted with nostalgia, but this does not encompass the whole of PM. It is important to consider the negative and positive implications of nostalgia, and also to recognise how it might colour recollection. But PM studies aim to generate a critical practitioner history rather than an elegy to some idealised past.

POLITICAL ENGLISH TEACHING?

One consistent theme to emerge is the teachers' willingness to locate practice into a number of contexts, to 'politicise' it. They criticise the external imposition of 'professional standards'. They scrutinise and challenge policy initiatives and they are ready to take collective action to defend valued ways of working. They insist on locating practice, and student learning, into historical, social and cultural contexts. There is a collective sensitivity to issues of race, gender, and especially social class. These political realities are seen as challenges to be confronted, mostly from 'oppositional' ideological perspectives.

Once more conjunctural influences seem significant. Circumstances when they were growing up, and their professional development in the 1960s/1970s, were periods that influence a critical consciousness. They adopt particular discourses when recalling the past. They use words like 'radical', 'militant', 'movement', 'fight' or 'struggle'. To some extent these might be read as symptomatic of political allegiances – words like 'struggle' are often associated with a Marxist position. However, they need to be read cautiously – a way of speaking at the time with various intentions behind it. They cannot necessarily be interpreted as evidence of political affiliation. Rather, they may suggest the *climate* of the times. Yet the teachers still represent themselves as active agents for social change, prepared to challenge dominant orthodoxies. They also demonstrate a strong commitment to defending the rights of disempowered or disenfranchised groups. But how are these ideas located into current contexts? How have conjunctural circumstances changed?

In the 'cauldron', and the following period, various critical publications helped English teachers locate practice into different contexts.[1] By the 1990s however, Lawton (1996) stressed the need for teachers to remain critically vigilant. He traces different ideological perspectives in education from a belief that it should be 'private', to a 'minimalist' position (cheap, elementary, basic). There are 'pluralist' perspectives (different kinds of school and curricula for different 'types' of children); and a 'comprehensive' ideology. Lawton argues after 1979 education policy was produced out of a mixture of these clashing ideologies, but 'comprehensive' concerns disappeared,

During the 1960s and 1970s, the main debate was between the pluralists and comprehensive planners. But after 1979 there was a regression to older – some had thought obsolete – forms of educational thinking. A lesson to be learned... is that when ideologies such as privatising and minimalism seem to have disappeared, they have not necessarily gone forever – they have simply sunk into the deep structure of political and educational thinking. Certainly after the 1979 Election, Conservatives with extreme right-wing views on education felt fewer inhibitions about raising their voices. There were struggles between privatisers and minimalists within the Conservative Party, and between privatisers and pluralists; but there were no Tory comprehensive planners. (1996: 3)

The hostile 'neo-liberal' conjuncture that emerged in the 1970s has had a significant influence on dominant political discourses around educational processes and outcomes. Indeed, as McCulloch's (2000) argues, the 'cauldron' is often depicted as a period of 'failure and betrayal'. Having a critical understanding of the history of the subject is crucial for English teachers if they are to locate their work, and student learning, into wider contexts. But how have discourses changed? Concerns around social class, for example, have been abundant in education. Yet Wyness argues deliberate attempts have been made to de-sensitise or de-politicise these concerns in recent decades,

> Much has been written about the demise of social class and other meta-narratives such as gender and nationality. The advent of consumerism and globalisation and the decline of Marxism as a political and intellectual force worldwide have at the very least complicated the view that our social positions, identities and affiliations are governed by controversial material differences. Similarly in education, the conventional view that children of different class backgrounds are mapped on to different class trajectories as they move through the school system has been challenged by an educational establishment committed to raising the standards of all children and ensuring that at least half of all young people have access to higher education. (2008: 142)

Wyness argues that despite pronouncements about 'inclusion', many policy initiatives have created covert measures that actually reinforce class differences. The development of educational 'markets', he argues, implies a 'differentiated educational product' (2008: 151). The concepts of competition and choice themselves indicate a range of different opportunities and outcomes that some social groups will be able to exploit more than others. There is evidence to suggest social-class indeed plays a significant role in determining the type of school a parent can 'choose', and thus the potential educational outcomes.[2] These developments suggest a society stratified by patterns of consumption as much as education and employment.

In terms of English teaching, present circumstances can be seen to impact variously on children from different backgrounds. The National Curriculum, with its elitist focus puts some groups at a disadvantage. The teachers in this book highlight a number of

CHAPTER 7

political concerns. They argue for much greater emphasis on speaking and listening as the fundamental starting point for greater equity in English. They foreground a commitment to student-centred, comprehensive education. There is strong commitment to mixed-ability teaching and making curricula relevant to students' social, cultural and historical realities. They are sensitive to issues like class, race and gender. Their role, they claim, is to foreground issues such as 'class', 'ordinary lives' and 'giving voice'. In constructing this role for English practitioners, the teachers emphasise the importance of building strong relationships with students. They suggest teachers need to be involved holistically in all teaching and learning processes. This means having the power to design relevant curricula. It means working collaboratively with colleagues and exam boards to generate progressive and adaptable ways of working. They echo the Bullock Report's insistence that no child should have to leave their culture, language and history 'at the school gate'. Indeed Steve claims Bullock embodied the work these teachers did: 'you've only got to read the Bullock Report and you've got a...massive definitive, descriptive account of what was going on'.

Yandell (2011) also returns to Bullock to argue that the concept of 'inclusion' in English should not simply be about 'admissions procedures' or 'pupil grouping arrangements' as it is sometimes understood. Instead, inclusion that builds on Bullock's account must be 'about knowledge itself – about whose knowledge counts, whose voice is heard' (2011: 162). Yandell echoes the teachers' views when they insist on giving students a 'voice'. However, this alone appears insufficient. Allowing students a voice is one thing, but they suggest this is valueless if it is not accompanied with the necessary cultural tools to critically examine social relationships, cultural differences, historical conditions and so on. To do this means building mutually meaningful relationships with students, families and communities. Steve claims he 'lived thirty seconds from the school in a big, filthy old council block'. He was 'so involved in the public life in the community that I couldn't go anywhere without being recognised or known. So I had a different relationship with my kids'. Ann describes her first department as innovative and creative, but working in the ways they did was only possible because of 'strong relationships, of course'. Liz and her department wanted to 'celebrate ordinary lives'. The teachers endeavoured to build positive relationships and work in 'inclusive' ways.

Yandell (2011: 62) argues 'inclusion' is really about the 'ethical implications of teachers' practice'. But current accountability models scrutinise teacher abilities to deliver a pre-determined curriculum. Little, if any, attention is paid to the wider social, historical and cultural implications of what teachers and children do in classrooms. Yandell insists,

> Following the line taken by the Bullock Report, I am suggesting that part of the respect that teachers owe their students is to attend to their lives, cultures, histories and experiences beyond the school gates, to see these out-of-school identities as integral to the students' identities within the classroom. And this does mean that teachers should make it their business to find out about their

students, to find out about their other languages and literacies, to find out about the 'funds of knowledge' that are valorised within their communities. Teachers' knowledge of their students is, of course, a very different kind of knowledge from the subject knowledge acquired on a degree course – but it is just as vital an ingredient in teaching. (2011: 162)

This argument suggests teacher professionality needs to be re-defined. Present models encourage teachers to construct deficit views of students, with little incentive to consider the various cultures and histories found in classrooms. Yandell argues the starting point for any teacher is the question: 'who are the students and what do they know?' Yet despite high-profile policy initiatives which ostensibly appear 'inclusive' (like *Every Child Matters),* the 'emphasis is on remediation – the teacher as social worker' (2011: 163). But Yandell proposes a model which sees,

...teachers as ethnographers, finding out about the histories, cultures and values of their students. The model involved in *Every Child Matters* is, in effect, one of deficit, to be addressed through a range of interventions; the model that can be traced back to the Bullock Report is one of dialogue. (2011: 163)

It is important for English teachers to understand different cultures and histories as fundamentally underpinning children's learning abilities. Yandell argues 'any account of schooling that neglects these forces is inadequate' (2011: 163). Learners arrive in English classrooms with knowledge constructed through a mosaic of experiences, contexts, and institutions. A one-size-fits-all model is impossible because children construct meaning differently in their different social realities, as Michael suggests. Instead, a dialogic, heteroglossial conception of the subject, which acknowledges the irreducibly social nature of language in use, is essential. Yandell (2008) argues that curriculum and assessment models in English reinforce the 'assumption that learning happens in the individual'. Instead he argues for a re-conceptualisation of 'learning as a fully social, distributed activity' (2008: 86).

This suggestion is of course political. Yandell is a conscious inheritor of a tradition he seeks to renew. He encourages English teachers to locate what they do into various contexts and urges the priority of collectivist rather than individualist principles. The teachers in this book make very similar arguments. They are critical of attempts to 'de-politicise' teaching. Is it possible that English teaching can be re-politicised in new ways for new times? PM studies can contribute to present and future debates by focussing research on practitioners, history and the collective memory of the subject. This can offer alternative narratives and discourses through which dominant political realities might be challenged.

Conclusion

Conjunctural circumstances have influenced the teachers' working cultures, identities and narratives. Their memories retain particular characteristics – self-

CHAPTER 7

teaching, militancy, rebelliousness, professional integrity, a commitment to developing 'English' as a subject. There is a strong commitment to students and locating learning into various social, cultural, political and historical contexts. The teachers generate 'oppositional' speech genres when recalling their work, which provide templates to challenge dominant discourses. The memories also highlight a struggle for identity. After many years of interpreting their experiences, it seems they have constructed 'realities' they are comfortable with. Narrative is integral to identity. Remember Bruner's argument,

> We construct a 'life' by creating an identity-conserving Self who wakes up the next day still mostly the same. We seem to be geniuses at the 'continued story'…we impose coherence on the past, turn it into history. (1996: 143–144)

The teachers have 'imposed coherence' on their collective past. Their story offers an alternative account of events, circumstances and developments in the 'cauldron'. This account represents the 'life' of English teaching – real teachers' stories, motivations, missions. Their collective experience foregrounds a number of concerns that might be taken up – locating English into political, cultural and ideological contexts; working to generate body of theory for English; working in collectivist ways. Analysing our own identities and the conjunctures we work in can result in a clearer, more critical sense of agency. In combining Bakhtinian theory with Williams' categories, practitioners would have a strong theoretical base through which to engage critically with a range of discourses, social relationships and power relations. This engagement might foreground, as Dixon did, a 'new starting point' for debates in English teaching. Dominant perspectives can only be challenged through dialogue and the active confrontation of discourses, speech genres and working cultures located in conjunctural circumstances. Re-conceptualising English through these processes can lead to an improved future in which practitioners collaborate to generate new narratives and possibilities.

ACKNOWLEDGEMENT

Sections of this chapter have appeared, in other forms, in Tarpey, P. (2015). Professional memory in context: Can it help counter the "counter-revolution". *Changing English, 22*(4), 382–392; and Tarpey, P. (2017b). Disrupting continuities: Re-thinking conceptions of 'growth' in English teaching. *English in Education, 51*(2), 157–169.

NOTES

[1] See for example Grace (1978, 1987); Lawn and Grace (1987); or Lawton (1975, 1977, 1980).
[2] See Ball, Bowe and Gewirtz (1995); Ball (2006, 2008); Burgess, Briggs, McConnell and Slater (2006); Coffey (2001); West, Hind and Pennell (2004); Burgess, Propper and Wilson (2007).

CHAPTER 8

CONCLUSIONS, IMPLICATIONS, DESTINATIONS

WHERE TO NEXT?

The spirit of this book is, I hope, one that encourages dialogue and co-operation. The evidence and analyses presented are not complete, but hopefully exemplify how the collective PM of practitioners might be recovered and understood. Like Dixon fifty years ago, I hope the book might serve as a 'starting point' for discussions around the subject, from which further ideas, evidence and discourses might emerge. The teachers' PM foregrounds their priorities, identities and working practices – it provides an alternative layer of narrative about various developments and the aims of English in the 'cauldron'. But what about English in present circumstances? What are current practitioners' motivations and priorities? In exploring professional lives through PM, it might be possible to generate alternative narratives to challenge dominant discourses around the subject. Far from unifying English teaching, dominant discourses often create pressure, division or resentment. Yet the act of challenging these discourses is extremely difficult because we *live* them. However, by critically confronting our ways of talking, the discourses and speech genres we draw on, the cultural perspectives we promote, it is possible to locate their origins in numerous contexts, as social constructions.

PM studies can shed light on how teacher memories and narratives are mediated through a range of discourses, circumstances and expectations. Gergen argues that confronting the discourses and circumstances we exist within can result in 'a greater knitting of human community' (1999: 63), because 'we are challenged to step out of the realities we have created' (1999: 62). Doing this means various assumptions can be re-imagined – for instance Gergen poses a number of questions about what discourses imply, who benefits, who loses out, whose voices are heard, what values and traditions are maintained, which are marginalised, what kind of future is being created? Language constitutes social reality. But re-defining and re-describing definitions, discourses and cultures means that different possibilities can be generated to forge a different future. Gergen urges us to interrogate language,

> If language is a central means by which we carry on our lives together – carrying the past into the present to create the future – then our ways of talking and writing become targets of concern. It is not only our grand languages of self, truth and morality at stake; our futures are also fashioned from mundane exchanges in families, friendships, and organizations, in the informal comments, funny stories and the remainder of the daily hubbub. (1999: 62)

CHAPTER 8

How are lives mediated by different forces – the discourses and social conventions that shape identities, ideological perspectives and actions? I have attempted to explore how various factors, in different periods of the teachers' lives, have influenced their attitudes to English teaching. They foreground an ambitious project for English in the 'cauldron', connecting it with human relationships and trying to make them as positive, equal and mutually fulfilling as possible. This was an oppositional stance at the time. But what are the dominant discourses in English teaching currently? What alternatives are up for debate? I encourage practitioners to join in the debate, to generate their own PM studies and define professional identities, missions and practices on their own terms.

WHAT IS PM AND HOW MIGHT IT BE SIGNIFICANT?

The term 'professional memory' is generally used to refer to memories of professional practice in different ways. Cunningham (2007) relates it to conflicting practitioner perspectives on the Plowden Report. Ben-Peretz investigates how memory influences 'personal professional knowledge', constituting a 'central part of the wisdom of practitioners' (1995: 7). She foregrounds the intrinsic role memory plays in developing professional practice, competence and expertise. Professional memory means experience can be shared with others. And in learning from experience, Ben-Peretz argues practitioners can develop an 'awareness that something is missing, a sense of dissonance between expectations and reality' (2002: 318).

PM studies can contribute to these processes and I acknowledge Ben-Peretz's contributions. But my conception of PM is located in collective memory. Understanding it requires an analysis of conjunctural circumstances and a consideration of how memory is constructed through social-relational processes. It generates collective accounts of personal and professional development by exploring how practitioners are socialised into the subject and their early professional practice – to consider how these experiences influence current attitudes. PM might be described as the trans-individual, collective body of knowledge and experience of a generation of practitioners. PM in English teaching seeks to understand how practitioners construct professional identities by focussing on events, practices, developments and circumstances at a given point in the history of the subject. PM is a relational process through which identity-conserving narratives are constructed. It represents an ideological and circumstantial struggle to generate discourses, values, missions and practices. It foregrounds accounts of practice from different perspectives: pedagogically, socially, culturally, theoretically, ideologically. It locates lived experience into history by adding the collective voice of practitioners.

The PM presented here offers a practitioner account of English in the 'cauldron'. Such accounts can provide teachers with opportunities to locate themselves into the history of the subject, and strengthen professional identity. PM studies might provoke critical self-reflection among practitioners – to consider their own backgrounds, motivations, practices, and explore how language, culture and history influence

CONCLUSIONS, IMPLICATIONS, DESTINATIONS

memory, identity and action. What influence does professional experience have? How does what we inherit in English teaching influence particular types of practice? These are not insignificant matters. The evidence presented promotes a collectivist understanding of professionalism, and a dialogic, heteroglossial approach to practice in English. Yet this conception of the subject, and teachers from this generation, are largely ignored in dominant discourses. In these circumstances, it is crucial that new practitioners are 'apprenticed' into the Professional Memory of the subject. As Steve argues, younger teachers would benefit from 'reflective interaction' with older practitioners. But where older generations of teachers are absent, accounts of English generated through PM can recapture their various concerns and priorities. This can offer templates and examples to be learned from.

The practices, struggles and values described by the teachers in this book provide evidence that dominant structures and discourses can be confronted and changed. They offer critical perspectives to teachers who may indeed 'want to react' against particular limitations on their practice. So PM studies can create unifying connections between past and present – examples of practice, methods and motivations to be re-imagined for new times.

WHAT PRACTICAL CONTRIBUTION MIGHT PM STUDIES MAKE?

I want to discuss the radical problematising of existing theoretical frameworks in English teaching. The dominant paradigm in English only really makes sense against a background of highly selective views of inherited traditions. At any given point, elements of one, several or indeed all of these traditions might apply. PM studies can generate a more complete sense of English teaching than current dominant perspectives suggest. They can highlight the richness and complexity of previous versions of English, some of which are air-brushed from accounts of the subject. Models of English drawn from PM can highlight positions from which to critique and reconceptualise the theoretical frameworks that underpin current definitions and approaches.

To explain this potential contribution of PM studies, I want to draw on the work of Louis Althusser.[1] In *Reading Capital* (2009) Althusser problematises certain 'epistemological propositions' in Marx's political economy, arriving at some theoretical conclusions. He highlights a specific section in Engels's preface to volume two of *Capital*. In it, Engels offers a discussion of 'Marx's utterances on surplus-value'. Engels argues that Marx re-imagined the concept of surplus-value in such a new way that it 'struck home like a thunderbolt out of a clear sky'. To illustrate his point, Engels analyses of a revolutionary moment in the history of chemistry. I need to re-cap the story briefly here.

Engels focuses on the well-known story of eighteenth century chemists, Joseph Priestley and Carl Scheele (see Lane, 2002; Datta, 2005). He explains how both men discovered a type of 'pure air' in a period when 'phlogistic theory' dominated the discipline. This theory posited a supposed substance called 'phlogiston' ignited when it separated from a combustible body, thus creating fire. The new air seemed to make combustion more effective and longer-lasting. This led Priestley and Scheele to believe that the air mixed with phlogiston and improved combustion; thus both assumed they had solved a problem. Priestley referred to the gas as 'dephlogisticated air', and Scheele called it 'fire air'. In fact, Engels points out, both men had 'produced oxygen without knowing what they had laid their hands on'. His point is that the two men had constructed such definitive ideas about their own work and inherited knowledge that they 'remained prisoners' to prior theoretical understandings that were flawed. He argues,

> The element that was destined to upset all phlogistic views and to revolutionise chemistry remained barren in their hands. (cited in Althusser, 2009: 165–166)

Priestley eventually disclosed his discovery to a French colleague, Antoine Lavoisier, who problematised the issue and concluded that the 'dephlogisticated' air was in fact a 'new' chemical element, 'oxygen'. Engels argues that Lavoisier,

> ...was the first to place all chemistry, which in its phlogistic form had stood on its head, squarely on its feet. (cited in Althusser, 2009: 166)

This reconceptualisation of a chemistry problem transformed the epistemological landscape of the science. Engels then argues that Marx's genius (like Lavoisier's) in generating new knowledge was not to seek *solutions*, but to look instead for *problems*. This is the point Althusser takes up in his analysis. It is not Marx's re-imagined concept of surplus-value that is important, but the processes he put in place in order *to do the re-imagining*. Althusser argues Marx initiated a revolution not only in the science of history and philosophy, but also 'in the history of the *theoretical*' (2009: 169). This development makes it possible to challenge existing ideological perspectives, critical analyses and objective definitions, but also the theoretical bases that underpin them. New theoretical perspectives can be generated through the dialectical act '*of posing as a problem* what had hitherto been given as a *solution*' (2009: 170). Doing this makes it possible to generate a new 'theoretical *problematic*' (2009: 170). Objects of study are inevitably defined in particular ways in the history of a given discipline. These definitions create objective, theoretical and social understandings of the objects themselves. Althusser argues Marx's re-constitution of the 'theoretical matrix' means that new questions put to an object must change '*the reality of the object: its objective definition*' (2009: 171). And so,

> To cast doubt on the definition of the object is to pose the question of a differential definition of the *novelty of the object* aimed at by a new theoretical problematic. In the history of the revolutions of a science, every upheaval in the theoretical practice is correlated with a transformation in the definition of the object, and therefore with a difference which can be assigned to the *object* of the theory itself. (2009: 171)

If the object of the theory is to problematise rather than seek to describe solutions then it follows that the object under scrutiny can no longer exist in its current definition. What is needed to achieve this are new questions generated from a new 'theoretical problematic'. Althusser argues,

> To change theoretical base is therefore to *change theoretical problematic*, if it is true that the theory of a science at a given moment in its history is no more than the *theoretical matrix of the type of questions* the science poses its object – if it is true that with a new basic theory a new organic way of putting questions to the object comes into the world, a new way of posing questions and in consequence of producing new answers. (2009: 170)

Althusser demonstrates how Marx re-imagined the concept of surplus-value and in doing so reconstituted the problematic in contemporary political economy. Marx therefore provided 'an answer which does not correspond to any question posed' (2009: 29). By taking this example and applying it here, it is possible to see how the current problematic in English teaching might be re-conceived for new times. The teachers' PM represents 'oppositional' or 'alternative' ways of working in English that have been successful in the past. PM studies can help inspire new questions directed at current conceptions of the subject that indeed produce new answers. Althusser's ideas can be applied in a number of ways. For example, the underlying theoretical base in English teaching is predicated on imperatives like the National Curriculum, standardised assessment, SATs, aims and objectives, functional skills and external accountability. Also, the canon, Standard English and 'correctness' in grammar contribute to the 'objective definition' of the subject. These underlying ideas influence the construction of practitioner identities, particular ways of working and expected outcomes. Yet many of the contradictions between these imperatives and the lived experience of teachers and students in classrooms are overlooked. For example, despite centralised control of the curriculum and teacher professionality, ideas like 'individual' or 'personalised' learning are promoted. But as Michael suggests, what does personalised learning mean 'if you spend your time coaching kids for SATs?'

The current theoretical base in English teaching also conceptualises learning as an individual, psychological process – it takes place 'in the head'. Learners are viewed as individuals responsible for their own 'deficits'. 'Failure' is associated with lack of ability, poor application or with poor teaching. But from a social constructionist and heteroglossial perspective this model is woefully inadequate. If, like Gergen argues, we are 'all made up of each other' then responsibility for any 'failure' among learners is much more widespread. It is dispersed socially, culturally, politically. If ideas like these can challenge the theoretical base in English teaching then learning might be re-conceptualised in more democratic ways – in Yandell's terms 'as a fully social, distributed activity' (2008: 86).

Another pervasive idea in recent times is 'reflective practice'. English teachers are encouraged and expected to reflect critically on their work, to continually improve practice (Green, 2011). But what are the structural and theoretical bases that inform 'reflection'? What is the purpose of it? Current definitions of English influence professional action. If the purpose of 'reflective practice' is to consider how to match-up to external accountability measures – an Ofsted inspection let us say – then pre-determined solutions provide answers to supposed problems in practice. This model can never be progressive. A more challenging way for teachers to reflect critically on practice would not be to seek solutions in this way, but to interrogate the theoretical reality, and the objectified definitions of English that helped create the 'problem' in the first place. Practitioners can benefit from having alternative models of theory and practice, understood through PM, to help challenge existing professional expectations.

The teachers in this book present a picture of professionalism that makes current conceptions seem inadequate. They talk of 'full professionalism', by which they mean practitioners being involved holistically in all aspects of teaching: from curriculum design, to developing practice and assessment methods. They insist practice must be located into the various contexts in which it occurs. They insist on developing children's confidence in their own identities and backgrounds; they are committed to social justice and enhancing children's agency. There is a commitment to oral work, with learning understood as a socially mediated process. They argue professional development opportunities must be available for teachers in and outside the classroom. The evidence highlights a PM of collective concerns and a strong co-operative ethos.

A comprehensive body of PM can help English teachers re-define their work and re-construct the theoretical templates that underpin practice and professional responsibilities. A new 'theoretical problematic' can pose new questions to English teaching that create new answers in different conjunctures. Questions should challenge the aims and content of English teaching. They should challenge current inspection arrangements. Do current models work in the best interests of students and teachers? The evidence in this book emphasises positive relationships and co-operation. Supportive advisory and inspection systems helped teachers create and share good practice. And importantly, the evidence foregrounds teachers who located their work into broader social, cultural and political contexts in order to define their own professionalism. In Steve's terms, these issues need to be 'put back on the agenda again'. This can only be done by practitioners forcing that agenda.

In present circumstances, PM studies are unlikely to find their way into teacher training standards. But if practitioners start to produce their own critical narratives, their own PM projects, then there is potential for a powerful body of evidence to emerge. Althusser (2009) points out Marx's theoretical break went largely unnoticed at the time,

> ...the event took place, the break took place, and the history which was born with it is grubbing its subterranean way beneath official history: 'well grubbed, old mole!' One day the official history of ideas will fall behind it, and when it realises this it will be too late for it unless it is prepared to recognise this event and draw the consequences. (2009: 169–170)

Residual cultures in English teaching, like those of the teachers in this book, are 'grubbing their way beneath official history'. Understanding these cultures can help practitioners generate new questions about their professional roles.

PM AND HISTORY OF EDUCATION

PM studies bring together history and memory. Accounts of English must acknowledge teacher memory as valid evidence. And memory must be historically located, as Gardner (2010) argues,

> If memory settles only on identity, it opens itself to the perils of wilful manipulation or organised forgetting. If history settles only upon its own claims to truth, it closes its eyes to its own boundedness. If history deprecates memory, it lays waste to its wellspring. If memory ignores history, it squanders its credibility. (2010: 115)

So accounts of the educational past must explore the relationship between history and memory – what I have called PM. McCulloch (2000) stresses the importance of challenging existing orthodoxies by re-evaluating different versions of the 'past': official, private, public. By doing this, it is possible to publicise the past, hold it up to public scrutiny and generate alternative, critical versions of events. Recalling the public past makes it possible 'to educate the public about the nature of education, and to provide independent and informed critiques which will challenge received orthodoxies and stimulate debate' (2000: 16). PM studies can contribute to this process by adding the collective voice of practitioners. As well as publicising the past, Aldrich (2000) argues historians of education can improve teachers' professional status by enhancing,

> ...professional confidence and expertise by providing a nuanced and cumulative context for the distillation of the best educational theory and practice at a particular point in history, both past and present. (2000: 76)

Robust evidence can help strengthen teacher identities. Yet much history of education in recent times has been marginalised or manipulated. As McCulloch (2000) argues there has been a trend in recent decades for historical context to be neglected in policy developments. Wendy Robinson (2000) agrees and argues the results of this neglect have produced three pernicious educational realities: first, the state has engineered a much more dominant position over teaching and teachers; second, there is a 'much more mechanical, technicist discourse of teacher training and pedagogical practice' (2000: 62); and third, a 'steady devaluing of teachers' capabilities, autonomy and independence has left a legacy of professional discontent' (2000: 62). Robinson argues policy initiatives have created uncertainty over future prospects for teachers, schools and children. She insists policy makers must 'take something from our historical past' (2000: 62). However, in present circumstances, policy makers demonstrate little appetite for this. Teachers must force these issues

CHAPTER 8

onto the agenda themselves. Robinson argues that accounts of the 'educational past' must include explorations of teacher training, pedagogy and professional identity. As the evidence in this book has shown, PM studies can contribute in all of these ways. But what are the audiences for history of education?

William Richardson (2000) laments the diminishing influence of histories of education aimed at 'professional audiences'. He distinguishes 'educationists specialising in history' from 'academic historians'. It is the educationists, whose audiences have traditionally been professional groups (teachers), who have lost influence. A key reason for this, Richardson argues, is the decline of history of education modules on teaching training programmes. With diminishing audiences for their work, educationists specialising in history have seen their territory encroached upon by academic historians, who have successfully managed to locate educational history as 'primarily a part of mainstream history…aimed at students of history and the lay public' (2000: 34). Richardson argues this shift has produced anodyne, 'coffee table' histories of the educational past. Instead, what are needed are accounts of historical events and circumstances that offer practitioners alternative perspectives through which to reflect critically on their working lives.

Richardson argues education professionals are disadvantaged by histories that do not contemplate the implications for practice. Histories of education should be more firmly located into educational studies. This can offer practitioners a clearer sense of identity and agency. After all, as Foucault suggests, 'knowledge is not made for understanding: it is made for cutting' (1986: 88). And because current practitioners do not necessarily have this type of historical knowledge, Richardson argues they are 'hemmed in by government' (2000: 35). The consequence of this is that, 'in such a situation, educationists specialising in history have no clear constituency or ready audience for their work' (2000: 35). In these circumstances PM studies can contribute to history of education. Practitioners themselves can recover and document their collective voices, priorities and concerns. When located into various contexts, circumstances and conjunctures, these narratives would have an existing audience: for practitioners by practitioners. Building alternative layers of narrative in this way can help challenge existing accounts in the ways McCulloch suggests. PM studies can also generate first-hand accounts of teacher training, pedagogy and professional identity that can be held up to scrutiny. By having a clear understanding of historical developments in English, practitioners would be in a stronger position from which to construct a consciously critical professional identity.

PM, TEACHER EDUCATION AND PROFESSIONAL DEVELOPMENT

Today, once again, there is a public debate about whether teachers are 'born' or 'made'. The discourses generated on this issue are not always well-informed but are potentially damaging to teacher professionalism. Recent initiatives mean some schools (academies, free schools) can employ 'unqualified teachers'. This not only undermines hard-won concessions to make teaching an all-graduate, certified profession, it also makes assumptions about teacher knowledge. In 2012 the Department for Education announced,

> Independent schools and free schools can already hire brilliant people who have not got QTS [Qualified Teacher Status]. We are extending this flexibility to all academies so more schools can hire great linguists, computer scientists, engineers and other specialists who have not worked in state schools before. (Gov.UK, 27 July, 2012)

What are the implications of 'extending this flexibility'? These proposed changes came at a time when all schools were pressured to become academies and national pay-bargaining was under threat. But there is an assumption here that 'brilliant' people might somehow 'impart' knowledge to others 'naturally'. This simplistic model of practice conveniently neglects the social, cultural, historical and political contexts that educational processes are framed within, making it intensely ideological. The implication is that teacher training programmes matter little in the development of effective practitioners, that subject knowledge and experience are the only requirements. But excellent subject knowledge alone is insufficient for making good teachers. Practitioners need a wide range of other skills and knowledge, not least the ability to understand their pupils, and as Yandell suggests, this is 'a very different kind of knowledge from the subject knowledge acquired on a degree course – but it is just as vital an ingredient in teaching' (2011: 162).

In that case, what are the best ways for these 'vital' skills to be acquired? William Pinar (2004) differentiates between teacher 'training' and 'education', with 'training' viewed through the same 'technicist' lens that Robinson (2000) identifies. Pinar insists teachers 'must be granted greater academic freedom, must be granted some control over the curriculum and the means by which it is taught and tested' (2004: 229). Teacher 'education' is closer to the 'full' professionalism Michael talks about,

> Teacher education (if it remains at all) must be reconceived from a skill-identified induction into school bureaucracy to the interdisciplinary, theoretical, and autobiographical study of educational experience in which curriculum and teaching are understood as complicated conversations toward the construction of a democratic public sphere. (2004: 229)

Pinar's conception of educational processes and structures is evidenced in the teachers' PM. Their approach *is* interdisciplinary, theoretical and autobiographical. They understand the complexities and challenges of teaching and they are prepared to struggle with them. They understand that curriculum can emerge from negotiation, collaboration and creativity. These were realities for them. And they can be, in different ways, for current practitioners. English teachers should make it their business to force their skills and knowledge (not just subject knowledge) into the discourse – to punctuate it with their professionality. And this means starting with ourselves. Jane Miller understood the importance of 'autobiography' in teacher professional development, claiming, 'teachers…must insert what they know into

CHAPTER 8

public discussions of education, and to do that they need to begin from their own histories' (1995: 26). PM studies like this can help English teachers to do just that. Any kind of teacher 'education' must include broad theoretical perspectives to help practitioners understand how their beliefs, attitudes and practices are mediated through various conjunctural circumstances. The evidence presented in this book adds weight to the arguments outlined above and the principles that Yandell and Pinar demand. However, teacher voices are largely side-lined in dominant debates about working practice and professional standards.

PM studies can re-insert teacher voices back into the debate and help practitioners re-conceptualise how they view and represent themselves as a collective professional group. Yes, this study relocates a small number of professional voices into a historical timeframe. This is important for broadening understandings of English in the 'cauldron'. But this study is also about challenging current dominant perspectives: to use our collective knowledge to demand greater agency and professional autonomy. But this potential will go unrealised without a comprehensive body of evidence, so further PM research is needed. Evidence from different groups of teachers will make it possible to define and articulate the common concerns, values and priorities shared across generations. This can help define a theoretical base from which to agitate for the kinds of skills, knowledge and professional development opportunities that English teachers demand.

PM, ENGLISH TEACHING AND COLLECTIVE MEMORY

The teachers in this book view practice in English similarly to the likes of Dixon, Rosen and Britton. That is, teaching and learning are viewed as collaborative processes located in specific social, cultural, historical and political contexts. Because of this, they are critical of current policy initiatives (centralised control, external accountability, standardised tests). They claim to have worked in 'oppositional' or 'militant' ways in order to define the conditions for their own practice, and they represent themselves as capable, energetic and politically engaged. But how is all this relevant in current contexts?

PM studies can benefit English teachers in a number of ways. A comprehensive body of PM could help practitioners locate their work into broader historical trajectories, to underpin practice with the weight of precedent. It might function similarly to a concept like 'case-law'. A profession like Law uses historical precedent effectively to maintain standards, professional integrity, identity and autonomy. A similar circumstance could prove valuable for English teachers. If practitioners were 'apprenticed' into the historical developments of the subject – practices, traditions, debates – they would be better positioned to demand a greater voice in the subject's evolution and their own professional development. Current practitioners work in very different circumstances to the teachers in this book, who suggest a sense of 'activism' has been eroded. But if PM studies can provoke critical reflection, it might be that English teachers are motivated to confront the various circumstances and speech genres that influence their professional identities. Making meaningful connections with the past can foreground common concerns and priorities in the present. This can provoke new questions to be put to the current 'theoretical problematic' in English teaching.

The PM presented in this book explores teacher identities, attitudes to practice and professional responsibilities. It helps us to understand how identities and working cultures have been constructed, as well as how they have been influenced, and influential, in different ways. PM can say *what* teacher identities look like, as well as *how* they emerge by highlighting the complicated circumstances that affect them. As a relational phenomenon, PM is constructed in social, cultural and historical contexts. As Gergen argues, memory is not a 'specific kind of process in the head of the individual' (1999: 134). Instead, PM looks to find connections between historical circumstances, the ways in which individuals remember the past and ultimately how they represent it through narrative. All memory is collective because of the social and cultural artefacts that enable its construction and subsequent narration. Inguez, Valencia and Vasquez (1997) state,

> We agree with Connerton (1989) who stated that the idea of an individual memory completely separate from social memory is a meaningless abstraction… different social groups, categories, and collectives, each with its own past, will surely have different social memories that shape and are shaped by their own intersubjectivity. Every memory, as personal as it may be – even of events that are private and strictly personal and have not been shared with anyone – exists only through its relation with what has been shared with others: the language, idiom, events and everything that shapes the society of which individuals are part. (1997: 250)

It is useful to remember Shotter's argument that social narratives are designed to 'constitute and sustain one or other kind of social order' (1990: 122–123). The teachers in this book sustain an oppositional stance. But more PM studies need to be done with different generations of teachers, in different contexts. This can contribute further evidence to the historical and autobiographical memory of English teaching. PM studies can generate new discourses that mean practitioners can indeed 'step out of the realities we have created'.

MORE PM STUDIES?

PM research is time-consuming. It relies on the goodwill of participants. I was very lucky to find teachers from the 'cauldron' who willingly gave their time and spoke persuasively, energetically and enthusiastically. Thank you. But further work needs to be done. It is important to build a more comprehensive body of evidence and locate the PM of these teachers alongside others. Different generations will recall different experiences, values and motivations and it is important to find out what English teachers say they share in common. PM research does not offer simple solutions, easily reducible into statistical data or soundbites. It explores people's lives and all the complexities involved. But one of the study's strengths, I hope, is its depth. I wanted the teachers' voices to be heard. It is crucial in present circumstances that the collective voice of practitioners is heard more emphatically. This requires active participation and organisation.

It is useful to re-locate teacher voices back into historical contexts because this can help to broaden understandings of English teaching. But for PM studies to reach their potential they need to be practical. This requires active organisation. Researchers and teachers should work collaboratively to generate evidence that poses new questions to dominant perspectives. I encourage teachers to conduct their own PM projects, to explore their own practices and attitudes, to locate these into various conjunctural circumstances – a continuous process with each generation contributing to our collective knowledge. It might be that projects can be organised through subject associations like LATE and NATE? More PM projects can produce a robust body of evidence that connects teacher identities, working cultures, practices, speech genres, values and conjunctural circumstances. Such a body of evidence could help re-define English teaching on practitioners' own terms.

I set out on a journey intending to tell the stories of six English teachers. But this has potential to snowball and further evidence needs to be gathered. PM studies can bring research back to the level of the teacher. Practitioners should make it their business to define professional identities on their own terms. And in learning from the past, it might be possible to generate new conceptions of professional identity and behaviour that can redirect the gaze away from the limitations of current models. This is not an outlandish or expensive idea. All that is required for this to work is an understanding of theory, time and effort. If closer links can be made between researchers and practitioners through PM studies, there is real potential that English teachers will have a stronger voice in discussions about their own professional destiny.

ACKNOWLEDGEMENT

Sections of this chapter have appeared, in other forms, in Tarpey, P. (2015). Professional memory in context: Can it help counter the "counter-revolution". *Changing English, 22*(4), 382–392; and Tarpey, P. (2017b). Disrupting continuities: Re-thinking conceptions of 'growth' in English teaching. *English in Education, 51*(2), 157–169.

NOTE

[1] Althusser was a Marxist critic and controversial thinker. He attempted to 'recharge' Marxist theory for a post-war generation grown weary of the politics of the French Communist Party, and the intellectual style of existentialist thinkers like Sartre. He appealed to some critics in English in the 1970s, particularly Terry Eagleton (1976, 1983). Yet he attracted criticism from theorists who found his work unrelentingly abstract and lacking in historical specificity – for example Raymond Williams (1977) and E.P. Thompson (1978). These disputes generated theoretical discussions that inspired influential figures in English teaching such as Harold Rosen.

REFERENCES

Abbs, P. (1969). *English for diversity.* London: Heinemann.
Aldrich, R. (1982). *An introduction to the history of education.* Sevenoaks: Hodder & Stoughton.
Aldrich, R. (2000). A contested and changing terrain: History of education in the twenty-first century. In D. Crook & A. Aldrich (Eds.), *History of education for the twenty-first century* (pp. 77–78). London: Institute of Education.
Aldrich, R. (Ed.). (2002). *A century of education.* London: RoutledgeFalmer.
Aldrich, R. (2006). *Lessons from history of education: The selected works of Richard Aldrich.* London: Routledge.
Allen, D. (1980). *English teaching since 1965: How much growth?* London: Heinemann Educational Books.
Althusser, L. (1969). *For Marx* (B. Brewster, Trans.). London: Allen Lane/Penguin Press. (Original Edition, 1969)
Althusser, L. (2009a). The epistemological propositions of capital. In L. Althusser & E. Balibar (Eds.), *Reading capital* (pp. 160–173). London: Verso Books.
Althusser, L. (2009b). From capital to Marx's philosophy. In L. Althusser & E. Balibar (Eds.), *Reading capital* (pp. 11–75). London: Verso Books.
Althusser, L., & Balibar, E. (2009). *Reading capital.* London: Verso Books.
Apple, M. W. (1979). *Ideology and curriculum.* London: Routledge & Kegan Paul.
Bakhtin, M. M. (1981). *The dialogic imagination.* Austin, TX: University of Texas Press.
Bakhtin, M. M. (1986). *Speech genres and other late essays.* Austin, TX: University of Texas Press.
Bakhurst, D. (1990). Social memory in Soviet thought. In D. Middleton & D. Edwards (Eds.), *Collective remembering* (pp. 203–226). London: Sage Publications.
Ball, S. (2006). *Education policy and social class: The selected works of Stephen J Ball.* Abingdon: Routledge.
Ball, S. (2008). *The education debate.* Bristol: Policy Press.
Ball, S., Bowe, R., & Gewirtz, S. (1995). Circuits of schooling: A sociological exploration of parental choice of school in social class contexts. *The Sociological Review, 43*(1), 52–78.
Ball, S., & Goodson, I. (1985). *Teachers' lives and careers.* London: Falmer Press.
Ball, S., & Goodson, I. (1985). Understanding teachers: Concepts and contexts. In S. Ball & I. F. Goodson (Eds.), *Teachers' lives and careers* (pp. 1–26). London: Falmer Press.
Ball, S., Kenny, A., & Gardiner, D. (1990). Literacy, politics and the teaching of English. In I. F. Goodson & P. Medway (Eds.), *Bringing English to order* (pp. 47–86). Lewes: Falmer Press.
Barnes, D. (1976). *From communication to curriculum.* London: Penguin Books.
Barnes, D. (1988). The politics of oracy. In M. Maclure, T. Phillips, & A. Wilkinson (Eds.), *Oracy matters* (pp. 45–54). Milton Keynes: Open University Press.
Barnes, D., Britton, J., & Rosen, H. (1969). *Language, the learner and the school.* Harmondsworth: Penguin Books.
Barnes, D., & Todd, F. (1977). *Communication and learning in small groups.* London: Routledge & Kegan Paul.
Barstow, S. (1960). *A kind of loving.* London: Michael Joseph.
Benn, C., & Chitty, C. (1996). *Thirty years on: Is comprehensive education alive and well or struggling to survive?* London: Davis Fulton Publishers.
Benn, C., & Simon, B. (1972). *Halfway there: Report on the British comprehensive school reform* (2nd ed.). London: Penguin Books.
Ben-Peretz, M. (1995). *Learning from experience: Memory and the teacher's account of teaching.* Albany, NY: State University of New York Press.
Ben-Peretz, M. (2002). Retired teachers reflect on learning from experience. *Teachers and Teaching, 8,* 313–323.

REFERENCES

BERA. (2011). *Ethical guidelines for educational research*. London: British Educational Research Association. Retrieved from http://www.bera.ac.uk/publications/Ethical%20Guidelines

Berger, P. L., & Luckmann, T. (1966). *The social construction of reality: A treatise it's the sociology of knowledge*. New York, NY: Anchor Books.

Bergson, H. (2004). *Matter and memory*. New York, NY: Dover Classics.

Bernstein, B. (1971). *Class, codes and control*. London: Routledge & Kegan Paul.

Beynon, J. (1985). Institutional change and career histories in a comprehensive school. In S. Ball & I. F. Goodson (Eds.), *Teachers' lives and careers* (pp. 158–179). London: Falmer Press.

Billig, M. (1990). Collective memory, ideology and the British royal family. In D. Middleton & D. Edwards (Eds.), *Collective remembering* (pp. 60–80). London: Sage Publications.

Bourdieu, P. (1986). The forms of capital. In J. Richardson (Ed.), *Handbook of theory and research for sociology of education* (pp. 241–258). New York, NY: Greenwood Press.

Bowles, S., & Gintis, H. (1976). *Schooling in capitalist America: Educational reform and the contradictions of economic life*. New York, NY: Basic Books.

Boyson, R. (1975). *The crisis in education*. London: Woburn Press.

Braudel, F. (1995). 'History and the social sciences: The longue duree', annales ESC 13 (S. Matthews, Trans.). In J. Revel & L. Hunt (Eds.), *Histories: French constructions of the past, postwar French thought* (Vol. 1). New York, NY: The New Press. (Originally published in 1958)

Bray, C. (2014). *1965: The year modern Britain was born*. London: Simon & Schuster.

Britton, J. (1970). *Language and learning*. London: Allen Lane.

Britton, J. (1982). *Prospect and retrospect*. London: Heinemann.

Britton, J. (1993). *Literature in its place*. London: Cassell.

Bruner, J. (1986). *Actual minds, possible worlds*. Cambridge, MA: Harvard University Press.

Bruner, J. (1990). *Acts of meaning*. Cambridge, MA: Harvard University Press.

Bruner, J. (1996). *The culture of education*. Cambridge, MA: Harvard University Press.

Bullock, A. (1975). *The Bullock report – A language for life, department for education and science*. London: HMSO.

Burgess, S., Briggs, A., McConnell, B., & Slater, H. (2006). *School choice in England: Background facts* (CMPO Working Paper Series No. 6/159). Bristol: University of Bristol.

Burgess, S., Propper, C., & Wilson, D. (2007). The impact of school choice in England. *Policy Studies, 28*(2), 129–143.

Burgess, T. (1996). A different angle: English teaching and its narratives. *Changing English, 3*(1), 57–77.

Burgess, T. (2002). Writing, English teachers and the new professionalism. In V. Ellis (Ed.), *When the hurly burly's done: What's worth fighting for in English teaching?* Sheffield: NATE Publications.

Burgess, T., & Hardcastle, J. (2000). Englishes and English: Schooling and the making of the school subject. In A. Kent (Ed.), *School subject teaching: The history and future of the curriculum* (pp. 1–27). London: Kogan Page.

Burr, V. (2003). *Social constructionism*. Hove: Routledge.

Butt, R., Raymond, D., McCue, G., & Yamagishi, L. (1992). Collaborative autobiography and the teacher's voice. In I. F. Goodson (Ed.), *Studying teachers' lives*. London: Routledge.

Callaghan, L. J. (1976, October 18). *A rational debate based on the facts'* (The Ruskin Speech). Oxford: Ruskin College. Retrieved from http://www.educationengland.org.uk/documents/speeches/1976ruskin.html

Cameron, D. (1995). *Verbal hygiene*. London: Routledge.

Chitty, C. (2004). *Education policy in Britain*. Basingstoke: Palgrave Macmillan.

Chitty, C. (2007). *Eugenics, race and intelligence*. London: Continuum.

Chomsky, N. (1965). *Aspects of the theory of syntax*. Cambridge, MA: MIT Press.

Clements, S., Dixon, J., & Stratta, L. (1963). *Reflections: An English course for students aged 14–18*. Oxford: Oxford University Press.

Coffey, A. (2001). Parents, consumers and choice. In A. Coffey (Ed.), *Education and social change*. London: Open University Press.

Cohen, L., Manion, L., & Morrison, K. (2011). *Research methods in education* (7th ed.). Abingdon: Routledge.

REFERENCES

Corrigan, P. (1979). *Schooling the smash street kids*. London: Macmillan Press.
Coser, L. A. (1992). Introduction. In M. Halbwachs (Ed.), *On collective memory* (pp. 1–34). Chicago, IL: University of Chicago Press.
Cox, C. B., & Dyson, A. E. (1969a). *The fight for education*. London: Critical Quarterly Society.
Cox, C. B., & Dyson, A. E. (1969b). *The crisis in education*. London: Critical Quarterly Society.
Cox, C. B., & Dyson, A. E. (1971). *The Black papers on education*. London: Davis-Poynter.
Coultas, V. (2013). English for the few or English for the many? In M. Allen & P. Ainley (Eds.), *Education beyond the coalition: Reclaiming the agenda* (pp. 46–60). London: Radicaled Books.
Crook, D., & Aldrich, A. (Eds.). (2000). *History of education for the twenty-first century*. London: Institute of Education.
Crotty, M. (1998). *The foundations of social research*. London: Sage Publications.
Cunningham, P. (2002). Primary education. In R. Aldrich (Ed.), *A century of education* (pp. 9–30). London: RoutledgeFalmer.
Cunningham, P. (2007). Plowden in history: Popular and professional memory. *Forum, 49*, 21–32.
Cunningham, P., & Gardner, P. (2004). *Becoming teachers: Texts and testimonies 1907–1950*. London: Woburn Press.
Datta, N. C. (2005). *The story of chemistry*. Hyderabad: Universities Press.
Davies, C. (1996). *What is English teaching?* Buckingham: Open University Press.
Davies, C. (2000). "Correct" or "appropriate"? Is it possible to resolve the debate about which should be promoted in the classroom? In J. Davison & J. Moss (Eds.), *Issues in English teaching*. London: Routledge.
Davis, J. (2002). The inner London education authority and the William Tyndale junior school affair, 1974–1976. *Oxford Review of Education, 28*(2–3), 275–298.
Davison, J. (2011). Literacy and social class. In J. Davison, C. Daly, & J. Moss (Eds.), *Debates in English teaching* (pp. 169–187). London: Routledge.
Davison, J., Daly, C., & Moss, J. (2011). *Debates in English teaching*. London: Routledge.
Davison, J., & Moss, J. (2000). *Issues in English teaching*. London: Routledge.
DES. (1965). *Circular 10/65: The organisation of secondary education*. London: HMSO.
DFE. (2012, July 27). *Academies to have same freedoms as free schools over teachers*. Retrieved from https://www.gov.uk/government/news/academies-to-have-same-freedom-as-free-schools-over-teachers
Dhunpath, R. (2000). Life history methodology: "Narradigm" regained. *Qualitative Studies in Education, 13*(5), 543–551.
Dixon, J. (1967). *Growth through English*. Huddersfield: NATE Publications.
Dixon, J. (1975). *Growth through English: Set in the perspective of the 1970s*. Oxford: Oxford University Press.
Dixon, J. (1991). *A schooling in English*. Milton Keynes: Open University Press.
Dixon, J. (2013). Developing English: Lessons from the sixties. *NATE at 50: A Teaching English Special Supplement, 2013*, 23–28.
Donnelly, M. (2005). *Sixties Britain*. Harlow: Pearson Education.
Eagleton, T. (1976). *Marxism and literary criticism*. Los Angeles, CA: University of California Press.
Eagleton, T. (1983). *Literary theory: An introduction*. Oxford: Blackwell.
Ellis, T. (1977). *William Tyndale: The teachers' story*. London: Writers and Readers Publishing.
Ellis, V. (2000). What has sexuality got to do with English teaching? In J. Davison & J. Moss (Eds.), *Issues in English teaching* (pp. 212–223). Abingdon: Routledge.
Findlay, K. (2010, September 1–4). *The professional identity of English teachers in the secondary school*. Paper presented at the Annual Meeting of the British Educational Research Association, Coventry, UK.
Fliesser, C., & Goodson, I. F. (1992). Negotiating fair trade: Towards collaborative relationships between researchers and teachers. In I. F. Goodson & J. M. Mangan (Eds.), *History, context and qualitative methods in the study of education* (Vol. 3, pp. 35–52). London & Ontario: RUCCUS.
Foucault, M. (1986). *The Foucault reader*. Harmondsworth: Penguin Books.
Francis, P. (2001). *The best policy? Honesty in education, 1997–2001*. Shropshire: Liberty Books.
Freeman, M. (1993). *Rewriting the self: History, memory, narrative*. London: Routledge.
Freire, P. (1970a). *Pedagogy of the oppressed*. London: Penguin Books.

REFERENCES

Freire, P. (1970b). *Cultural action for freedom*. Cambridge, MA: Harvard University Press.
Freire, P. (1973). *Education for critical consciousness*. New York, NY: Seabury Press.
Freire, P. (1976). A few notions about the word "concientization". In R. Dale, G. Esland, & M. Macdonald (Eds.), *Schooling and capitalism*. London: Taylor & Francis.
Galton, M. J., Simon, B., & Croll, P. (1980). *Inside the primary classroom*. London: Routledge.
Gardner, P. (2003). Oral history in education: Teacher's memory and teacher's history. *History of Education, 32*, 175–188.
Gardner, P. (2010). *Hermeneutics, history and memory*. Abingdon: Routledge.
Gardner, P., & Cunningham, P. (1998). Teacher trainers and educational change in Britain, 1876–1996: "A flawed and deficient history"? *Journal of Education for Teaching, 23*(3), 231–255.
Gergen, K. (1999). *An invitation to social construction*. London: Sage Publications.
Gergen, K. (2001). *Social construction in context*. London: Sage Publications.
Gibbons, S. (2009). Lessons from the past? *English Teaching: Practice and Critique, 8*(1), 64–75.
Gibbons, S. (2013). *The London association for the teaching of English 1947–67*. London: Trentham Books.
Gill, S., & Goodson, I. F. (2011). Life history and narrative methods. In B. Somekh & K. Lewin (Eds.), *Theory and methods in social research*. London: Sage Publications.
Gillard, D. (2006). *The Hadow reports: An introduction*. Retrieved from http://www.educationengland.org.uk/articles/24hadow.html
Glaser, B. G., & Strauss, A. L. (1967). *The discovery of grounded theory: Strategies for qualitative research*. New York, NY: Aldine.
Goffman, E. (1959). *The presentation of self in everyday life*. New York, NY: Doubleday Anchor.
Goodson, I. F. (1983). *School subjects and curriculum change: Case studies in curriculum history*. Beckenham: Croom Helm.
Goodson, I. F. (1991). History, context and qualitative methods. In I. F. Goodson & R. Walker (Eds.), *Biography, identity and schooling: Episodes in educational research*. Basingstoke: Falmer Press.
Goodson, I. F. (Ed.). (1992a). *Studying teachers' lives*. London: Routledge.
Goodson, I. F. (1992b). Studying teachers' lives: An emergent field of enquiry. In I. F. Goodson (Ed.), *Studying teachers' lives*. London: Routledge.
Goodson, I. F. (1994). Exploring teachers' professional knowledge: Constructing identity and community. *Teacher Educational Quarterly, 21*, 85–105.
Goodson, I. F. (1999). The educational researcher as public intellectual. *Journal of British Education, 25*, 277–297.
Goodson, I. F. (2003). *Professional knowledge, professional lives*. Maidenhead: Open University Press.
Goodson, I. F. (2004). Understanding curriculum change: Some warnings about restructuring initiatives. In F. Hernandez & I. F. Goodson (Eds.), *Social geographies of educational change* (pp. 15–27). Dordrecht: Kulwer Academic Publishers.
Goodson, I. F. (2005a). *Learning, curriculum and life politics*. Abingdon: Routledge.
Goodson, I. F. (2005b). Long waves of educational reform. In I. F. Goodson (Ed.), *Learning, curriculum and life politics*. Abingdon: Routledge.
Goodson, I. F. (2013). *Developing narrative theory: Life histories and personal representation*. Abingdon: Routledge.
Goodson, I. F., & Choi, P. L. (2008). Life history and collective memory as methodological strategies: Studying teacher professionalism. *Teacher Education Quarterly, 35*(2), 5–28.
Goodson, I. F., & Cole, A. L. (1992). Exploring the teacher's professional knowledge: Constructing identity and community. In I. F. Goodson & J. M. Mangan (Eds.), *History, context and qualitative methods in the study of education*. London & Ontario: RUCCUS.
Goodson, I. F., & Hargreaves, A. (1996). *Teachers' professional lives*. London: Falmer Press.
Goodson, I. F., & Mangan, J. M. (Eds.). (1992). *History, context and qualitative methods in the study of education*. London & Ontario: RUCCUS.
Goodson, I. F., & Medway, P. (1990). *Bringing English to order*. Lewes: Falmer Press.
Goodson, I. F., Moore, S., & Hargreaves, A. (2006). Teacher Nostalgia and the sustainability of reform: The generation and degeneration of teachers' missions, memory, and meaning. *Education Administration Quarterly, 42*(1), 42–61.

REFERENCES

Goodson, I. F., & Rudd, T. (2012). *Studying historical periodisation* (Riaipe3 Project). Retrieved from https://www.researchgate.net/publication/291243172_Studying_Historical_Periodisation

Goodson, I. F., & Rudd, T. (2016). Restructuring, reform and refraction: Complexities of response to imposed social change. *Educational Practice and Theory, 38*(2), 2–21.

Goodson, I. F., & Sikes, P. (2001). *Life history research in educational settings*. Buckingham: Open University Press.

Goodson, I. F., & Walker, R. (Eds.). (1991). *Biography, identity and schooling: Episodes in educational research*. Basingstoke: Falmer Press.

Goodwyn, A. (2012). The status of literature: English teaching and the condition of literature in schools. *English in Education, 46*(3), 212–227.

Gordon, P. (2002). Curriculum. In R. Aldrich (Ed.), *A century of education*. London: RoutledgeFalmer.

Gove, M. (2013, May 9). What does it mean to be an educated person? *Speech given at Brighton College*. Retrieved from https://www.gov.uk/government/speeches/what-does-it-mean-to-be-an-educated-person

Grace, G. (1978). *Teachers, ideology and control*. London: Routledge & Keegan Paul.

Grace, G. (1987). Teachers and the state in Britain: A changing relation. In M. Lawn & G. Grace (Eds.), *Teachers: The culture and politics of work*. London: Falmer Press.

Gramsci, A. (1985). *Selections from cultural writings*. London: Lawrence & Wishart.

Green, A. (2004). Individual remembering and 'collective memory': Theoretical presuppositions and contemporary debates. *Oral History, 32*(2), 35–44.

Green, A. (Ed.). (2011). *Becoming a reflective English teacher*. Maidenhead: Open University Press.

Gretton, J., & Jackson, M. (1976). *William Tyndale: Collapse of a school – or a system?* London: Allen & Unwin.

Hadow, W. H. (1931). *The Hadow report: The primary school*. London: HMSO. Retrieved from http://webarchive.nationalarchives.gov.uk/20101007105102/ http://www.ttrb.ac.uk// viewArticle2.asx?contetId=15840

Halbwachs, M. (1992). *On collective memory*. Chicago, IL: University of Chicago Press.

Hall, S. (1987, June). Gramsci and us. *Marxism Today*, pp. 16–21.

Halliday, M. A. K. (1973). *Explorations in the functions of language*. London: Edward Arnold.

Halliday, M. A. K. (1975). *Learning how to mean*. London: Edward Arnold.

Hardcastle, J. L. (2008). Four photographs in an English course book: A study in the visual archeology of urban schooling. *Changing English, 15*(1), 3–24.

Hardcastle, J. L. (2016). The dramas themselves. *Changing English, 23*(2), 112–127.

Hardcastle, J. L., & Medway, P. (2013). English for the post-war age. In G. Snapper (Ed.), *NATE at 50: A teaching english special supplement* (pp. 29–40). Sheffield: NATE Publications.

Hargreaves, A. (1994). *Changing teachers, changing times: Teachers work and culture in the postmodern age*. London: Continuum.

Hargreaves, A. (2000). Four ages of professionalism and professional learning. *Teachers and Teaching: History and Practice, 6*(2), 151–182.

Hargreaves, A., & Moore, S. (2005). Voice, Nostalgia and teachers' experiences of change. In F. Bodone (Ed.), *What difference does research make and for whom?* New York, NY: Peter Lang Publishing.

Hargreaves, D. (1967). *Social relations in a secondary school*. London. Routledge & Kegan Paul.

Harris, J. (1991). After Dartmouth: Growth and conflict in English. *College English, 53*(6), 631–646.

Hartley, D. (2009). Personalisation: The nostalgic revival of child-centred education. *Journal of Education Policy, 24*(4), 423–434.

Heath, S. B. (1982). What no bedtime story means: Narrative skills at home and school. *Language in Society, 11*(1), 49–76.

Heath, S. B. (1983). *Ways with words: Language, life, and work in communities and classrooms*. New York, NY: Cambridge University Press.

Helsby, G., & McCulloch, G. (1996). Teacher professionalism and curriculum control. In I. F. Goodson & A. Hargreaves (Eds.), *Teachers' professional lives*. London: Falmer Press.

Hoggart, R. (2009). *The uses of literacy: Aspects of working class life*. London: Penguin Classics. (Originally published in 1957)

Holbrook, D. (1961). *English for maturity*. Cambridge, MA: Cambridge University Press.

REFERENCES

Holbrook, D. (1964). *English for the rejected*. Cambridge, MA: Cambridge University Press.
Holbrook, D. (1967). *Children's writing*. Cambridge, MA: Cambridge University Press.
Holbrook, D. (1972). *The secret places*. London: Methuen.
Howlett, J. (2013). *Progressive education: A critical introduction*. London: Bloomsbury.
Hoyles, M. (Ed.). (1981). *The politics of literacy*. London: Writers and Readers Publishing.
Hymes, D. H. (1972). On communicative competence. In J. B. Pride & J. Holmes (Eds.), *Sociolinguistics*. London: Penguin Books.
Illich, I. (1971). *Deschooling society*. New York, NY. Harper & Row.
Inguez, L., Valencia, J., & Vasquez, F. (1997). The construction of remembering and forgetfulness: Memories and histories of the Spanish civil war. In D. Pennebaker, D. Paez, & B. Rime (Eds.), *Collective memory of political events*. Mahwah, NJ: Earlbaum.
Jones, K. (1983). *Beyond progressive education*. London: Macmillan Press.
Jones, K. (1989). *Right turn: The conservative revolution in education*. London: Hutchinson Radius.
Jones, K. (2003). *Education in Britain – 1944 to the present*. Cambridge: Polity Press.
Jones, K. (2013). The Long counter-revolution. In M. Allen & P. Ainley (Eds.), *Education beyond the coalition: Reclaiming the agenda* (pp. 156–177). London: Radicaled Books.
Jones, K. (2014). Conservatism and educational crisis: The case in England. *Education Inquiry, 5*(1), 89–108.
Keddie, N. (1971). Classroom knowledge. In M. F. D. Young (Ed.), *Knowledge and control*. London: Macmillan Press.
Keddie, N. (Ed.). (1973). *Tinker, tailor: The myth of cultural deprivation*. London: Penguin Books.
Kellner, D. (2000). Multiple literacies and critical pedagogies: New paradigms. In P. P. Trifonas (Ed.), *Revolutionary pedagogies: Cultural politics, instituting education, and the discourse of theory*. London: Routledge.
Kent, A. (Ed.). (2000). *School subject teaching: The history and future of the curriculum*. London: Kogan Page.
Labov, W. (1969). *The study of nonstandard language*. Washington, DC: NCTE.
Labov, W. (1972). *Language and the inner city: Studies in Black English vernacular*. Philadelphia, PA: University of Pennsylvania Press.
Lane, N. (2002). *Oxygen: The molecule that made the world*. Oxford: Oxford University Press.
Laszlo, J. (1997). Narrative organisation of social representations. *Papers on Social Representations, 6*(2), 155–172.
Lawn, M., & Grace, G. (1987). *Teachers: The culture and politics of work*. London: Falmer Press.
Lawton, D. (1975). *Class, culture and the curriculum*. London: Routledge & Kegan Paul.
Lawton, D. (1977). *Education and social justice*. London: Sage Publications.
Lawton, D. (1980). *The politics of the school curriculum*. London: Routledge & Kegan Paul.
Lawton, D. (1996). *Beyond the national curriculum: Teacher professionalism and empowerment*. London: Hodder & Stoughton.
Legg, S. (2005). Contesting and surviving memory: Space, nation and nostalgia in Les Lieux de Memoire. *Society and Space, 23*(4), 481–504.
Lennon, J. (1965). *A spaniard in the works*. London: Jonathan Cape.
Lichtman, M. (2013). *Qualitative research in education* (3rd ed.). Thousand Oaks, CA: Sage Publications.
Loach, K. (2013). The spirit of '45 [DVD documentary]. London: Fly Film Company/Film4.
Lowe, R. (2007). *The death of progressive education: Hoe teachers lost control of the classroom*. Abingdon: Routledge.
Marenbon, J. (1994). The new orthodoxy examined. In S. Brindsley (Ed.), *Teaching English*. London: Routledge.
Marx, K. (1972). *The Marx and Engels reader* (R. C. Tucker, Ed.). New York, NY: Norton.
Maude, A. (1971). The egalitarian threat. In C. B. Cox & A. E. Dyson (Eds.), *The black papers on education*. London: Davis-Poynter.
McCallum, A. (2012). *Creativity and learning in secondary English*. London: Routledge.
McCulloch, G. (2000). Publicizing the educational past. In D. Crook & A. Aldrich (Eds.), *History of education for the twenty-first century*. London: Institute of Education.

REFERENCES

McCulloch, G. (2002a). Secondary education. In A. Aldrich (Ed.), *A century of education*. London: RoutledgeFalmer.

McCulloch, G. (2002b). Local authorities and the organisation of secondary schooling, 1943–1950. *Oxford Review of Education, 28*(2–3), 235–246.

McCulloch, G. (Ed.). (2005). *The RoutledgeFalmer reader in history of education*. London: Routledge.

Measor, L., & Sikes, P. (1992). Visiting lives: Ethics and methodology in life history. In I. F. Goodson (Ed.), *Studying teachers' lives*. London: Routledge.

Medway, P. (1980). *Finding a language: Autonomy and learning in school*. London: Writers and Readers Publishing.

Medway, P. (1990). Into the sixties: English and English society at a time of change. In I. F. Goodson & P. Medway (Eds.), *Bringing English to order*. Lewes: Falmer Press.

Medway, P., & Hardcastle, J. L. (2013). English for the post-war age: English teachers, freedom and change. *NATE at 50: A Teaching English Special Supplement, 3*, 23–40.

Medway, P., Hardcastle, J. L., Brewis, G., & Crook, D. (2014). *English teachers in a Postwar democracy: Emerging choice in London schools, 1945–1965*. New York, NY: Palgrave Macmillan.

Meredith, S. (2011). *Forever churchfileds: Churchfields comprehensive school, West Bromwich, the journey of a well-loved school*. West Midlands: Sandra Meredith Publications.

Middleton, D., & Brown, S. D. (2005). *The social psychology of experience*. London: Sage Publications.

Middleton, D., & Edwards, D. (1990). Conversational remembering: A social psychological approach. In D. Middleton & D. Edwards (Eds.), *Collective remembering*. London: Sage Publications.

Middleton, S. (1992). Developing a radical pedagogy: Autobiography of a New Zealand sociologist of women's teaching. In I. F. Goodson (Ed.), *Studying teachers' lives*. London: Routledge.

Miller, J. (1995). Trick or treat? The autobiography of the question. *English Quarterly, 27*(3), 22–26.

Misztal, B. (2003). *Theories of social remembering*. Maidenhead: Open University Press.

Mortimore, P. (2008, June 3). In memoriam: 20 years ago they killed off ILEA. Why? *Guardian*. Retrieved from http://www.guardian.co.uk/education/2008/jun/03/schools.uk1

Morton, A. (1997). *Education and the state from 1833*. Richmond, VA: Public Records Office.

Nelson, M. (1992). Using oral case histories to reconstruct the experiences of women teachers in Vermont, 1900–1950. In I. F. Goodson (Ed.), *Studying teachers' lives*. London: Routledge.

Newbolt, H. (1921). *The teaching of English in England*. London: HMSO. Retrieved from http://www.educationengland.org.uk/documents/newbolt/newbolt1921.html

Newson, K., & Mansfield, R. (1965). *The art of English: A general course for secondary schools*. London: Schofield & Sims.

Nora, P. (1989). Between memory and history: Les Lieux de Memoire (Representations No. 26, Special Issue: Memory and Counter Memory, pp. 7–24). Berkeley, CA: University of California Press.

Norwood, C. M. (1943). *Curriculum and examinations in secondary schools: Report of the committee of secondary examinations council appointed by the president of the board of education in 1941* (The Norwood Report). London: HMSO.

Ornstein, A. C., & Levine, D. U. (2000). *The foundations of education* (7th ed.). Boston, MA: Houghton Mifflin Company.

Orr, J. E. (1990). Sharing knowledge, celebrating identity: Community memory in a service culture. In D. Middleton & D. Edwards (Eds.), *Collective remembering*. London: Sage Publications.

Padden, C. A. (1990). Folk explanation in language survival. In D. Middleton & D. Edwards (Eds.), *Collective remembering*. London: Sage Publications.

Pinar, W. F. (2004). *What is curriculum theory?* Mahwah, NJ: Lawrence Erlbaum Associates.

Plowden, B. (1967). *Children and their primary schools: A report of the central advisory council for education* (The Plowden Report). London: HMSO.

Postman, N., & Weingartner, C. (1969). *Teaching as a subversive activity*. New York, NY: Dell Publishing.

Poulson, L. (1998). *The English curriculum in schools*. London: Cassell.

Radley, A. (1990). Artifacts, memory and a sense of the past. In D. Middleton & D. Edwards (Eds.), *Collective remembering*. London: Sage Publications.

Richardson, W. (2000). History, education and audience. In D. Crook & A. Aldrich (Eds.), *History of education for the twenty-first century*. London: Institute of Education.

REFERENCES

Richmond, J., & Eyers, S. (1982). *Becoming our own experts: Studies of language learning.* London: Talk Workshop Group. Retrieved from http://www.becomingourownexperts.org/sites/www.becomingourownexperts.org/files/downloads/ecomin%20our%20own%20experts.pdf

Robinson, W. (2000). Finding our professional niche: Reinventing ourselves as twenty-first century historians of education. In D. Crook & A. Aldrich (Eds.), *History of education for the twenty-first century.* London: Institute of Education.

Rosen, H. (1972). *Language and class: A critical look at the theories of Basil Bernstein.* Bristol: Falling Wall Press.

Rosen, H. (1975). Out there or where the masons went. *Theory Into Practice, 14*(5), 338–342.

Rosen, H. (1981). *Neither Bleak house nor liberty hall: English and the curriculum.* London: University of London Institute of Education.

Rosen, H. (1998). *Speaking from memory: The study of autobiographical discourse.* Stoke-on-Trent: Trentham Books.

Russell, B. (1984). *A history of western philosophy.* London: Routledge.

Sachs, J. (2003). *The activist teaching profession.* Buckingham: Open University Press.

Sampson, G. (1921). *English for the English.* Cambridge: Cambridge University Press. Retrieved from http://archive.org/details/englishforenglis00samprich

Schudson, M. (1990). Ronald Reagan misremembered. In D. Middleton & D. Edwards (Eds.), *Collective remembering.* London: Sage Publications.

Schwartz, B. (1982). The social context of commemoration: A study in collective memory. *Social Forces, 61,* 374–402.

Schwartz, B. (1990). The reconstruction of Abraham Lincoln. In D. Middleton & D. Edwards (Eds.), *Collective remembering.* London: Sage Publications.

Searle, C. (1975). *Classrooms of resistance.* London: Writers and Readers Publishing.

Sharp, P. (2002). Central and local government. In R. Aldrich (Ed.), *A century of education.* London: RoutledgeFalmer.

Shayer, D. (1972). *English in schools 1900–1970.* London: Routledge & Kegan Paul.

Shotter, J. (1990). The social construction of remembering and forgetting. In D. Middleton & D. Edwards (Eds.), *Collective remembering.* London: Sage Publications.

Simon, B. (1953). *Intelligence testing and the comprehensive school.* London: Lawrence & Wishart.

Simon, B. (1955). *The common secondary school.* London: Lawrence & Wishart.

Simon, B. (1985). *Does education matter?* London: Lawrence & Wishart.

Simon, B. (1991). *Education and the social order: 1940–1990.* London: Lawrence & Wishart.

Simon, B. (1994). *The state and educational change.* London: Lawrence & Wishart.

Simon, B. (2005). Can education change society? In G. McCulloch (Ed.), *RoutledgeFalmer reader in history of education.* Abingdon: Routledge.

Tarpey, P. (2009). Professional memory and English teaching. *English Teaching: Practice and Critique, 8*(1), 52–63.

Tarpey, P. (2015). Professional memory in context: Can it help counter the "counter-revolution". *Changing English, 22*(4), 382–392.

Tarpey, P. (2016). "Fire Burn and Cauldron Bubble": What are the conjunctural effects on English teacher professional memories, identities and narratives? *Changing English, 23*(1), 77–93.

Tarpey, P. (2017a). "We not I" not "I me mine": Learning from professional memory about collectivist English teaching. *Changing English, 24*(1), 103–117.

Tarpey, P. (2017b). Disrupting continuities: Re-thinking conceptions of 'growth' in English teaching. *English in Education, 51*(2), 157–169.

Teaching London Kids. (1973). Protest in the staffroom. *TLK,* p. 2.

Teaching London Kids Editorial. (1982). The case of the half-bakered report. *TLK,* p. 15.

Thomas, G. (2009). *How to do your research project.* London: Sage Publications.

Thompson, E. P. (1978). *The poverty of theory and other essays.* London: Merlin Press.

Trier, J. (2010). Representations of education in HBO's the wire, season 4. *Teacher Education Quarterly, 37*(2), 179–200.

REFERENCES

Trudgill, P. (1974). *Sociolinguistics: An introduction to language and society*. Harmondsworth: Penguin Books.
Trudgill, P. (1975). *Accent, dialect and the school*. London: Edward Arnold.
Volosinov, V. N. (1973). *Marxism and the philosophy of language*. Cambridge, MA: Harvard University Press.
Vygotsky, L. (1978). *Mind in society*. Cambridge, MA: Harvard University Press.
Vygotsky, L. (1986). *Thought and language*. Cambridge, MA: Massachusetts Institute of Technology.
Walker, R., & Goodson, I. F. (1991). Stations: Episodes in a teacher's life. In I. F. Goodson & R. Walker (Eds.), *Biography, identity and schooling*. Basingstoke: Falmer Press.
Wardle, D. (1976). *English popular education 1780–1975*. Cambridge: Cambridge University Press.
Watts, R. (2002). Pupils and students. In R. Aldrich (Ed.), *A century of education*. London: RoutledgeFalmer.
Wertsch, J. (2002). *Voices of collective remembering*. Cambridge: University of Cambridge Press.
West, A., Hind, A., & Pennell, H. (2004). School admissions and "selection" in comprehensive schools: Policy and practice. *Oxford Review of Education, 30*(3), 347–369.
Whitty, G. (2000). Teacher professionalism in new times. *Journal or In-Service Education, 26*(2), 281–295.
Whitty, G. (2002). *Making sense of educational policy*. London: Paul Chapman Publications.
Whitty, G. (2006). Educational research and educational policy making: Is conflict inevitable? *British Educational Research Journal, 32*(2), 159–176.
Williams, R. (1958). Culture is ordinary. In B Highmore (Ed.), *The everyday life reader* (pp. 91–100). London: Routledge.
Williams, R. (1977). *Marxism and literature*. Oxford: Oxford University Press.
Williams, R. (1981). *Culture*. Glasgow: Fontana Paperbacks.
Williams, R. (1993). *Culture and society*. London: Chatto & Windus. (Originally published in 1958)
Williams, R. (2011). *The long revolution*. London: Chatto & Windus. (Originally published in 1961)
Willis, P. (1977). *Learning to labour: How working class kids get working class jobs*. Farnborough: Saxon House.
Wilshaw, M. (2012). *High expectation, no excuses*. Retrieved from http://webarchive.nationalarchives.gov.uk/20141124154759
Woodin, T. (2005). Muddying the waters: Class and identity in a working class cultural organisation. *Sociology, 39*(5), 1001–1018.
Woodin, T. (2007). Working class education and social change in nineteenth and twentieth century Britain. *History of Education, 36*(4–5), 483–496.
Woodin, T. (2008). "A beginner reader is not a beginner thinker": Student publishing in Britain since the 1970s. *Paedagogica Historica. 44*(1–2), 219–232.
Woodin, T. (2009). Working class writing, alternative publishing and audience participation. *Media, Culture and Society, 31*(1), 79–96.
Worpole, K. (1977a). *Local publishing and local culture: An account of the work of the Centreprise Publishing project*. London: Centreprise Publications. Retrieved from http://hackneyhistory.wordpress.com/2011/06/27/centreprise-working-class-history-and-localpublishing
Worpole, K. (1977b). Beyond the classroom walls. In M. Hoyles (Ed.), *The politics of literacy*. London: Writers and Readers Publishing.
Wyness, M. (2008). Schooling and social class. In D. Matheson (Ed.), *An introduction to the study of education*. Abingdon: Routledge.
Wyse, D., Jones, R., Bradford, H., & Wolpert, M. A. (2013). *Teaching English, language and literacy* (3rd ed.). London: Routledge.
Yandell, J. (2008). Mind the gap: Investigating test literacy and classroom literacy. *English in Education, 42*(1), 70–87.
Yandell, J. (2011). English and inclusion. In J. Davison, C. Daly, & J. Moss (Eds.), *Debates in English teaching*. London: Routledge.
Yandell, J. (2013). Curriculum, pedagogy and assessment: Of rigour and unfinished revolutions. In M. Allen & P. Ainley (Eds.), *Education beyond the coalition: Reclaiming the agenda* (pp. 5–23). London: Radicaled Books.

REFERENCES

Yglesias, J. R. C., & Holman, D. K. J. (1961). *Pleasure in English*. London: Longman.
Young, M. (1971). *Knowledge and control*. London: Macmillan Press.
Young, M. (2008). *Bringing knowledge back in: From social constructivism to social realism in the sociology of education*. Abingdon: Routledge.
Young, R., & Collin, A. (2004). Introduction: Constructivism and social constructionism in the career field. *Journal of Vocational Behaviour, 64*, 373–388.

INDEX

A

Abbs, Peter, 28, 88, 89
Academy Schools, 125
Accountability, 1, 3, 24, 38, 119, 124, 125, 127–132, 143, 164, 171, 172
Activist teachers, 32, 33, 110, 114
Advisers, English teaching, 12, 13, 107, 112, 115, 136, 158, 162
Allen, David, 18, 31, 154
Althusser, Louis, 5, 169–172, 178n1
Annales historians, 4
Anti-Nazi League, 108
Anti-racism, 71
Anti-sexism, 33
Art of English, the, 87, 88

B

Bachelor of Education (B Ed), 13, 77
Bakhtin, Mikhail, 3, 55–57, 59, 65, 71, 138, 151–154
Bakhurst, David, 50, 51
Ball, Stephen, 5, 15n1, 18, 25, 36, 38–40, 65, 110, 166n2
Barnes, Douglas, 96, 100, 120, 133, 155
Beatles, the, 94
Ben-Peretz, Miriam, 15n2, 132, 168
Bergson, Henri, 47, 49
Bernstein, Basil, 42
Billig, Michael, 50, 52
Black Papers, 40, 41, 43, 154
Bourdieu, Pierre, 75
Boyson, Rhodes, 41
Braudel, Fernand, 4
Britton, James, 2, 21, 31, 37, 38, 40, 83, 112, 120, 133, 134, 155, 176
Bruner, Jerome, 60, 61

Bullock Report, 2, 18, 36–38, 104, 120, 129, 142, 164, 165
Burgess, Tony, 2, 15n1, 18, 37, 40–42, 112, 113, 166n2
Burr, Vivien, 58
Burt, Cyril, 23

C

Callaghan, James, Ruskin College Speech, 18
Centerprise, 32, 33, 99
Certificate in Education (Cert Ed), 12, 13, 77, 78
Child-centred teaching, 19, 21, 22, 27, 30, 32, 87, 140, 141, 161
Churchfields School, 12, 93
Circular 10/65, 2, 23
Clarendon Report, 22
Clements, Simon, 28
Collectivism, 43, 49, 61, 87, 113–115, 121, 138, 143, 146, 155, 165, 166, 169
Comprehensive Schools, 2, 7, 24, 35, 38, 67, 123, 155
Conjunctures, 4, 5, 7–9, 12, 17–43, 54, 56, 67, 77, 79, 83, 86, 106, 110, 114, 124, 126, 145, 155–157, 163, 166, 172, 174
Conscientization, 3, 97
Constructivism, 46, 58, 59
Coultas, Valerie, 1, 18, 54, 137, 148, 149
Counterculture, 7, 32, 155
Cox, Charles Brian, 17, 31, 32
Crosland, Anthony, 23, 85
Crotty, Michael, 58, 59

INDEX

Cultures, 6, 8, 18, 26, 28, 31–34, 37–39, 41, 42, 51, 57–60, 68, 76, 77, 93–96, 100, 103, 109, 114, 128, 134, 145–151, 156, 158, 164–168, 178
  emergent, 146–149, 152
  residual, 146–148, 150, 152, 173
Cunningham, Peter, 2, 81, 95

D
Dartmouth Conference, 28
Davies, Chris, 18, 37
Davison, John, 25
Department for Education (DfE), 117, 175
Dialogism, 49, 55, 151
Dixon, John, 6, 7, 18, 21, 27–32, 40, 55, 65, 77, 83, 88, 89, 101, 108, 115, 118, 133, 149, 150, 155, 158, 166, 167, 176
Dyson, Anthony, 17, 32

E
Education Act 1944, 5, 20, 23
Education Reform Act 1988, 24, 135, 158
Eleven plus test, 23
English, 1–15, 17, 18, 21, 24–34, 36–43
  aims of, 6, 27, 87, 127, 154, 157, 167
  associations, 2, 28, 48, 89, 90, 92, 107, 112, 114, 127, 128, 130, 131, 133, 134, 136, 178
  curriculum, 25, 27–29, 76, 85, 89, 90, 94, 95, 97, 99–102, 104, 108, 117–120, 122, 123, 125–127, 129, 133, 134, 137–139, 141–143, 146, 148, 149, 157, 158, 163–165, 171, 172, 175
  inspectors, 35, 107, 109, 127, 128, 131, 134, 141, 153, 162
  'new', 6, 149, 151
  resources, 1, 2, 7, 8, 13, 14, 27, 28, 103, 117, 121

English and Media Centre, 11, 14, 84, 89
English Centre, 2, 7, 11–14, 36, 43, 83, 87–89, 106–112, 114, 129, 130, 133, 134, 155, 159, 162
English for Diversity, 88
English for Maturity, 88
English for the English, 25
English for the Rejected, 88
Every Child Matters, 165

F
Findlay, Kate, 149, 151
Foucault, Michel, 174
Free Schools, 174, 175
Freire, Paulo, 3, 24, 80, 97, 119, 127

G
Gardiner, D., 18, 25, 38, 39
Gardner, Philip, 2, 15n2, 53, 173
Genealogy of context, 5, 8, 9, 17, 21, 63, 82
Gergen, Kenneth, 46, 47, 55–59, 167, 171, 177
Gibbons, Simon, 2, 6, 18, 21, 23, 39–41
Goffman, Erving, 57
'Golden age', 17, 18, 156, 161
Goodson, Ivor, 2, 4, 8–12, 15n2, n3, 17, 18, 22, 38, 63, 81, 151, 153, 156, 160
Gove, Michael, 125, 129, 139, 148, 149
Grace, Gerald, 41, 66, 72, 127, 159, 166n1
Grammar, 6, 17, 18, 23, 26, 28, 55, 56, 67, 124, 137, 143, 148, 149, 152, 154, 157, 158, 171
Grammar Schools, 12–14, 17, 23, 26, 38, 39, 65, 66, 68, 69, 74, 75
Gramsci, Antonio, 18
Growth, 5, 27–32, 43, 61, 87, 92, 108, 132, 138, 148, 149, 151, 152, 166, 178
Growth Through English, 27, 28, 148

190

H

Hadow Report, 19
Hackney Downs school, 33, 125
Halbwachs, Maurice, 8, 48, 49, 52, 59
Hall, Stuart, 5
Hardcastle, John, 5, 6, 18, 28, 37, 42, 67, 133, 134
Hargreaves, Andy, 2, 15n2, n3, 127, 132, 160
Hargreaves, David, 24, 86, 104, 106
Hartley, David, 161
Heteroglossia, 49, 55, 56, 138, 151, 165, 169, 171
History of education, 13, 85, 112, 134, 135, 173, 174
Hoggart, Richard, 23, 69, 95
Holbrook, David, 28, 88, 100
Holland Park School, 13, 112
Holloway School, 14, 88, 105, 108, 112
Howlett, John, 19, 20, 125, 139, 140

I

Inner London Education Authority (ILEA), 2, 7, 10–14, 34–36, 43, 43n1, 83, 87, 89, 105–114, 123, 127, 145, 155, 159, 162
Inner speech, 54–57, 59, 151, 153
Institute of Education, 3, 11, 13, 14, 37, 83, 107

J

Jones, Ken, 5, 17, 18, 20–24, 31, 35, 36, 90, 105, 124–126, 130, 156, 158, 159

K

Keddie, Nell, 24, 86, 106
Kenny, A., 18, 25, 38, 39
Kinnock, Neil, 76

L

Labour Party, 99, 109, 110, 159
Labov, William, 42, 69
Lawton, Denis, 127, 162, 166n1
Learning from experience, 132, 135, 143, 168
Leigh, Mike, 106
Lennon, John, 52, 94
Life history, 2, 8, 9, 12, 81, 103, 136
Loach, Ken, 155
London Association for the Teaching of English (LATE), 2, 6, 7, 14, 27, 28, 32, 37–39, 83, 90, 107, 112, 127, 145, 155, 158, 159, 178
London County Council, 6, 27
London Drama Magazine, 13, 112
Longue durée, 4
Lowe, Roy, 7, 17, 18, 24, 27, 32, 36, 39, 65, 69, 77, 137

M

Marx, Karl, 75, 103, 147, 162, 163, 169–172
Maude, Angus, 32
McCallum, Andrew, 25, 27
McCulloch, Gary, 15n2, 19, 22, 23, 85, 125, 154, 163, 173, 174
Medway, Peter, 6, 18, 21, 26–28, 32, 39, 66, 67, 90, 133, 134
Memory, 1, 2, 4, 5, 8–11, 14, 15, 34, 41, 43, 45–61, 63–67, 69–73, 77, 81, 82, 106, 111, 114, 115, 125, 128, 129, 136, 142, 143, 145–169, 173, 176–178
  autobiographical, 52–54, 59, 175, 177
  collective, 2, 4, 8–10, 14, 46, 48–54, 57–59, 81, 125, 165–167, 176, 177
  historical 52–54, 177
Middleton, David, 8, 15n3, 49, 54
Militancy, 7, 35, 105, 109, 119, 121, 126, 127, 137, 146, 154, 166
Miller, Jane, 100, 175
Mixed-ability teaching, 3, 37, 38, 91, 103–106, 114, 121–123, 127, 164

INDEX

Mode Three Certificate of Secondary Education (CSE), 101, 102
Mortimore, Peter, 34

N
National Association for the Teaching of English (NATE), 28, 90, 92, 114, 127, 145, 178
National Curriculum, 18, 24, 56, 89, 117, 122, 126, 158, 163, 171
National Front, 108
National Health Service, 6
National Union of Teachers (NUT), 35, 105, 159
Neil, A. S., 19
Newbolt Report, 25
Newcastle Commission, 22
Nora, Pierre, 52
Norwood Report, 22, 23, 26
Nostalgia, 2, 52, 121, 160–162

O
Office for Standards in Education (Ofsted), 56, 124, 125, 128, 141, 153, 172
Official past, 19, 125, 173
Oral history, 49
Oral work and talk, 37, 42, 49, 81, 91, 92, 96–98, 104, 114, 120, 136, 141, 157, 172

P
Personalisation, 137, 141, 161, 171
Pinar, William, 175, 176
Pleasure in English, 28
Plowden Report, 20, 37, 81, 94, 155, 168
Popular culture, 7, 29, 42, 77, 93–96, 114
Positive Images Campaign, 36
Postgraduate Certificate in Education (PGCE), 14, 75, 80, 83, 84
Postman, N., 24, 80, 96, 119, 127
Praxis, 3, 132, 142, 160

Professional development, 9, 12, 34, 36, 106, 108, 111–114, 127, 129, 130, 135, 136, 145, 162, 168, 172, 174–176
Professionalism, 2, 9, 12, 24, 130–133, 153, 156, 159, 169, 172, 174, 175
Progressive education, 17–19, 41, 121, 139, 141, 149
Primary schools, 19, 20, 23, 25, 45, 64, 94
Public past, 173

Q
Qualified teacher status (QTS), 175

R
Radical teachers, 18–21, 35, 41, 109, 123, 159
Reading Capital, 169
Reflections, 28, 40, 63, 67, 88
Refraction, concept of, 150, 151
Relational self, 58
Richardson, William, 174
Robinson, Wendy, 1, 173–175
Rosen, Harold, 6–8, 18, 21, 27, 28, 31, 40, 42, 59, 83, 112, 120, 133, 134, 155, 176, 178n1
Russell, Bertrand, 47

S
Sachs, Judyth, 110, 111
Sampson, George, 25
Schudson, Michael, 52
Schwartz, Barry, 52
Shayer, David, 18, 40, 113, 157
Shotter, John, 8, 50, 129, 177
Simon, Brian, 6, 18–20, 22, 23, 28, 43n1, 65, 85
Social constructionism, 14, 46, 49, 57–59
Social justice, 3, 6, 32, 65, 71, 77, 79, 82, 86, 99, 106, 114, 129, 141, 146, 155–157, 172

192

Social Relations in a Secondary School, 106
Socialism, 6, 9, 14, 41, 75, 86, 87, 90, 119, 122, 141, 145, 148, 168
Socialist Workers' Party, 14, 159
Speech genres, 49, 54–57, 59, 71, 81, 87, 90, 125, 126, 142, 150–154, 166, 167, 177, 178
Spens Report, 22
Standard English, 26, 56, 99, 137, 141, 148, 157, 158, 171
Standardised Assessment Tasks (SATs), 123, 124, 161, 171
Stratta, Leslie, 28, 88
Summerhill School, 19

T
Taunton Commission, 22
Teacher education, 85, 112, 174–176
Teacher shortages, 112
Teacher training, 3, 9, 35, 63, 69, 71, 72, 74–79, 83, 105, 134, 158, 172–175
Teacher training college, 69, 71, 72, 74–79, 83
Teachers' centres, 7, 34, 114, 146
Teaching London Kids (TLK), 14, 32, 33, 36, 86, 99, 105, 112, 113
Thatcher, Margaret, 14, 36, 122, 127

Theoretical problematic, 170–172, 177
Tripartite system of secondary schools, 5, 6, 22, 23, 67, 75

U
Utterance, 46, 51, 55–57, 65, 82, 125, 151–154, 157, 169

V
Volosinov, Valentin, 14, 49, 51, 54, 55
Vygotsky, Lev, 3, 49–51, 54, 55, 141

W
Walworth School, 6, 27, 67
Weingartner, Charles, 80, 96, 119, 127
Welfare state, 5, 7, 39, 64, 65, 155
Wertsch, James, 52
Whitty, Geoff, 24
'William Tyndale affair', 18, 43n1
Williams, Raymond, 3, 6, 18, 22, 26, 65, 69, 146, 147, 148, 150, 166, 178n1
Wilshaw, Michael, 124, 125, 129
Woodin, Tom, 65
Worpole, Ken, 33, 34, 99

Y
Yandell, John, 38, 54, 149, 164, 165, 171, 175, 176